THE MYSTERY OF CHRIST, OUR HEAD, PRIEST AND KING

THE MYSTERY OF CHRIST
Our Head, Priest and King

BY

REV. C. V. HÉRIS, O.P.

Translated by

REV. DENIS FAHEY, C.S.Sp.

1950

NEWMAN PRESS
WESTMINSTER, MARYLAND

PRINTED IN GREAT BRITAIN
BY WILLMER BROS. AND CO. LTD.,
62-68 CHESTER STREET, BIRKENHEAD.

FOREWORD

Father C. V. Héris, O.P., whose work *Le Mystère du Christ* is translated by Dr. Fahey in this volume, is a distinguished member in a very ardent group of French Dominican theologians. For close on thirty years now he has done an immense amount of work for the propagation of Thomism. Besides his work as a Professor, he has contributed consistently through these years to scientific publications like the *Revue des Sciences Philosophiques et Théologiques*, the *Bulletin Thomiste*, and *Le Vie Intellectuelle*. But he has also had the ambition (so clearly in accordance with the desire of the Church) to initiate the general public into the splendours of Thomistic thought.

Thomistic thought is essentially the thought of Jesus Christ. The devotion that runs through St. Thomas's own marvellous life is devotion to Jesus Christ, "for love of whom," he protested on his death-bed, "I have studied and kept vigil, toiled, preached and taught." Archbishop Vaughan is right in saying of him: "It was the Christ-principle which filled his whole life and bore him up out of this visible scene into those expanding realms of light, from which light comes into the minds of men."[1] Father Héris shows himself a true Thomist in that he has devoted himself particularly to making known to the world Our Lord Jesus Christ.

He has done this in the first place by translating and commenting on that part of the *Summa Theologica* which deals with the Incarnation; then by numerous articles such as *Le Christ notre Chef, La Royauté du Christ*, but chiefly by this book, already translated into Italian, in which, under the title *Le Mystère du Christ*, he gives us a splendid synthesis of the Third Part of the *Summa Theologica*.

The aim of all this writing—as of the present translation—is to help us to realize that Christ means everything to us, that to be a Christian in the full sense of the word is to belong wholly to Christ, who becomes, as St. Thomas himself put it, the total principle of our life and actions. *Totum Principium vitae nostrae et operationis nostrae est Christus.*[2] Hence we are able to say with St. Paul: "I live, now not I, but Christ liveth in me."[3]

How Christ Himself brings about this glorious consummation is the special theme of this book. Dr. Fahey has been moved to undertake its translation because, as he himself puts it: "Our Lord Jesus Christ, Head of the Mystical Body, is both Priest and King, and Fr. Héris develops admirably the relation between the two functions."

---

[1] *Life and Labours of St. Thomas of Aquin*, Vol. II, pp. 923-924.
[2] *Comment in Epist. ad Philipp.*, C. I, lect. 3.
[3] *Epist. ad Galat.* II, 20.

If Christ lives in us, it is because He has given His life in sacrifice for our redemption. If He is King of Glory, King whose Law of Love rules, by possessing, the very hearts of His subjects, it is because, being lifted up on Calvary, He has drawn those hearts to Himself. The very Kingship of Christ is explained by His Priesthood and Sacrifice. "Above all else, is Jesus the Sovereign Priest of humanity," Fr. Héris will write. And, incidentally, he surpasses himself in those pages in which he treats of the sovereign act of the Sovereign Priest—that act which gives its name to the *Actio* of the Mass.

Dr. Fahey, to whom we are already so greatly indebted for his magnificent work in the same cause as that to which Fr. Héris has devoted his life, leaves us, by this translation, much more his debtors. The writer is happy to think that even these few lines that it is his privilege to contribute as a Foreword to this volume may be taken as token payment, in his own name and in the name of those Thomists on whose behalf he may presume to speak, of some part of that debt.

Fr. Aegidius doolan, o.p.

St. Mary's, Tallaght,
Feast of SS. Peter and Paul, 1948.

CONTENTS

PART II

CHRIST IN US

INTRODUCTION

"The mystery which had been hidden from ages and generations, but now is manifested to his saints . . . which is Christ, in you the hope of glory."[1] These few words from St. Paul seem to express perfectly the sublime grandeurs of the Mystery of Christ. Christ is ours and we are His. Christ is ours because God, in His eternal designs, willed that the Word should become man to raise fallen humanity, to restore to it the Divine Life of Grace, and to give in its name to God's sovereign Majesty, the homage of praise and glory which sin had made impossible. We are Christ's, because through Him, and Him alone, henceforth we have access to the throne of God: by Him we may hope to possess one day the happiness of heaven; finally, by Him we can send up the homage of our grateful adoration to the God of Infinite Goodness. He is the mighty arch linking heaven to earth, the Supreme Pontiff of fallen humanity, the High Priest who by His Priesthood restores between God and creatures the union which had been rudely shattered. The union of the two natures, the Divine and the human, in Jesus, and by Jesus—that is the mystery of Christ: it is all summed up in the phrase that it is the mystery of His Priesthood.

Anyone who has only a superficial acquaintance with the Third Part of the *Summa Theologica*, dealing with the Incarnate Word and His mission of redemption, is surprised at the small space which the Angelic Doctor assigns to the study of the Priesthood of Christ. He devotes to it just one 'Question' and a few 'Articles,' and that, though the subject had not been specifically dealt with by him in his previous works. This superficial view is, however, far from the truth. Through St. Thomas's scholastic treatise there runs a unifying thought, which is the *leit-motiv* linking together the questions dealt with in this part of the *Summa* and delineating the different traits of the Priesthood of Christ. We shall endeavour, in the course of this work, to bring out this underlying unity and show how in studying the Priesthood of Christ we get a synthetic view of the main aspects of Thomistic Christology.

"For every high-priest," says St. Paul in the *Epistle to the Hebrews*, "taken from among men, is ordained for men in the things that appertain to God, that He may offer up gifts and sacrifices for sins. . . . Neither doth any man take the honour to himself, but he that is called by God, as Aaron was."[2] Such is the

---

[1] *Epistle to the Colossians*, I, 26. The French version of the last part of the text may be rendered as follows: "in whom you have the hope of glory."

[2] *Epistle to the Hebrews*, V, I-4.

general idea of the priesthood which we propose to use as our
basis for the study of the Mystery of Christ. To explain the
implications of such a definition, we shall first however treat
briefly of the rôle of religion and of the priesthood in the moral
life of humanity.

Of all the beings to be found in our material universe, man
alone, because of the fact that he is endowed with intelligence,
is capable of knowing God, and of realizing his dependence on
Him. The superiority of his nature, which enables him to
transcend the domain of material things and rise to what is
spiritual and invisible, imposes on him the duty of acknowledging
the rights of the Creator, of returning thanks for all the benefits
he receives from Him, and of asking Him for whatever is necessary
for his further progress in this life. This recognition of God as
Author and Absolute Master of all things, Dispenser of every
gift, finds expression with man in adoration, thanksgiving and
petition. These relations of man with his Creator are the essential
constituents of his religion and his worship.

Though man has a spiritual soul, he is also sentient and corporeal. He must therefore exteriorize the sentiments of his soul in
an appropriate way. God has given him power over the world of
inferior creatures. They are at his disposal, and he has the right to
use them for the preservation and development of his physical
life. He can, accordingly, employ them also as the visible signs
of his homage and his cult. This is the reason for the exterior
liturgy, composed of oblations and sacrifices, which is to be met
with in most religions, and which for man is the natural expression
of his interior worship.

Again, man is by nature a social being. He is incapable of
procuring by himself the multiple goods that help him along the
path of progress and perfection. He necessarily forms part of
groups that are organized and graded in a visible, exterior
manner, family, tribe, people or nation. He must therefore offer
homage to God not only as an individual, but also as a member of
a duly-constituted society, for he owes to God the homage of his
whole being, social as well as individual. Nay more, as part of a
whole, his external acts have a repercussion on the whole and by
that very fact come under the control of an organized group.
Thus it is easy to understand that the exterior religion of a man
can be established in stable fashion only in the form of a social
cult uniting in the same act of homage every individual of the same
group.

We thus come to the first idea of the priesthood. As man in his
social capacity has to render to God an external cult, this cult
like society itself, must be organized, and must be carried out in
the name of all by someone specially authorized, who will
gather, as it were, into his own hands, the prayers of all, to
present them to God. "The priest is ordained for men in the things
that appertain to God." If we were to restrict ourselves to natural

religion, it would seem the normal thing for the head of the family, or the patriarch of the tribe, or the prince of the people, thus to approach God in the name of all those subject to Him.

But we must take account of Revelation and the supernatural order to which it has pleased God to raise His rational creatures. On this new and higher plane on which man finds himself from the beginning, it is no longer to God as known by reason that he must give homage, but to God as revealing Himself to man in the profound mystery of His Inner Life and demanding a corresponding faith on man's part. The essential conditions of man's worship of God are not thereby subverted; they are only transposed and adapted to the new order of things. Man, instead of approaching God in a servile attitude, with the fear and lowly submission of a creature to his Creator, offers his adoration in faith, hope and charity, with the childlike sentiments of one specially loved and cared for by God, and destined to live for ever in the divine intimacy. He will still continue, of course, to express his worship of God exteriorly and in socially organized fashion, but by man's elevation to the supernatural state the priesthood will have gained in worth and dignity. It will belong to God, if such is His good pleasure, to determine the liturgical forms of supernatural worship. It will equally belong to Him to set up the requisite hierarchy, and to designate and consecrate the priest who is to offer oblations and sacrifice in the name of the people. Thus in the Mosaic Law, we find God Himself instituting the Levitical cult and establishing the priesthood of Aaron. Hence St. Paul writes in the *Epistle to the Hebrews:* "Neither doth any man take the honour (of the priesthood) to himself, but he that is called by God as Aaron was."

There is besides another element which gives a very special character to the worship rendered by man to the God of Revelation. I refer to sin. Man is a sinner, and he has to present himself as such before God. Before he can be certain that his homage and adoration are acceptable to Him whom he has offended, and before he can claim the right to ask for fresh gifts in prayer, it is indispensable that he should obtain pardon. Hence the sacrifices for sin, the expiations and the purifications which characterize his worship. Sin places man more completely still at the mercy of God. God is the Master, offended in His Honour and His Beneficence. He has the right to exact reparation to the full extent He deems sufficient. He Himself has consequently the right to determine the type and the number of victims whose oblation will constitute in His eyes a genuine satisfaction for sin. Above all He has the right to designate the priest who can represent sinful humanity with some hope of seeing his intercession and his worship favourably received. No one could dare presume himself worthy to intercede with God for fallen humanity, if he were not so authorized by God Himself. The priest must then of a truth, be he who, "taken from among men, is ordained for men in the things that appertain to God, that he may offer up gifts and sacrifices for sins."

Now the High-Priest thus chosen by God to pray in the name of fallen humanity, and to present to Him the sacrifice of intercession and pardon, is Jesus Christ. He alone has power to draw near to God in order to obtain our return to grace. He alone can institute that perfect worship by which our homage and adoration can once more ascend to the Most High and be certain of finding favour in His sight. It is true that before the coming of Christ, God allowed man to pay Him homage and offer Him worship, especially in accordance with the rite established by the Mosaic Law. But such worship derived all its value from the future religion of Christ, of which it was the forerunner and the symbol. "For the Law brought nothing to perfection, but a bringing-in of better hope, by which we draw nigh to God."[1] With the coming of Christ, symbols disappeared to make way for reality. There was henceforth but one Priest and one form of worship by which humanity could definitively bring about its return to God.

In these pages we shall apply ourselves to the study of this Sovereign Priesthood of Jesus Christ. Our first task will be to discover whence came this prerogative to Christ, what is its basis, and what are the powers conferred on Him by it, for "Christ did not glorify himself that He might be made a High-Priest." Then we shall examine how Christ exercised the functions of His Priesthood, and how He instituted the worship which He offers to God on behalf of the human race. Lastly, we shall see how this worship and this Priesthood are perpetuated here below amongst us, and how they find their consummation in the glory of the elect in heaven, who are eternally united with their High-Priest, with Him to sing for ever the praises of the all-merciful God.

---

[1] *Epistle to the Hebrews*, VII, 19.

PART I

CHAPTERS I-VI

OUR DESTINY IN CHRIST.

> "But of Him are you in Christ
> Jesus, who of God is made unto us
> wisdom, and justice, and sanctifica-
> tion, and redemption."
> (*First Epistle to the Corinthians, I, 30.*)

CHAPTER I

THE PRIESTLY VOCATION OF CHRIST

An Inquiry into the Purpose of the Incarnation.

If we are to understand the place of honour which Christ's Priesthood holds in His life-work, it is of supreme importance to study first of all the ends which God had in view in the Incarnation. In point of fact, on the motive that induced God to come down and dwell in our midst, must depend the signification and nature of the mission confided to Christ, as well as His rôle with regard to men. It may perhaps be objected with St. Paul that "the judgments of God are incomprehensible and His ways unsearchable." Doubtless they are. And yet the Apostle does not hesitate to write in the same passage: "God hath concluded all in unbelief, that He may have mercy on all,"[1] thus casting a vivid light on the profound reason for the Incarnation of the Son of God.

The plans of God cannot remain entirely hidden from us. His aims are necessarily in conformity with what He Himself is, and when we know Him, we can always ascertain to some extent at least, the nature and general import of His works. Moreover, every effect, when carefully examined, infallibly reveals in some degree the intention of its author. The workman cuts stones in different sizes according to the place they are destined to occupy in the building. Creatures likewise have their place assigned them in the order of the universe according to their nature; this rank determines the rôle they are to fulfil here below. It is very much to the point, then, to understand the nature of the Incarnation if we are to appreciate the purposes which God had in view in bringing it about.

The Meaning of an End and a Determining Motive.

It is one thing to aim at an end, and quite another to make up one's mind to pursue it for some special motive. In all our proceedings we seek what we consider to be *good* for us. The good is the end which determines our activities. At the same time the ways of attaining it are so numerous that our choice of a course of action from among them must be for well-defined motives. Such and such an end, considered in itself, would not be sufficient in most cases to spur us on to action, if it were not presented to us surrounded by attractive features which influence us. The child determines to be good because he knows that some reward will recompense his efforts; the student who is impelled by ambition, applies himself to study with more ardour.

---

[1] *Epistle to the Romans*, XI, 32. The Westminster version has: "God hath imprisoned all alike in disobedience."

The fact is that every concrete work which demands the application of our energy presents itself to us attended by ever-varying circumstances of which we must never lose sight. These circumstances affect our decision all the more forcibly according as the task in hand offers less attraction. They furnish, then, the *determining motive* for our action. Thus the study of science is good, because it develops my mind, but if I am already equipped with some knowledge, it is not indispensable for me. However, if there are uneducated people around me whom I can instruct, my taste for teaching and my desire to be of use furnish a motive which incites me to fresh endeavours. Even while I seek an altruistic end, I none the less pursue my own chief object which I find it impossible to renounce, namely, my own intellectual perfection; and, beyond that again the *good* pure and simple.

The motive, then, which calls forth our activity, without in any way turning us aside from our ultimate object, imprints on our efforts its own particular character and gives them a special stamp: it makes them disinterested or selfish, noble or vulgar, it increases their good or lessens it. Above all it helps to modify the details of their realization in practice, by directing them towards the ultimate end according to a plan in complete harmony with the exigencies of that end.

These observations concerning human psychology have their proportionate application to the works of God. The ends which govern the divine activity here below in no way detract from God's absolute liberty. God is Himself His own end, but He is not bound to pursue this end by the production of created things. If He does so, it is for a motive He Himself freely selects, and this motive will be connected with the providential circumstances in which He has placed His creatures. "God sometimes decides," says St. Thomas, "to save a sinner because of the prayer of a just man."[1] In the same way God wills the Incarnation for some very special reason which it is important to determine.

Accordingly, the problem of the eternal designs of God with regard to Christ resolves itself first of all into an inquiry into the supreme ends to which by its very nature the Incarnation is ordained. But it is especially important to discover the motive for which God willed this mystery, for it is this motive which will determine the concrete mode of realization of the divine work and its distinctive traits.

The Ends for which God Works.

The works of God have as their source His goodness, infinitely fruitful and bountiful. The fact alone that God is *good* does not explain His producing creatures. It is because He is *Being* that God creates things, for creation means conferring existence, and one can do this only in the measure in which one exists oneself. But it is the good which is aimed at, that controls action; it

---

[1] *Summa Theol.*, IIIa P., Q.I., a. 3, ad. 4.

draws to itself the beings that possess it only in germ, and when it has been successfully assimilated, it inclines them to diffuse goodness to others. Love is the word for this double movement by which a being, under the influence of the good, progresses towards its perfection and then proceeds in its turn to communicate its goodness to others.

For God of course, there can be no question of progress; all goodness and perfection are concentrated in Him. But if it is true that the perfect being, by reason of its inherent goodness, is impelled to pour out the excess of its treasures upon others, must we not thereby conclude that God will communicate His goodness to others with a lavishness and a prodigality in harmony with His perfection? Let there be no misunderstanding, however. We have already pointed out that God is supremely free with regard to the production of beings outside Himself; of course, His infinite perfection seems to call for a display of infinite fruitfulness, but it is in the bosom of the Divine Essence, by the Trinity of Persons, that this infinite fecundity is realized. The mysterious relations, by which the Father begets the Son, and the Father and the Son breathe forth Subsistent Love, the Holy Spirit, give full satisfaction to the longing for diffusion which springs from the possession of Infinite Goodness. Thus, thanks to revelation, we see in the Blessed Trinity the normal and necessary blossoming forth, so to say, of the Divine Nature.

Accordingly, creation cannot be considered as the inevitably necessary result of the goodness of God communicating itself. Since God communicates Himself infinitely and incessantly in the Blessed Trinity, the limitless exigencies of Divine Goodness are satiated. Nothing can compel God to operate outside Himself, and the difficulty really is to find a legitimate and sufficient reason for creation. It is to be noted, however, that to do so we have not to abandon the principle already stated: "goodness is essentially diffusive of itself." After having given Himself in the measure of His capacity, that is, without measure, there still remains for God the possibility of giving Himself outside the circle of His own Being, within limits imposed, of course, not by the nature of the Divine Goodness, but by the inherent conditions of created beings.

The infinite communication which takes place within the bosom of the Divinity, does not change the nature of God. He always remains Goodness Itself, whose nature it is to bestow. This gift of Himself outside Himself is unnecessary, and, as it were, useless, from God's point of view. But it is not utility which a loving heart and, above all, He who is Love Itself, has in view when He gives Himself to others. It is the giving purely and simply, and, even when there is no necessity to exercise His beneficence, love impels Him to bestow and to express the inner feelings of His Heart, because of His own very plenitude and superabundance. So that, though there is nothing in God to render creation compulsory, nor is there even a positive fitness or congruity that He should create, nevertheless, it is obvious that His exterior works are a possible expression of His Goodness and of His Love, and that they cannot be explained in any other way.

Thus creation is a work of love, but of a love transcendent, absolutely free and disinterested. If we add to that the fact that in drawing close to creatures, God does not cease to love Himself, we have thus reached the supreme end which guides Him in all His works. God certainly loves Himself, and because He loves Himself, He bestows goodness in creating, for He is Infinite Goodness, and it is of the nature of goodness to diffuse itself. It is impossible for Infinite Love to have as object anything other than Infinite Goodness. God simply cannot give and show love without having Himself as end. God gives and by the communication He makes of Himself to creatures, He draws them to Himself who is the sole possible end of every being. The first gift of God to His creature—existence—is also the first step it makes towards Him, by its ascent from nothingness to reality; all the other perfections with which He adorns it as time goes on are but successive stages in its steady return to Him.

Thus all nature having come forth from the Goodness of God, turns back unceasingly towards this same Goodness, to manifest and proclaim it. The glory of God is nothing else than this manifestation. It finds expression in the essential movement of all that is, by which it is ordained to God, a movement of love, a song of praise, provoked by Infinite Goodness, the principle and the term of all goodness and all love.

The Ends of the Incarnation.

These general remarks on the works of God will help us straightway to a sound appreciation of the ends of the Incarnation. Looking at things solely from the point of view of Divine Wisdom, one naturally hesitates to think that it would be becoming for God, after having created intellectual natures, to raise them by grace or by the Hypostatic Union, to the supernatural order for which, of themselves, they were not fitted. Without presuming to sit in judgment on the Divine Plan, does it not seem that a universe, where intelligent beings could normally and harmoniously develop all their faculties, govern the beings inferior to them, and direct them towards their end would be a perfect image of Infinite Wisdom?

Such problems are readily solved when we put ourselves at God's point of view—that of Goodness and Love. Above and before all, God made creatures in order to communicate Himself to them. That, however, in no wise excludes the rights of His Wisdom, but His Wisdom is primarily at the service of His Love. Looking at creation in this light one cannot see what could hold God back in the out-pouring of His benefits. Created natures have their limits which they cannot overstep, but God can open out fresh fields to their activity. And if, in this, Divine Goodness shows Itself more than liberal, is not such liberality worthy of It? For example, is it not fitting that God's grace should elevate intellectual creatures to an assimilation with the Divinity, by which they become participants in the Nature and the Inner Life of their own Creator?

Nay, more: the order of grace, lofty though it be, only assimilates us creatures to God in a purely relative way, in the order of knowledge and love. We do not become God: we are divinized only in our spiritual operations. Our participation in the Divine Nature is, ontologically, but an accident. Is it possible to dream of a more perfect union of man with God, a union which will be not merely accidental but substantial? Can man be God without ceasing to be man; can he be at the same time God and man?

Faith answers that this is possible, and we shall see later on how it is to be understood without running the risk of contradiction. Since it is possible, it is in harmony with the tendency of Divine Goodness. Divine Wisdom will also approve, but above all Divine Love will find satisfaction therein, for it will be for God the sovereign communication of Himself to His creatures, the highest degree of the diffusion and gift of Self.

The Incarnation, then, like all that comes from the hand of God, has its source and *raison d'être* in His Infinite Goodness. It has its final end there, too, or rather, on account of the unity of the divine work, the Incarnation synthesizes and completes in marvellous fashion the ascent of all creatures towards God. In Christ, as Cajetan, the celebrated commentator on St. Thomas, remarks, all creation—material, organic and spiritual—is substantially united to the Divinity, because man is an epitome of all creation. St. Paul says that it was God's good pleasure to "re-establish all things in Christ, that are in Heaven or on the earth";[1] He is the summit of the holy mountain towards which the beings of all time and place converge, to give utterance to that "praise of His glory,"[2] so completing the inevitable tendency of every diffusion of the Divine Goodness.

This elevation of Christ by the Hypostatic Union, to the highest pinnacle of creation, evidently procures for His Humanity an unparalleled glory. Not only does it confer on Him a primacy of pre-eminence over all creatures, but even a primacy of finality.[3] As St. Thomas loves to repeat, the imperfect is for the perfect, the inferior creatures are at the service of the superior ones. By

[1] *Epistle to the Ephesians*, I, 10.

[2] *Ibid.*, I,12.

[3] The elevation of Christ's Human Nature by its personal union with the Eternal Son of God not only confers on Him a pre-eminence over all creatures but even effects that it is through Him and by Him they attain their final end. (Translator's note).

the Incarnation all things are subject to Christ and Christ to God.[1] Thus we have a clear view of the essential elements of the Divine Plan concerning the mystery of the Incarnation. We can see that the Incarnation seems ordained to a twofold end; one immediate and intrinsic so to speak, to the divine work—the glory of Christ; the other more extrinsic but supreme and the reason of the former—the glory of God.[2]

The Incarnation was not Necessary.

It must be remarked that the two ends mentioned above are imposed by the very nature of the mystery, independently of the particular way in which God determined to realize it. Supposing that man had not sinned, and that God had sent His Son into the world to crown the work of creation by becoming incarnate, these two ends, the glory of Christ and the glory of God would still have been attained. God would not have willed the Incarnation without at the same time aiming at His glory, through the glory of Christ. But that does not imply that we can consider the Incarnation as necessarily willed by God, or hold that He was obliged to crown and complete the work of creation by the Hypostatic Union. God cannot be forced to produce anything outside Himself. His liberty in respect to what is extrinsic to Him is absolute. Certainly there exists between certain creatures a necessary relation of which Providence must take account; if God creates corporeal living beings, He owes it to Himself to provide them with the nourishment they require for their subsistence. But such a relation does not exist between Christ and the world. The Hypostatic Union belongs to the Supernatural Order. It

---

[1] Cf. *I Epistle to the Corinthians*, XV, 27, 28.

[2] In the *Epistle to the Hebrews*, I, 3, St. Paul, after having said that God, who had spoken in the past by the prophets, had spoken to the Apostles' generation by His Son, continues as follows: "Who being the brightness of His glory, and the figure of His substance, and upholding all things by the word of His power, making purgation of sins sitteth on the right hand of the majesty on high." In his Commentary on this verse St. Thomas writes: "Three things render a man fit to attain a lofty dignity. The first is Wisdom. 'The wise shall possess glory.' (Proverbs, III, 35). The Apostle therefore extols the wisdom of Christ as the splendour of God's glory. According to St. Ambrose, glory is a clear perception of excellence expressing itself in a spontaneous song of praise and jubilation. It is as it were a manifestation of what one has come to know of somebody's goodness. We know that God is Goodness Itself. He is essentially good, all other things being entitled to be called good owing to their having some share in that goodness of which He is the Source. Thus to God alone glory belongs *par excellence*. Now the Word of God is the splendour or effulgence of the Wisdom by which God knows Himself. Therefore the Apostle calls the Son the splendour of glory, that is the dazzling manifestation of the perfect knowledge which God has of His own Goodness. If the 'sitting on the right hand' refers to Our Lord's Divine Nature, the meaning is that He is co-equal with the Father. If it refers to Our Lord's human nature, the meaning is that He is in enjoyment of all the most precious gifts the Father can bestow, as He is the one mediator with royal dignity drawing all things lovingly to God" (*Comment. in Ep. ad Hebraeos*, Cap. I., Lect. II., passim). (Translator's note).

transcends the power and natural desire of all creatures. It even transports us beyond the realms of Sanctifying Grace. Accordingly, just as it is not imperative for the divine wisdom to perfect the order of nature by the order of grace, so is it in no way imperative that both these orders receive their consummate perfection by the Hypostatic Union. As we have already seen, the Incarnation finds its *raison d'être* not so much in Creative Wisdom as in Divine Love, a Love essentially communicative of Itself. But this Divine Love, by reason of the plenitude of the Divine Essence and the perfection of the Three Persons, finds complete happiness in the bosom of the Divinity, and has absolutely no need to pour Itself out on extrinsic objects.

The theologians and pious authors, who follow Duns Scotus and the Franciscan School, appear to be in error, then, in declaring that the limitless love of the all-wise God demanded the realization of the Incarnation, and that, even without the Fall, it was fitting that God should crown His work by uniting Himself personally to human nature. This seems in some degree to run counter to that sovereign liberty of God, who brings into existence the world He wishes, and can in no way be obliged to create the best possible world.

The Divine Decree concerning the Incarnation.

One might, indeed, be inclined to think that the act of the Divine Will concerning the Incarnation had of itself complete efficacity, independently of the circumstances in which the mystery was to be realized. Thus God, having decreed the Incarnation, could not fail to bring it about in any event. This line of reasoning is, however, completely at fault with regard to the nature of the Divine Decrees.

Even in the order of our human activity, in which prudence must govern our lives and guide us in fulfilling the rational ideal which we are meant to attain, our determinations to act are never really effective except we take into account all the possible lines of conduct. At the root of all prudent action, there must be a knowledge and love of the end which we pursue; but before the knowledge and desire can realize the longed-for ideal, they must discover the means of reaching it. They must make a choice between the different ways that lie open, foresee the circumstances that are likely to present themselves, and the obstacles that may impede progress. And when this preliminary work has been accomplished, when the plan of action has been drawn up and determined upon, there still remains for us the necessity of a definite decision to go ahead and execute it. It is in presence of this final decision, which brings to a head all the preceding considerations—and in it alone—that we are face to face with the effective determination to realize the plan proposed at the outset.

To God, of course, we do not ascribe those successive acts of intelligence and will that mark our advance towards a final decision. God has not to pick and choose amongst the means that lead to the end He sets before Himself. At a single glance, He sees both the end and the means that procure it. At the same time it is none the less possible, according to our way of looking at things, to conceive a distinction in God between the willing of an end, which logically comes first, and the willing of the means, and to assert that the Divine Will is really efficacious only on condition of embracing at the same time both means and end. God knows and wills the end of all His operations—the communication of His goodness. He is perfectly well aware of the multiple ways of attaining that end. Amongst them He selects those that suit Him, and arranges them according to His good pleasure. At the same instant He has before Him in the fullest detail the circumstances that will arise, circumstances which He either wills or permits, and which He incorporates into the plan outlined by His immeasurable wisdom. It is in presence of this whole synthesis of things foreseen and determined that God decides to act, that is to say, to create or to produce. This decision represents the Divine Decree of His Providence or His Predestination.

Thus the decree by which God decides effectively to realize something presupposes the arrangement of the plan of its realization in its minutest details. If God contented Himself with merely conceiving or simply willing the end and the means in a general way, without descending into the details of the plan for execution, He would only have what theologians call an *antecedent will*, which does not imply fulfilment. It is in this sense that we say that God wishes all men to be saved, although in actual fact all are not saved .. As long as God's will is not expressed in a decree of His Providence, it is not really efficacious; it is not a *consequent* will.[1]

Conversely, every efficacious act of willing an end on the part of God is realized. It may happen in the sphere of our activity that, after having really willed to achieve some end, we are

---

[1] To explain God's manner of willing, we, on account of the limitations of our minds, have to think of God's will as if it had certain divisions, though in reality it has none. Theologians speak of God's Antecedent and Consequent Will. The *Antecedent Will* (*voluntas antecedens, voluntas secundum quid*) is exercised when God wills something in the abstract and apart from its concrete circumstances. It is conditional, that is, it will produce its full effect if certain conditions are fulfilled. By the *Consequent Will* (*voluntas consequens, voluntas simpliciter*), God wills something in its concrete circumstances, and apart from these He would not have wished it. This act of will is absolute.

It should not be thought, however, that the Antecedent Will is a mere sterile desire producing no effect. For instance God wills the salvation of all men (antecedently), and He prepared means of salvation that are sufficient for all. God willed that the Jewish Nation would accept His Son (Antecedent Will), and He gave them sufficient grace to do so, but they rejected Him, and God permitted that rejection (Consequent Will). What God permits He does not really want to happen, He merely wishes not to hinder its occurrence. Cf. Ia P., Q. XIX, A. 6, ad. 1; in I Sent., dist. 46, a. 1; dist. 47, a 1-3; De Veritate, 23, 2; 28, 3, ad. 15 (Translator's Note).

brought to a standstill by unexpected difficulties in carrying out our plans and lack the courage to persevere. Again, obstacles, which could not have been foreseen, may force us to modify our entire plan, just when we were ready to proceed to action. This is due to our inability to have present before our mind's eye the whole order and sequence of our enterprises, as well as to the instability of our wills. The lack of certitude in our intelligence is, of course, a source of weakness for the will. "For the thoughts of mortal men are fearful and our counsels uncertain."[1] But at the eternal instant that God decides to take action, He does so with full knowledge of the means He will adopt and the circumstances in which that action will take place. What He once resolves upon, He infallibly brings to pass.

On the question of the Incarnation, then, we must hold that God efficaciously willed this work of love only in the particular manner in which it came about. The mode of its realization was that the Word should be united to a body capable of enduring suffering and death; that, after a life of labour and apostleship for us, He should suffer and die to reconcile us with God. Such was the plan of the Incarnation, including within its scope both sin and the redemption of mankind. What God willed effectively in the eternal decree of His Providence was not the Incarnation considered in the abstract, but the Incarnation of the Word, in a human body exposed to suffering and death, therefore in the conditions brought about by the Fall. Hence the Incarnation as decreed in the concrete was directed towards the redemption and the salvation of the human race by the suffering and death of the Cross. Sin is no mere accidental circumstance, overlooked by Divine Providence, coming as it were from outside to compel modification of the plan. Such an anthropomorphic way of looking at things will not meet with favour in theology. If there is sin in the world it is because God has allowed it. He neither causes nor wills sin, but He permits it for mysterious reasons known only to His Infinite Wisdom. Sin, in a certain sense, enters into the decree of Divine Providence concerning the world, as a circumstance foreseen and permitted by God that He may win glory thereby. It is an occasion for God to manifest to the world His wonderful love by raising up sinful man by the sublime expedient of the Redemption. Accordingly, to envisage the Incarnation as capable of realization under other conditions means deviating from the plan drawn up by God and leaving the decree of His Providence out of account. It results merely in the formulation of a pure supposition.

The Glory of Christ in the Incarnation.

Nevertheless, even if the Incarnation, in its concrete reality, was decreed in view of original sin and for the salvation of the

---

[1] *Book of Wisdom*, IX, 14.

fallen human race, it none the less retains its supreme ends in the eyes of God. Glory obviously accrues to God from such a mystery of love and mercy, and likewise to Christ. The view we have expressed is sometimes criticized as if it lowered the Word Incarnate by assigning to Him the rôle of Saviour of a creature of inferior dignity, instead of taking due account of the fact that man is Christ's and "Christ is God's."[1] When, however, we examine things closely we cannot fail to see that the actual, integral plan of the Incarnation, instead of diminishing or obscuring the glory of Christ, increases it.

"It is certain," St. Thomas says, "that God loves Christ, not only more than the whole human race, but even more than all creatures taken together; this is proved by His decreeing for Him a greater good, assuming His human nature into union with the Divinity and giving Him 'a name that is above every other name.' This excellence is in no way diminished by the fact that God delivered Him over to death for the salvation of mankind; on the contrary, He has thereby become a glorious conqueror, and as Isaias says, 'the government is upon his shoulder' (Isaias. IX, 6)."[2]

So far as our weak intelligence can pierce into the secrets of the Divine Omnipotence, there would seem to be three chief ways in which God could realize the Incarnation.

Assuming that man had not sinned, God could have created a glorious Christ, who, by the Hypostatic Union, would have had over creation a double primacy of pre-eminence and of finality, both being indissolubly linked together. Or in the same hypothesis of sin being absent and original justice being retained by man, He could have given to Christ, in addition to that double primacy, one of efficiency, which would have enabled Him to merit grace for every spiritual creature and to be the Dispenser of all the gifts of God. In the latter case, Christ would evidently have had more glory. Or lastly, in the event of sin, God could have given Christ a primacy of efficiency—not in the sanctification of innocent creatures, as in the previous hypothesis, but in the justification of a sinful race. It is this latter plan that has been adopted and realized. In it, Christ does not effect our supernatural sanctification starting from a state of natural justice but raises us up from the state of sin into which we had fallen through the disobedience of our first parents. Such a process of justification is beyond all dispute superior to the other. If there is already a gulf, which Divine Power alone can bridge, between the natural and the supernatural orders, between nature and grace, what a yawning abyss must lie between a nature in revolt against God and the divine life of charity! A sinless creature presents no obstacle to God in the production of grace; all that is required is that the

---

[1] *First Epistle to the Corinthians*, III, 23.
[2] *Summa Theologica*, Ia P., Q. 20, a. 4, sol. 1.

Divine Power should intervene to draw the creature to God, to Whom it already tends after a certain fashion. But in the case of the sin-stained soul, God has to overcome the resistance which sin has rooted in it and which turns it away from Him. This work of mercy is more stupendous, according to St. Thomas, than creation itself.[1] And the same saint adds that "An equal gift of grace is of greater value to a sinner who has merited punishment than to a just man; just as a hundred pieces of gold is a greater gift to a beggar than to a king."[2]

Christ accomplished this work of mercy in the Redemption, not only as efficient cause, principal and ministerial, but also by His merits and satisfaction. The resultant glory far surpasses anything He could have achieved in a sinless world. What does it matter if He has not, as the Angelic Doctor teaches, a primacy of efficiency in regard to the first sanctification of the Angels and of Adam? Such a primacy would be far inferior to that conferred on Him by the Redemption. The agony and death by which Christ saves us, give Him additional glory and enhance His triumph. In the words of St. Paul: "We see Jesus who was made a little lower than the angels, for the suffering of death, crowned with glory and honour, for it became Him for Whom are all things, who hath brought many children into glory, to perfect the author of their salvation by His passion."[3] Thus the glory of Christ is so closely linked with the Redemption that without it His glory would be distinctly less.

Accordingly, the conclusion follows necessarily. Christ, the object of the Divine Plan and of the providential decree of God, is the Christ whose Incarnation in a mortal body subject to suffering is essentially ordained to the Redemption of mankind. By it He enjoys the highest glory and the triple primacy of pre-eminence, finality and efficiency in justification. The Incarnation and Redemption redounding to the glory of Christ and thence to the glory of God, such is in its full reality, the order established by God in the world.

The Determining Motive of the Incarnation.

If it is possible for us, by the study of what it necessarily entails, to get into their proper perspective the different elements of the Divine Plan, we cannot say the same about the question of the motive that impelled God to act as He did. If we take the four essential elements of the Divine Design, we can, however, exercise a certain discrimination between them with regard to this problem.

First of all, then, the Incarnation in a body subject to suffering, could not have been in God's eyes a sufficient motive for the existence of Christ. We know, of course, that it is in its concrete

---

[1] *Summa Theologica*, 2a 2ae, Q. 113, art. 9.
[2] *Summa Theologica*, 2a 2ae, Q. 20, art. 4, sol. 4.
[3] *Hebrews*, II, 9-10.

mode of realization, and not in the abstract, that we must examine the mystery of the Word made Flesh. The object of the efficacious will of God is certainly a mortal Christ capable of suffering, not Christ without any reference to concrete circumstances. The Incarnation in this light was meant essentially for the Redemption of man and the ulterior glory of Christ; it could not have been decreed for itself, as it is only a means to an end. Consequently, the only motives for which God could have decided to decree the Incarnation are: either His own glory, in the most perfect way, as the supreme manifestation of His love; or the glory of the Christ-Saviour, in Whom the perfection of the created universe would attain its zenith; or lastly, the redemption and salvation of mankind. The question then, is which of these three motive was for God the determining one.

It is very much to the point here to recall the statement of St. Thomas on the motive of the Incarnation: "Everything that depends exclusively on the Will of God, and to which the creature has no right, can be known to us only to the extent we are informed of it by Holy Scripture, because it is through the Scripture that the Divine Will is manifested to us."[1] God could have brought about the Incarnation as it has actually been realized, to set up at the summit of all creation a perfect Christ, triumphant and glorious. He could also have done so either to show forth His infinite Love, or to redeem man from his state of degradation and sin. Amongst those different hypotheses, God alone can indicate to us the secret motive that inspired Him.

Let us turn, therefore, to Revelation. To avoid mistakes, however, it is well to recall that what we want to discover is the determining motive of the Incarnation, and that, in consequence, it is absolutely necessary that Scripture or Tradition should point out exactly why the Word became Flesh. It will not be enough to find in Holy Writ texts declaring that Christ has been made "head over all the Church" (*Ephesians*, I, 22), that He is the "first-born amongst many brethren" (*Romans*, VIII, 29), that "all things are made subject to Him" (*I Corinthians*, XV, 27), that "God so loved the world as to give His only-begotten Son" (*St. John*, III, 16), in order to conclude that the primacy of Christ or the glory of God is the determining motive of the Incarnation. We are quite certain that the Incarnation has for inevitable result this primacy and this glory, all the more so, since it is realized in a body subject to suffering and death. But in the mind of God, is it precisely for the primacy and glory of Christ that the Word was made Flesh? The simple affirmation that Christ is the Head of humanity and of the entire universe and that the Incarnation is the work of Divine Love, is not sufficient to prove it. In the same way, if it were only revealed that God desired the ransom of mankind through Christ, we could not deduce from

---

[1] *Summa Theologica*, IIIa P., Q. 1, art. 3.

this that the Redemption is the determining motive of the Incarnation. Perhaps the Franciscan school of thought has not paid sufficient attention to that point. To strengthen their case they bring forward all the scriptural references to the primacy of Christ and the glory of God. To be conclusive, their argument should show us texts in which God declares explicitly that He intends to bring about the Incarnation precisely on account of the glory it gives Him, or the primacy it confers on Christ.

Everywhere both in Scripture and Tradition, we find it affirmed that the Word became Flesh for our salvation. Never do we find it said that it was precisely for the sake of the glory accruing from it to Christ and to God that God permitted sin and willed the Redemption. St. Paul is quite definite that "God hath concluded all in unbelief, that He may have mercy on all."[1] The mercy which the Apostle has in mind is the Redemption of mankind by Christ. "For whom He foreknew, He also pre-destinated to be made conformable to the image of His Son; that He be the first-born among many brethren."[2] This Divine Criterion, however, though really present, is, as it were, secon-dary. It fades into the background before the insistence with which we find it repeated that Christ came among men to redeem them from sin. A rapid survey of the scriptural texts dealing with the question will dispel all doubt on this point.[3] One cannot fail to notice how the idea of salvation is brought into relief by the four Evangelists. "I came not to call the just but sinners,"[4] said Our Lord. He could have asked His Eternal Father to save Him from the sorrowful hours of His Passion, but" for this I came into the world."[5] "It is quite certain," writes Pere Lagrange, in his commentary on this text, "that 'for this' must not be understood of what is to come after, that is to say, of the glorification, but of the death immediately foreseen, of which His trouble of soul is, as it were, the forerunner." The very name of Jesus, imposed by God, and expressing the Divine Will with regard to Christ, means Saviour. "God," says St. John, "sent not His Son into the world, to judge the world, (a prerogative of His primacy), but that the world may be saved by Him."[6]

St. Paul, speaking of the reign of Christ, conceives it as a reign at once militant and life-giving, which is to come to an end with the world. He stresses this aspect, leaving in the background the triumphant reign in heaven, as if it were the less important and as if the essential rôle of Christ was to be Saviour of mankind.[7]

---

[1] *Epistle to the Romans*, XI, 32.
[2] *Ibid.* VIII, 29.
[3] These texts are to be found in the *Dictionnaire de Théologie catholique*, article *Incarnation*, col. 1483 and foll.
[4] *St. Mark*, II, 17.
[5] *St. John*, XII, 27.
[6] *St. John*, III, 17.
[7] *Epistle to the Corinthians*, XV, 20-28. Cf. article of Pere Lemonnyer, *Xenia Thomistica*, II, pp. 311-318.

Patristic texts are in no way less precise than those of Scripture.[2] It is easy to understand why the Church, the authentic exponent of Revealed Truth, expresses her faith in the following terms in the Nicene Creed: "I believe . . . in the only Son of God, who . . . *for us men and for our salvation,* came down from heaven, and was made man."

We may conclude then that, so far as the Divine Intentions have been made known, the redemption of the human race is the veritable motive which induced God to will the Incarnation of His Son. Such is the opinion of St. Thomas: "Since throughout the Scriptures the motive given for the Incarnation is the sin of the first man, it is preferable to say that the Incarnation was ordained by God as a remedy for sin, in such a way that were it not for sin there would have been no Incarnation."[2] Our minds find complete satisfaction in this solution. Certainly, if the primary determining motive of the Incarnation were to procure the highest possible glory for Christ, then we would be forced to admit that God permitted sin—sin with its dreadful appanage of suffering, death and danger of eternal damnation,—for no other reason than to procure the glory of a specially favoured being, to set up as Head of the universe a perfect Christ, but a Christ owing His perfection in part to our fall.

How much more convincing is the doctrine that sees in the salvation of man the chief motive of the Incarnation! God allowed us to fall, it is true, but the heart of God was immediately moved at the sight of our misery. It provoked mercy, and Divine Mercy decreed the Incarnation. "But when the goodness and kindness of God our Saviour appeared, He saved us, not by the works of justice, which we have done, but according to His mercy,"[3] God stooped down to His sinful creature; through pity for him He determined that Christ should suffer, and, by suffering, gain a glory calculated to elevate Him above men and angels, for "it became God, for Whom are all things, and by Whom are all things, who hath brought many children into glory, to perfect the author of their salvation, by His passion."[4] So that in the last analysis we must always return to the explicit statement of the Apostle: "God hath concluded all in unbelief, that He may have mercy on all."[5]

The Motive of the Incarnation and the Priesthood of Christ.

In spite of its great length, this study of the plan governing the Incarnation has not led us away from the subject of our work—

---

[1] Cf. *Dictionnaire de Théologie,* Art. *Incarnation.*
[2] *Summa Theologica,* IIIa P., Q. 1, art. 3.
[3] *Epistle to Titus,* III, 4-6.
[4] *Epistle to the Hebrews,* II, 10.
[5] *Rom.* IX, 32. Commenting on this verse and the preceding one in his *Commentary on the Epistle to the Romans,* St. Thomas writes: "Because God wanted His mercy through Christ to be exercised towards all kinds of men, He allowed the whole human race, Jews and Gentiles, to be enchained in incredulity, to be bound as it were with a chain of error." (Translator's note).

the Priesthood of Christ. On the contrary, it will help us to a fuller understanding of the pride of place which His Priesthood holds in the Divine Plan. If it is correct—and we think we have proved it—that the chief purpose of Christ's coming is to redeem us, it is lawful to conclude that Jesus, by the providential decree of God in His regard, is before all else Sovereign High-Priest of humanity. The rôle of Redeemer and Saviour is properly that of Priest. What exactly is the rôle of Christ on earth? He is called upon to repair, to the full extent demanded by justice, the offences committed by man. He has to offer to God, through the suffering and death of the Cross, a complete satisfaction which will make the dew of Divine Mercy descend upon sinful humanity. Finally, as well as satisfying the demands of God's justice, Christ has to merit for man and confer on him those divine graces and benefits which will restore to him the supernatural holiness he had forfeited.

Jesus, therefore, fulfils to the letter the rôle of Mediator. He stands between God and man to send up to God the sinner's cry for pardon and to call down on man the benefits of Divine Mercy. Now what else is a priest but an official mediator, chosen by God to link together earth and heaven?

Expressed in still more precise terms, the mission of salvation confided to Christ by God consists in this—that He should unite all men with Himself in the union of His Mystical Body, and after purifying them from sin and sanctifying them by grace, that He should cause to ascend towards God that praise of His glory which every creature owes to its Creator, and which man must necessarily express in an exterior way by the offering of sacrifice. Now only a priest who is acceptable to God can offer the sacrifice and institute the worship, due from humanity; for, by definition, the priest "is ordained for men in the things that appertain to God, that he may offer up gifts and sacrifices for sins."[1]

The eternal destiny of Christ, by dedicating Him to the salvation of men, makes of Him the one perfect Priest of humanity. "Wherefore when He cometh into the world he saith, 'sacrifice and oblation thou would'st not, but a body thou hast fitted to me: holocausts for sin did not please thee. Then said I: behold I come: that I should do Thy will, O God'. . . . In the which will we are sanctified by the oblation of the body of Jesus once: for by one oblation, He hath perfected forever them that are sanctified."[2]

It stands out clearly, then, that the real motive of the Incarnation is the Priesthood of Christ. In saying this, we give to the mystery its full value and its complete significance, for Christ, through His Priesthood, has not only to redeem and sanctify humanity, but also to lead it to the feet of God and offer it in homage to His Sovereign Majesty for His greater glory. By

[1] *Epistle to the Hebrews*, V, 1.
[2] *Ibid.* X, 5-14.

making the Priesthood of Christ the determining motive of the Incarnation, we make clear the fact that the Incarnation is immediately ordained to the Redemption: but we do not fail to point out that it is directed no less to the supreme ends, towards which all Divine Action necessarily aims.

The mission of Christ is sacerdotal, His vocation, that of High-Priest: The Incarnation is decreed by God to enable Him to fulfil His sublime rôle. This is the inevitable conclusion that must be drawn. It remains for us, however, to consider the intimate relation existing between the priestly vocation of Christ and His Incarnation. It is not without very special and very profound reasons that God decided that He who was to be vested with the dignity of Sovereign Priest, should in His human nature be personally united to the Second Person of the Blessed Trinity. In His providential designs, God does not generally confer a dignity or a mission without simultaneously elevating the recipient to a state of perfection and sanctity suited to the rôle he is called upon to play. Christ was the one perfect Priest of the only religion now possible. As He was destined to promote the glory of God by redeeming the human race, it was fitting that He should be consecrated by God as Supreme Priest, that He should be clothed with the sanctity befitting His office, that He should be equipped with the powers required for the fulfilment of His function. The Incarnation was, in fact, perfectly adapted to these different requirements, and we shall now turn to the consideration of them.

Chapter II

THE SACERDOTAL CONSECRATION OF CHRIST

The Divine Sonship of Christ and His Priesthood.

"Christ," says St. Paul," did not glorify Himself that he might be made high-priest. He received this glory from Him who said Thou art my son."[1] Later in the same Epistle, the Apostle declares that "the law maketh men priests, who have infirmity: but the word of the oath, which was since the law, maketh the Son who is perfected for evermore."[2] These sentences from the Epistle to the Hebrews throw a vivid light on the Priesthood of Christ. By linking it with the Divine Filiation of Jesus, they set forth its essential foundation and ultimate basis. Jesus is Son of God, not in the same way as the elect are children of God through sanctifying grace, but in a sense that is unique and transcendent. He is Son, not only as God in all things like to His Father, but also as Man, being personally united to the Second Person of the Blessed Trinity. And on account of this Divine Sonship, whose splendour is shared by His human nature, He is constituted Priest of the Most High from the first moment of His conception. For, on the other hand, it is certain that the Priesthood of Jesus belongs to Him as Man and not as God. "Every high priest is taken from amongst men." He stands as official mediator between God and men; one cannot conceive God Himself in His Divinity acting as intermediary between Himself and His creatures. But it is no less certain, on the other hand, that if Christ, as man, has a right to the title of Son of God, this is because of the Hypostatic Union between the Word and human nature, brought about by the Incarnation. A study of the Hypostatic Union is, therefore, necessary for us, if we are to make manifest the relations between the Divine Sonship of Jesus and His Priesthood.[3]

The Hypostatic Union.

The Catholic Church, the sole authentic interpreter of the Revelation made by God to man, teaches us that in Jesus there are two natures, the Divine and the human, and that these two are substantially united in the Person of the Word, the Son of God, begotten of the Father by an eternal generation. This ineffable union is called the Hypostatic Union. It neither confuses nor destroys the natures, but unites them in such a way that there is but a single subsistent being, a single person.

---

[1] *Epistle to the Hebrews*, V, 5.
[2] *Epistle to the Hebrews*, VII, 28.
[3] The Hypostatic Union means the union of the Divine Nature and the human nature of Christ in the unity of His Divine Person. Hypostatic, therefore, is equivalent to personal. (Translator's Note).

From created things one may easily form some idea of what is meant by the union of different natures in the unity of a single person. Experience brings before us many individual substances displaying a well-defined unity and a real autonomy. Certain other substances on the contrary, seem to be what they are, only because they are linked with other substances and form with them a single independent whole. The eye, the hand, and the heart are examples of the latter class; they are not complete, autonomous substances, but rather substantial parts of a being in which they are united into the organic unity of the whole body. Men and animals, on the other hand, are substances in the full sense, complete and perfect, each in its own way lacking nothing of what is required for independent existence. Substances of this kind receive the name of *hypostases* or *supposita,* but the special name of *person* is reserved exclusively for intellectual substances, such as angels and men.

This *autonomy or independence in being and in action,* designated in most cases by the abstract term, *subsistence,* is therefore the special characteristic of a *suppositum* or a person, for to subsist means to exist in or by oneself. The substantial parts which go to make up a *suppositum* evidently do not exist by themselves. It is rather the *suppositum* which subsists in and by them, so as to form with them one being, an autonomous or independent whole.

Since there is question here of the unity of one real substantial being, it is important to distinguish clearly between unity of nature and unity of subsistence or unity of personality. The soul and the body are substantial parts of one and the same human being. Instead of each by itself being a complete nature, the result of their reciprocal tendencies and mutual union is the formation of a single human nature, the soul being related to the body as form is to matter, as actualtiy is to potentiality.[1] But at the moment that soul and body come together to form one nature, this union in point of fact results in the constitution of an independent autonomous being, a *suppositum,* a person subsisting by himself, a man. There is therefore realized in the union of the soul and the body both a unity of nature and a unity of subsistence or personality.

In the union of nature we are in the presence of a synthesis of the essential elements of a being, and which enter into its formal

---

[1] The words *matter* and *form* in Scholastic philosophy have a meaning quite different from that which they have in popular language to-day. The use has been almost inverted. People speak of *matter* as representing what is real, actual or important, as opposed to the *form,* which is considered to be something unreal and unimportant, or to imply some merely accidental change of the *matter.* For Aristotle and St. Thomas, on the contrary, *matter* meant the potential, the incomplete, the unrealized, while *form* was equivalent to full actuality, complete realization of being. It is in this latter sense that the words *matter* and *form* are used in the text. Historically, the change has been largely due to the influence of Kantian philosophy. Cf. *Psychology,* by Rev. M. Maher, S.J., p.. 560. (Translator's Note).

definition, so that if one were to suppress one of these elements, the being would lose its special nature. Thus man is essentially composed of an organized body and an intellectual soul: these two elements define the nature of man. If we suppress or change either of them, we are no longer dealing with a man. Unity of nature, then, is what makes a being indivisible in its essence and distinct essentially from others. This unity, be it remarked, in no way implies that the thing actually exists. Whether the being exists or not, its essence remains one, at least in our conception of it; it demands the combination of certain elements and excludes others. One can define it in the abstract, without raising the question of its actual existence.

Unity of subsistence, on the contrary, can only be conceived with reference to actual existence. It does not bring together the essential elements of a being: it supposes them to be present. But it has this result that, in its concrete realization, this being "stands on its own feet," that is to say, it exists without being linked up with any other substance. From the point of view of existence, unity of subsistence makes a being indivisible in itself and distinct from all others.

Subsistence, therefore, belongs to the order of realization of being: it is found in a nature or substance already complete in its essential elements. It confers on such a substance its proper mode of existence, namely, existence by itself and apart from any other substantial reality. Substance and existence are, in consequence, intimately connected. Everything that subsists, exists: and everything that exists, subsists, for, properly speaking, only substances exist, as an accident has no actuality other than that of inhering in a substance.[1] Subsistence is, in a word, the condition of unity in existing things.

These elementary philosophical notions are indispensable, if some light is to be thrown on the mystery of the Hypostatic Union. Of course, we must not expect them to apply rigorously and uniformly to the Word Incarnate: the mystery cannot be adequately expressed by human concepts. But by utilizing them we can at least form some idea of it, and by an analogous application of ideas taken from created things, we can reach the Uncreated, however inadequately.

We have said that in us body and soul come together to form a single subsistent being, a single hypostasis, a man. Similarly we can say that in Christ, the Divine and human natures are united in the unity of one subsistent being, one person—the Second Person of the Blessed Trinity. But there is a difference. The soul and the body, being incomplete natures, demand to be united essentially, before being united in the unity of a human person;

---

[1] A *Substance* is a being which by its nature demands to exist *in itself*. An *Accident* is a being which by its nature demands to exist *not in itself but in another thing*. An accident inhers in another being as in a subject, e.g. heat, colour, shape, etc. are accidents of some substance.

in Christ, on the other hand, the divine and human natures are complete and perfect: they cannot be united essentially but always remain distinct, even when they are personally joined together. Accordingly, in Christ there is not unity of nature, but unity of subsistence. Whence does this unity arise?

The human nature of Christ is essentially a complete nature and lacks no element required for its integral perfection. It possessess all the perfections which belong to it by right and which make it the most exquisite of all human natures. Of itself, like every other nature, it demands to subsist by itself, and yet, in point of fact, it does not so subsist. United to the Divine Nature, it is deprived of its proper subsistence in such wise that it forms with the Divine Nature, and in the Person of the Word, a single personal being, a single Suppositum, one Hypostasis. On its side, the Divine Nature of Christ forms with the Word but one Person; there is identity between the Person and the Nature of the Word, as there is identity between each of the Persons of the Blessed Trinity and the Divine Nature. The Three Divine Persons are one in the unity of the Divine Nature: they are really distinct as Persons but One in Nature. The Divine Nature of the Word does not lose its own personality when it is united with the human nature. On the contrary, while the Word subsists in the Divine Nature, It subsists also, from the moment of union, in the human nature. So, too, we can say that in a human being, the soul, the form of the body, of itself immortal, communicates to the body its own subsistence, and constitutes with it a human person.

At the same time it must be remarked that the soul has no existence previous to the body. At the very moment in which it is created by God, it is united to the body and subsists in it. The Word, on the other hand, pre-exists eternally in His Divine Nature, and it is only when the human nature of Christ is begotten in the womb of the Blessed Virgin Mary by the operation of the Holy Spirit, that He assumes it into the unity of His Person. The comparison best adapted to illustrate this mystery, and the one to which St. Thomas often appeals, is that of the union of the soul and body at the moment of the resurrection. The soul, which has not ceased to exist and subsist by itself, communicates to the body its own subsistence and unites it personally to itself. We must immediately add, however, that this personal union implies an essential one between soul and body, unlike the one effected in the Incarnation. Here again it is evident that every comparison is necessarily defective, when we are trying to bring home to ourselves the mysteries of God.

To sum up, then, the union of the Humanity to the Divinity is realized, in Christ, in the Person and with respect to the Person of the Word. Just as in us the soul is united to the body to form one subsistent human being, so the human nature is united to the Divine Nature, to form in the Word a single personal being at once divine and human.

The Personal Union of the Divine Nature and the Human Nature in Christ.

We would, however, have a very incomplete understanding of the Hypostatic Union if we failed to recognise that, according to Catholic doctrine, this union is substantial and not merely accidental or non-substantial. In a *suppositum* not all the component and determining elements which go to make it what it is are in it in the same way. Some of them make it a substantial whole, others give it certain secondary modifications. Thus human nature, essentially composed of a soul and a body, is constitutive of the human *suppositum* : it specifies it, making of it a real, genuine representative of the human family. Of course, the nature as such does not subsist, since of itself it has no actual and immediate relation to existence; but the *suppositum,* which subsists and exists of its own right, does so only in accordance with the essential determinations imposed upon it by the nature. The *suppositum* would be nothing itself without those determinations, which make it, as the case may be, an animal or a human or an angelic *suppositum*. But on the other had, since the *suppositum* belongs to the order of existence and realization, it gives to these determinations their actual reality. Though they specify it, it actualizes them by uniting them with itself in one subsistent whole. It subsists in them after the fashion their nature demands, in the unity of the same subsistence and the same existence. And what we say of the nature constitutive of the *suppositum,* is equally true of all the substantial parts which make of it an integral whole. The head, the hand, the eye, as well as the body, are component parts of the *suppositum;* they neither subsist nor exist by themselves, but the *suppositum* subsists in them, in accordance with the determinations they give it. It is the subsistence of the *suppositum* which confers upon them the unity of actual realization and existence that they have. And because subsistence is a modality of the substantial being, which it unifies in view of enabling it to exist, it follows that every substantial element—like the nature or the component parts of the *suppositum*—which will be united to the subsistent *suppositum,* will be substantially united to it. This substantial union in the order of subsistence is to be distinguished from substantial union in the order of essence. The latter tends to form a single nature, the former aims at constituting a substantial being with a single independent existence.

Accidental elements, like action, reaction, quantity, quality and place, which enter into the composition of a *suppositum,* are in a very different position. They are received into the *suppositum* and enjoy existence, only thanks to their inherence in it. That the *suppositum* receive these accidental elements it is necessary that it be itself already constituted and in the enjoyment of existence, so that the existence of the *suppositum* is at least prior in thought to that of the accidents which determine it. One cannot, therefore, conceive a *suppositum* to be constituted a subsistent being or given substantial existence, by an accident. The accident is superadded, so to speak, to the *suppositum*, and by qualifying or determining it in a new way, an accident adds to it a subsidiary kind of existence, but it does not give it its unity of subsistence or existence. Properly speaking, an accident does not exist; it is received into, it inheres in its subject, and all the reality it has is due to the fact that it so inheres. It modifies the subject from outside, so to say, without entering into its inner constitution, or helping to establish its subsistent unity. Once an accident is received into a *suppositum*, it is united to it merely by an accidental or non-essential union. An accident enters into union with a hypostasis or *suppositum* and forms part of the whole, but can never be the cause of the subsistence of the hypostasis or *suppositum*.

Once these distinctions are understood, it is an easy matter to see that the union of the Divine Nature and the human nature in Christ must necessarily be a substantial union. For this nature is, like any other human nature, a substance composed of a body and a soul. One can easily imagine an accidental union of the two substances, but that signifies merely an external relation of one to the other, a relation which does not destroy in them either essential unity or unity of independent existence. By an accidental or non-essential union a suit of clothes is united to the wearer of it, in the same accidental manner man is united to God by sanctifying grace. Clothes and wearer, man and God, each maintains its own subsistence, its own independent existence. This type of accidental union which Nestorius wished to apply to the Incarnation is manifestly a heresy, and has at different times been condemned by General Councils of the Church.

If there cannot be an accidental union between the Divine Nature and the human nature of Christ, then the union must be substantial. By this we mean that the human nature, like an essential element of a *suppositum*, helps to form the unique personal being called Christ. There is no question of attributing the human nature to the Person of the Word as we attribute an accident to its subject. No, the nature is united to the Word precisely from the point of view and by the bond of subsistence. In other words, the Word fulfils the same functions of subsistence in regard to the human nature and the Divine Nature, so that, being united according to one and the same mode of subsistence, they form but one and the same personal being. And since, on the other hand, a *suppositum* is determined and specified by the nature in which it subsists, where there are two natures, there are also two different determinations of a same *suppositum*. As by His Divine Nature, the Word is truly God, so by His human nature, He is truly man. The Word Incarnate is a single being, at once divine and human. He is God-made-Man, the Man-God.

Certainly, we do not mean to insinuate that by the Incarnation, the Word undergoes any change. As God, He is unchangeable. When Divine operations have a creature as object, they change the creature, not God. By the Hypostatic Union, the human nature is drawn upwards to God, comes under the influence of the Word. whose all-powerful action deprives it of its own subsistence, in order to unite it in personal union with Himself. The entire result is produced in the human nature, without any change in God. But just as we may call God Creator once He has drawn things out of nothing, though He Himself remains unchanged, so we can accurately say that the Word is man from the time He assumes human nature to subsist in it, and to unite it personally with Himself.

To sum up, we have in Christ Jesus, the Word Incarnate, a single person, subsisting from all eternity in the Divine Nature alone, then at a given point of time in a human nature also.

The Attributes of Christ's Divine and Human Natures.

A number of consequences flow from this doctrine of the Incarnation, and it is well to point them out now, as they will be of considerable help in understanding the nature of Christ's Priesthood, and its relations with the Hypostatic Union.

Firstly, since in Christ there are two natures in one Person, it follows that one may attribute to Him personally, the special attributes of each of these natures. It is equally correct to say: *Christ is eternal* and *Christ is mortal*. We have only to remember that each property is attributed to Him on account of one of the natures. Because Christ is God by His Divine Nature, and man by His human nature, and because again we speak of *Him* as *this God* or *this Man*, when we want to designate Him personally, it is possible for us to attribute to Him indifferently the properties of the two natures. We can say: *this God is man* or *this man is God; this God suffered and died*, or *this Man is the Creator of the world*. To suffer and die is proper to man but not to God, unless God be also man. But God is also man and the fact that in Christ there is but one Person, one subsistent being, as subject of all properties, now human, now divine, gives the rational explanation and justification of this manner of speaking, called in the technical language of Theology the "communication of idioms."

The Personal Attributes of Christ.

From another point of view, certain attributes of Christ belong directly to His Person, the Person of the Word, instead of owing their origin to either of His natures. Being personally the Word of God, Christ is, as such, the only Son of the Father, eternally begotten of Him. Accordingly, He is the Son of God in the strict sense of the term and in a way that surpasses that of any other adopted son. This Sonship is an attribute of His Person, and not of His nature, because in every case that which is born, that which comes into being, is the person and not merely or primarily the nature in which the person as it were clothes or manifests itself. It is therefore, the Word Himself, considered as a

Person begotten according to His Divine Nature, and not that nature itself, Who is, properly speaking, the Son of God. Therefore, as Christ is personally the Son of God, we meet His Divine Sonship wherever we find His Personality. As man, on the other hand, He is none other than the Person of the Word subsisting in a human nature, so that we say rightly that Christ as Man is really and truly the Son of God. We admit, of course, that this dignity is not His by His human conception in the womb of Mary, but by His Divine generation in the bosom of the Father. Nevertheless, on account of the Hypostatic Union, this title of Son of God belongs to Him not only as God but also as Man, for in Him both Man and God are one and the same Person, the Second Person of the Blessed Trinity.

Jesus, the Only Son of God.

We now see that the consequence of the mystery of the Incarnation is the sublime fact that a man is the only Son of God the Father. In this brief statement we condense, as it were, the full complexity of the marvellous unity of the Word with our humanity, while at the same time we express all the grandeur which this human nature has from its being assumed by the Second Person of the Blessed Trinity. The Man, Jesus, is the Son of God, in virtue of the Hypostatic Union, and therein lies His sovereign glory:"Who, being the brightness of his glory, and the figure of his substance, and upholding all things by the word of his power, making purgation of sins, sitteth at the right hand of the majesty on high: being made so much better than the angels, as he hath inherited a more excellent name than they. For to which of the angels hath he said at any time: 'Thou art my Son, to-day have I begotten thee?', and again, 'I will be to him a father, and he shall be to me a son.' "[1]

It is clear from the foregoing that the relation of the Priesthood of Christ to His Divine Sonship depends on its relation to the Hypostatic Union.

The Twofold Activity of Christ, Divine and Human.

To understand the principles which govern the exercise of His Priesthood, we must examine the twofold activity of the Son of God, His Divine Activity and His human activity. It is a universal law that, in order to act, a thing must exist. This is the sense of the saying of the Scholastic Philosophers "the mode of action follows the mode of being" or "as a thing is, so does it act." But we have seen that, strictly speaking, only substances exist, and these must subsist, if they are to exist. Genuine action, therefore, belongs exclusively to beings that subsist. Hence we have that other axiom: "Actions belong to subsistent beings."

We must not conclude, however, that, because it is subsistence that, properly speaking, constitutes the *suppositum,* that it, too, must

---

[1] *Epistle to the Hebrews,* I, 3-5.

be the source of its activity. Subsistence is a condition of action and not its source. As a simple modification of the substance, it enables a being to exist, and therefore to act. But if we are to discover the real principle of action, the primary source of activity, we must turn to the nature of the being. The nature alone possesses the powers or faculties capable of those actions by which the being reaches its perfection. St. Thomas, following Aristotle, often makes use of the expression: "the nature is the principle or source of movement."

We have already stated more than once that in a *suppositum*, it is the *nature* which plays the determining and specifying rôle. To be strictly accurate it is not the nature that subsists but the *suppositum* that subsists according to the determinations given by the nature. In a word, while the *suppositum* is "*that which*" exists, the nature is "*that by which*" or "*that in which*" something exists.

In regard to action, similar observations must be made. If the *suppositum* is "*that which exists*," it is also "*that which acts*." If the nature determines the *suppositum*, it also determines and specifies its action: the *suppositum* acts according to its nature. There is, however, this difference that, while the nature conditions the existence of the *suppositum*, the nature is not the source of that existence. Existence is due to the action of an external cause which places a being "in the world of existing things." Existence is not an essential element or a property of a thing's nature. The nature of a being, even apart from its existence, still answers to its proper definition. On the contrary, action springs from the nature as from its efficient cause. The power or faculty of acting is a property of the nature and cannot be separated from it without destroying the nature itself. With regard to the existence of the *suppositum*, the nature is, therefore, simply a condition: it is that "*by which*" the *suppositum* exists. With reference to action, on the other hand, the nature is the source from which the action flows, and which the *suppositum* utilizes. It is "*that by which*" the *suppositum* acts. In both cases, the *suppositum* exists and the *suppositum* acts: it is both subject of existence and subject of action. But, in the first case, existence comes from outside (in the case of a created *suppositum*), whereas, in the second, action has its origin in the nature itself.

The *suppositum*, acting 'according to what it is,' and by a power conferred on it by the nature, is the author of action, and, in the case of beings endowed with freedom, the responsible author. The acts of the being are attributed to it not merely morally but physically. Let us apply these principles to the case of Christ. His human nature, as we know, has no subsistence, and accordingly, no existence of its own. It is the Word that subsists and exists in and according to it. This, however, in no way implies that Christ's human nature is incomplete, because its existence is neither a component nor an essential part of a nature. There is but one existence in Christ. Christ's human nature, however, being a created nature, has the power of performing actions which have their origin in this nature. These could not be suppressed without impairing the nature itself. Of course, in order that the nature may be the source of action the Word must subsist in it, because there is neither action nor existence, if the being constituted by the nature is not subsistent. Needless to say, it is Christ, the Divine Person, who acts as man, by means of His human nature and by its faculties or powers. These faculties, none the less, continue to be human faculties. Christ, being at once God and Man, possesses different faculties of action and different kinds of action in accordance with each of His natures. The person acting is one because the *suppositum* is one: while there is a twofold action and two kinds of faculties, because of the two natures, the Divine and the human. It is true that in the Divine Nature the power of acting, the action and the *suppositum* are identically the same, but this does not lessen the distinction between action, faculty and *suppositum* in the case of the human nature, for the latter is united to the Divine Nature exclusively from the point of view of subsistence.

So in Christ we have two distinct forms of activity, corresponding to His two natures: the activity that is really and truly divine, and an activity that is really and truly human. We must guard, however, against conceiving the person as a third and higher source of activity, superimposing itself on the other two, and using them as instruments to attain its ends. The person, as a matter of fact is only a source of activity, *through* the nature by which it acts. In itself, its formal rôle is to perfect the substance in the order of being, to give it unity of subsistence. This unity is simply a condition of acting as well as of existing. So that, when we say the person or the *suppositum* acts, we mean that the concrete nature, the nature as subsisting in the person, acts, but the action emanates from the nature and not from the person.

Metaphysical Personality and Psychological Consciousness in Christ.[1]

The preceding section has prepared the way for the important distinction which must be made between the metaphysical personality of Christ and the psychological consciousness which He had of His *Ego*.[2] Human action is in the psychological order, and it is only natural that the consciousness which we have of our own inner unity and of the autonomy of our intellectual and volitional activity should give rise to what we may call our idea of ourselves. This idea is on the purely experimental plane. It does not go beyond the phenomena of consciousness, and can in no way reach the supra-experimental order which escapes our consciousness—the order of subsistence or metaphysical personality. Our

---

[1] See appendix at the end of the chapter.
[2] The word *Ego* means the whole man composed of body and soul.

activity, it is true, could never develop in its harmonious unity, without a deep foundation of being, wherein it plunges its roots and whose profound laws it reflects; our consciousness, however, perceives only the reflection. In the passing phenomena, it does not immediately grasp the substance and its metaphysical presuppositions. If our psychological consciousness is linked up with and based upon our metaphysical personality, the connection between them cannot be the subject of experimental investigation. It can only be arrived at by a process of reasoning.

Hence, when we speak of Christ's human activity, we do not deny that this intellectual and volitional activity is unified in a human, psychological consciousness, mistress of itself and able to guide itself autonomously by using all its inferior faculties. But this psychological consciousness, constituted by the phenomena of rational life, is quite a different thing from the metaphysical personality of Christ, which is constituted by the Word Itself. The rôle of the metaphysical personality is not to govern human action. That is the province of intellectual and volitional human consciousness. The Second Person of the Blessed Trinity knows and wills both by His human and His Divine Nature: apart from these natures, He does not act.[1] He is simply their principle of subsistence, their principle of unity and being.

When, therefore, Christ acts, it is unquestionably this Being, One and Subsistent, that acts. It is the Man-God, the Word, who acts, and the action belongs strictly to Him; He is its subject. This action, however, may come from the Divine or from the human nature. In the latter case, there is no reason to look for a special intervention of the Word, as God, by which He would take hold of the activity of Christ's human nature to direct it according to His good pleasure. God has only to accord to this activity the usual co-operation that He gives to every action on the part of a creature.

In other words, Christ, in acting humanly, acts as a real man. He has all the mental equipment of a perfect man; an intellect to point out the way to action, a will capable of coming to decisions freely and without constraint. Of course, this rich human activity belongs to the Word, who subsists in the nature from which they proceed. The Second Person of the Blessed Trinity, as Man, thinks with a human mind and wills with a human will, because the human nature, become His by the Hypostatic Union, enables Him so to act. We are thus in presence of psychological autonomy, but not of metaphysical autonomy. The presence of the former does not prevent the human action and will of Christ from being subject, as every creature is, to the Divine Action and the Divine Will; but they remain nevertheless conscious and free, the two natures having in Christ no other link than that of subsistence.

---

[1] We abstract here from the notional act by which the Holy Spirit proceeds from the Word, as well as from the Father.

The Submission of Christ to God.

We thus see clearly that Christ, as Man, by the very fact of His created nature, stands in regard to God in the same relation of submission and dependence as every other creature. He is "equal to God by His Divinity, inferior to God by His Humanity," as the Athanasian Creed puts it. Because He is Man, Christ owes submission and homage to God, just like other men. We may well marvel at the astonishing fact that the Word, in His human nature, owes to His Father, submission, praise and prayer. It is the realization of the paradoxical fact of God being subject to God. Such are some of the consequences which follow from this wonderful mystery of love called the Incarnation.

On consequences such as these are based the whole doctrine of the meritorious intercession of Christ and of His worship of God, in a word, the whole doctrine of His Priesthood. This Man, who is also the Son of God, is inferior to God. On the one hand, because He is Man, He can humble Himself and annihilate Himself before God and address His prayers and homage to the Divine Majesty; on the other hand, because He is God, His prayer cannot be unheard or fail to be acceptable to the Father. Magnificently did St. Paul express these sentiments, when he wrote: "(Christ), being made in the form of God, thought it not robbery to be equal to God; but emptied Himself, taking the form of a servant, being made in the likeness of men, and in habit found as a man; He humbled himself, becoming obedient unto death; even unto the death of the cross."[1]—"Who in the days of His flesh with a strong cry and tears offering up prayers and supplications to Him that was able to save Him from death, was heard for His reverence. And whereas He indeed was the Son of God, He learned obedience by the things which He suffered."[2]

The Humanity of Christ and His Priesthood.

From what has been already said, one may surmise something of the inner nature of the Priesthood to which Christ is destined by His Divine vocation. The Priesthood is for Him a function that pertains to His human activity. It belongs to His Humanity, not however as a property flowing from the very essence of a nature. It is a prerogative founded on the Hypostatic Union and results from the fact that He is at one and the same time Man and the Only Son of God. The Priesthood is the prerogative of Our Lord as Man, but its ultimate foundation lies in the personal union of His Humanity with the Divinity.

We know how intimately the Humanity and the Divinity of Christ are linked together by the Hypostatic Union. It is impossible to imagine a closer connection. By grace, that participation of the Divine Nature which enables us to perform

---

[1] *Epistle to the Philippians*, II, 6-7.
[2] *Epistle to the Hebrews*, V, 7-8.

divine actions, we are raised to a very high degree of union with God. Nevertheless, we never cease to be ourselves. We are divinized in our nature, but we do not become God. By the Hypsotatic Union, on the contrary, the human nature of Christ, even though it undergoes no essential change, no longer belongs to itself; the human being constituted by it is personally the Son of God; this Man, considered as a subsistent being, is really God. The union by grace remains an accidental one in the metaphysical sense of the term; the Hypostatic Union is substantial, as has been already explained. A more perfect union is beyond our power to conceive. We may attempt to imagine a complete absorption of the human nature by the Divinity, but this would be the destruction of one of the elements of the union, and, therefore, of the union itself.

Accordingly, it is clear that no creature can ever come into such close contact with God as Christ in His Humanity. Consequently, Christ, thanks to His human nature, occupies the highest place in the hierarchy of creatures, on the very confines of the Divinity, so to say. Such a position, conferred on Christ by the Hypostatic Union, makes Him the rightful Mediator between God and the world, and by that very fact, lays the foundations of His Priesthood. From one point of view, since He is elevated above all creatures, they are subject to Him; from another point of view, because of His personal union with God, He is sanctified and consecrated in His human nature by the Divinity, and, by the very fact, destined to offer divine worship to God. For, to be really Mediator and Priest, it is not sufficient to be placed by the Incarnation between God and creatures. This position must confer on Him the qualities and powers that such mediation demands. It must enable Him to represent men before God, to speak and act in their name; it must confer on Him also the right to give to God the worship He demands from His creatures, especially from fallen creatures. A mediator, as St. Thomas points out, is one who links together two extremes. He must be in contact with each precisely from the point of view of the mediation he is to exercise. A mediator between God and fallen man must be able both to represent the whole human race and to offer to God the homage He has a right to expect from it. Is this twofold aspect of Christ's mediation realized by the eminent place which the Hypostatic Union gives Him in the hierarchy of created being? That is the whole question.

The Mediation of Christ.

Looked at from man's side, the Incarnation, by raising Christ above all creatures, ordains all things to Him. The world of matter is subject to man so that he may use it for his spiritual advancement. The whole universe, including even those unhappy sinners who turn their backs on the Divine Life, is by God's Providence, directed to the world of grace. Finally, both the world of nature and the world of Grace are ordained to the Hypostatic Union. All things are subject to Christ and Christ to God. This is the established order of the universe, resulting not only from the Will of God, but from the very nature of things. Consequently, no creature can return to God, except through Christ. The perfection of His being demands this, not indeed that the human nature of Christ can be considered in itself the most perfect of creatures, but because its personal union with the Divinity confers on it a supernatural perfection that can never be surpassed, and because the whole order of the world must be judged from the standpoint of man's elevation to the Supernatural Life. Everything, therefore, is unified by and converges on Christ; He is the keystone where meet the arches that form the temple of the universe, and through Him, the homage of creation ascends to God.

From God's side too, Christ is specially designated as the Priest who can offer perfect worship in the name of the whole human race. The Hypostatic Union consecrates and sanctifies the Humanity of Christ in such a way that His whole being is dedicated to the service of God. In virtue of that Union, Our Lord's Humanity receives a true priestly consecration. This point is so important that a few additional words of explanation are indispensable.

The Nature of Holiness.

Sanctity or Holiness, according to St. Thomas, implies two characteristics—purity and stability.[1] By purity is meant separation from all that is not God or that is opposed to Him, with a view to a closer resemblance to His sovereign perfection. Stability is a certain immutability in this purity and union with God. These two elements of sanctity can be realized both in the order of being and in the order of action. A creature is holy in the order of being, when, apart from any activity of its own, it is united to God and taken possession of by Him in some special way. A creature is holy in the order of operation when, by its virtuous acts, it turns back to God and cleaves to Him of its own accord.

Sanctity in the Order of Being or Sanctity considered Statically.

Sanctity in the order of being is usually designated by the term consecration. Although one may speak of a kind of fundamental consecration of all creatures because of their absolute dependence on God, still the word is ordinarily reserved to express a certain taking over of a thing, by which it is withdrawn from every other use, and is destined exclusively for the service of God. Thus the objects used for Divine worship are said to be consecrated, because they are reserved for God's service.

---

[1] Cf. *Summ. Theol.*, IIa IIae, Q. 81, art. 8.

Since consecration consists in making over a thing exclusively to God, it follows that no consecration is valid unless it is accepted by God. By visible ceremonies, a man can signify his intention of despoiling himself of something in order to hand it over to God, but it is only God who can make the act of donation to be definitive, by accepting the object offered and making it His own. Divine acceptance is something active, that is to say, it produces in the object a new quality, by which it becomes really and physically a consecrated thing. St. Thomas continually insists that the love of God, when directed to a creature, produces in it the lovableness which makes it agreeable in His sight. God's love is effective before being affective, because the Divine Goodness cannot be attracted by anything outside Itself, and if God stoops to a creature, He does so with the intention of enhancing its perfection and of uniting it more closely to Himself. When God accepts and appropriates a thing to Himself, this mark of Divine predilection is realized in the creature by a new Divinely-produced character known as consecration. It is not a question of being deputed to God's service in a merely extrinsic fashion, but rather of the production of a definite reality in the object consecrated by which it is specially sanctified. Thomistic thought demands this supernatural realism. If man concurs in an act of consecration by rites and ceremonies, it is as a simple instrument of the Divine Goodness. Of course, consecration can assume different degrees and forms, according to the Divine use for which the consecrated object is intended. But always and in all cases, by appropriating a thing to God, consecration ordains it to His service and worship, and destines it to procure His glory.

Sanctity in the Order of Action or Sanctity considered Dynamically.

Sanctity in the order of operation has also as result the offering to God of genuine worship. But while consecration may be given to all creatures, even to purely material ones, sanctity in the order of action belongs exclusively to rational creatures. It presupposes that a man knows his final end—God—and that he freely determines to tend towards Him by a virtuous life. This turning to God is a voluntary homage offered to Him from whom man has received all that he possesses. It is a worship of glory by which he recognizes God's infinite Goodness and His supreme dominion over the world.

Sanctity and Religion.

It is obvious that sanctity, whether dynamic or static, whether in the order of action or being, is closely bound up with religion. The latter, in its deep and genuine sense, is an habitual disposition of the soul, which inclines man to render to God, by certain actions, the worship which is His due. These actions, of themselves, have no other aim than the recognition and proclamation of God's goodness: such are prayer, acts of oblation and sacrifice.

These acts are acts of worship in the strict sense, and if exterior, they constitute the visible, social religion proper to man. Issuing directly from the virtue of religion, they are holy with that active sanctity which aims at procuring the glory of God. With regard to the other actions of a virtuous life, even though their direct object is not the worship of God, they can still be brought under the influence of the virtue of religion, which can then command them and utilize them to offer homage to the Divine Majesty. The virtue of religion has, therefore, an essential rôle in the worship we give to God by holiness of life and action. It has also an essential rôle in the worship which is based on the consecration of man and the things he uses to give honour to God. For when a man is dedicated to God by a special consecration, he must fulfil the functions of his state of life with befitting dignity and religious reverence. This he can do only through the virtue of religion, which inclines him to serve God with all the requisite interior dispositions. Consecration gives him a right to come into the presence of God and to serve Him in the particular way indicated by the very nature of this consecration. Besides it is necessary that this worship be offered in a becoming and holy manner, and be the expression of genuine interior sentiments of submission and piety.

Religion, sanctity and consecration are, therefore, concepts, which, if not synonymous, at least involve one another, and which give man's worship of God all its value. They also participate in the two characteristic notes of sanctity, purity and stability: purity, because they express union with God and separation from all that is not God; stability, because on the one hand, the virtue that is implied in the concepts of religion and sanctity is a stable and habitual disposition; and because on the other hand, the consecration which comes from God lasts as long as the consecrated being, the gifts of God being without repentance.

The Sanctity of Christ in the Order of Being.

It only remains for us now to study the degree of sanctity conferred on the Sacred Humanity by the Hypostatic Union, in order to appreciate the sublime way in which this Humanity is dedicated to the worship of God, and to the glory of His Holy Name.

Tradition unanimously affirms that the Hypostatic Union confers on the Humanity of Christ a special and pre-eminent holiness, which is, however, different from our sanctification by grace. For the Fathers, this sanctification is an unction which the Humanity receives from the divinity, because of its substantial union with the Word. It makes of Christ the Anointed of God, the Holy One *par excellence*. "Christ," says St. Cyril, "is not anointed as saints and kings are anointed, but because He is the Word made Flesh."[1] And St. Gregory Nazianzen writes: "Christ

---

[1] *In Joann.* i, II, ch. X.

is called the Anointed or the Christ, because of His Divinity. The Divinity is the unction of His Humanity, not that it sanctifies Him actively as it does other saints, but because of its sanctifying presence."[1] The Council of Frankfort, in 794, confirmed this doctrine, when it taught: "Christ is anointed by nature, we by grace; for in Him dwells the plenitude of the Divinity."

The holiness of the Humanity of Christ, arising from His personal union with the Divinity, is not therefore produced by the Word in the same manner as that effected by the Holy Spirit in our souls by means of grace. There can be no question of our attaining the same kind of holiness with a mere difference in degree and in the fact that it is attributed not to the Word but to the Holy Spirit. Of course, the Humanity of Christ possesses sanctifying grace. But here we are dealing with something much more intimate, whereby the Word is not only the intrinsic cause of sanctification, but the formal reason of the sanctity of Christ whose Humanity is permeated through and through by the Subsistence of the Second Person of the Blessed Trinity. If it is true that a thing is holy in the measure in which it is united to God, what unique holiness must we not attribute to Christ? In Him there is perfect union of the divine and human natures in the Person of the Word. The human nature so belongs to God that it is *His*, subsisting as it does by Him. "In Christ," says St. Thomas, "in whom the human nature is joined to the Divinity in the unity of the Divine Person, there is full and perfect union with God, such a union, indeed, that all the acts of the Divine Nature and all the acts of the human nature are the acts of the Divine Person. Christ is full of grace, not in the sense that He has received a special, gratuitous gift, but in the sense that He is God Himself."[2] And again, "Christ was sanctified in a particular manner. God sanctifies others in order to make them adopted children; Christ, on the other hand, He sanctified to be His Son by nature, personally united to the Word."[2]

This union is in the order of being and not in the order of action, because the Humanity of Christ is united to the Divinity in a personal union or union of subsistence. The faculties or principles of action of Christ as Man, do not cease thereby to be human, and we shall see later that sanctifying grace is required, to enable them to act in a divine manner. What we behold here is a genuine consecration of the Humanity of Christ to the Divinity, a consecration which is substantial and whose immediate formal principle is the Second Person of the Blessed Trinity. This consecration has been aptly likened to an unction, because this term helps to signify the intimate nature of the compenetration of the Humanity by the Divinity.

---

[1] *Orat.*, 30, n. 21.
[2] *Comm. on St. John*, Ch. I, L. 8.
[3] *Comm. on St. John*, Ch. X, L. 6.

Thus consecrated to God in the substance of His Being, Christ in His Humanity is designated in a most absolute way for the service and worship of God. Other creatures are consecrated to God by a sanctification which is bestowed on them after they have been brought into existence, and this sanctification seems to be limited to the particular use God wishes to make of them. The Sacred Humanity of Christ, on the contrary, is consecrated to God from the very moment of His conception, for it exists and can exist only as united to the Word. Its consecration is absolute: there is nothing in it which does not belong to God, or which is not for His service. Christ, in His Humanity, does not belong to Himself: He belongs to God. His whole life, from the first moment to the last, all His movements, all His undertakings, all His sufferings, can tend only to give glory and homage to God, for they are the life and acts of the Son of God Himself.

The Sanctity of Christ in the Order of Action.

We know already that it does not suffice for the perfection of the worship of a rational creature that it should be consecrated to God in its substantial being. In addition, the acts by which it gives concrete expression to its worship must be elicited by a virtuous and holy will. Consecration designates a person specially for Divine service: holiness permits him to give to this service all the dignity and moral beauty which make it pleasing to God. The Hypostatic Union not only consecrates Christ to God but renders Him absolutely incapable of sinning. His human acts belong to the Person of the Word: it is the Second Person of the Blessed Trinity who is responsible for them. Of course, God the Son performs them by means of His human faculties, but it still remains true that, if they did not proceed from a virtuous will, the moral imperfections of Our Lord's human nature could be attributed to the Second Person of the Blessed Trinity. The Son of God owes it to Himself, therefore, to ensure the absolute impeccability of His human nature. Nevertheless, this impeccability is not in any way an obstacle to liberty. On the contrary, it gives Christ full control over the development of His life in the service of God, without His ever having to fear the slightest slip or defect. To explain the existence of such perfection, we have but to bear in mind that God bestows on Christ the efficacious graces and the enlightenment necessary to guide Him infallibly in the exercise of the most heroic virtues. We shall see later that sanctifying grace, in giving to Christ the Beatific Vision, further perfects His impeccability. For the moment, it is enough to remember that the Hypostatic Union, of itself, necessarily entails the perfect moral sanctity of Christ, and that, even apart from any elevation of His human nature by grace, Christ is the Holy One of God in the order of operation as in the order of being.

Christ, the Priest of God.

We see, then, that Christ's whole being glorifies and cannot but glorify God, that He renders to God the most perfect worship imaginable, inaugurating the unique religion, henceforth the only one acceptable to God. Christ, the Holy One of God, is the Worshipper of God *par excellence*. And if we remember, on the other hand, that the Hypostatic Union has placed Christ at the head of creation, ordaining all things to Him, we must of necessity conclude that Christ is the only possible Priest through whose hands creation's homage can pass, and that any form of worship other than the one inaugurated by Him means disorder.

The Hypostatic Union has made Christ as Man the only Son of God. This Sonship, in which are concentrated all the bonds of intimate union between Christ and God, is the foundation of all His rights and of all His powers of offering religious worship and universal homage to the Divine Majesty. His Sonship is thus the ultimate foundation of His Priesthood, so that St. Paul could write in all truth: "Christ hath received the honour of the priesthood from Him who said 'Thou art my Son' ... The word of the oath hath set up a Son whose perfection is for ever."[1]

Appendix.

Metaphysical personality belongs to a rational or intelligent subsistent being, that is, to a perfectly autonomous subject of action (the non-rational is not perfectly autonomous, for the animal cannot apprehend the order of being, it is acted upon rather than acting). Thanks to our psychological consciousness or our awareness of our mental states, we apprehend the *self* as the cause of subject of these states. We become aware of *ourselves*. We go as it were, beneath our states and actions and come face to face with the *self*, the *I*, who has these states and does these actions. Psychological consciousness immediately reveals the nature as rational. This is simply the basis for considering personality or the subsistence of a person as superior to the subsistence of an irrational animal. In order to form the concept of a person and to find that concept verified in the data of our experience, it is, therefore, absolutely essential that we be endowed with the faculty of intelligence, the spiritual power of forming abstract concepts; and secondly, that having formed the concept of person as "a rational or intelligent subsisting being," we be capable, by the exercise of reflex consciousness, of finding in our own mental life the data from which we can conclude that this concept of person is verified in each and every one of us.

The exercise of reflex consciousness also enables us to form a quasi-objective or historical view of our own personality as one of a number of similar personalities in the world. It is because this complex notion of my personality is an abstraction from my

[1] Cf. *Epistle to the Hebrews*, V, 5 and VII, 28.

remembered experiences that a perversion of imagination and a rupture of memory can sometimes induce the so-called illusions or alterations of personality. But this "personality" is not personality at all in the proper sense explained above. It is merely an *idea*, the notion we form of ourselves or the view we habitually have of ourselves. Cf. *Ontology*, by Rev. P. Coffey, pp. 273 and foll.[1]

---

[1] This Appendix has been added by the Translator.

CHAPTER III

THE PERFECTION OF CHRIST AS PRIEST

The Supernatural Character of Religion in the present Order.

Destined by His eternal vocation to be the High-Priest of humanity and consecrated such by the Hypostatic Union, it is indispensable for Christ to possess powers of action in keeping with the functions incumbent on Him as Priest. For, according to the Divine Plan, the mission of Christ on earth was to raise men from the fallen state resulting from original sin and to re-establish them in the Divine friendship they had lost. Such a friendship presupposes the Supernatural Life of Grace. It is the rôle of Jesus to communicate this Life to men, so that having made them just in God's sight, He can in their name, offer to God the worship of adoration and thanksgiving which His infinite Goodness and His merciful Love demand.

Grace penetrates into the depths of the soul and from it emanate certain divine faculties which enable man to know and love God as He is in Himself. Here below, it is true, this knowledge remains obscure, for, relying on the testimony of Revelation, it tends to God only by the confident adherence of faith. Our love is not fully satisfied either, because it possesses God only in hope. Yet this state of imperfection is but a passing one. By its nature grace is destined to enable the soul to enjoy the splendours of the Beatific Vision and rejoice in the happiness of the eternal possession of God. Besides God as known and loved under the vital influence of grace is not merely God as we know Him by the light of reason in His transcendent unity, but God as He reveals Himself to us in the Trinity of His Persons. Grace ordains us to a participation in His inner, mysterious Life. It enables us to penetrate the secrets of that Life and to enter into the family circle of the Father, the Son, and the Holy Ghost. Thus our worship of God is elevated to a new and supernatural plane. It is to the Triune God that our homage must henceforth ascend: it is to Him that our adoration must be directed. In the hypothesis of a purely natural order, it would have sufficed for man, instinctively religious, to direct his knowledge and love to the worship of God as the Creator of the world. But seeing that we are called to a life that is supernatural, it is essential that the virtue of religion, infused into our souls with grace, should direct our new powers of faith, hope and charity, to the worship of God in Three Divine Persons. Accordingly, we are meant to live our entire life in the presence of God, offering to His sovereign majesty an interior worship in spirit and in truth, a worship that will manifest itself externally by appropriate ceremonies.

The Life of Grace in its Fulness.

The sacerdotal rôle of Christ consists precisely in communicating Supernatural Life to men and in giving to God supernatural worship. It is evident that if Christ is to fill His rôle properly, He must Himself have the fulness of Supernatural Life. How can He render due homage to the Blessed Trinity in our name, if He cannot reach God in His mysterious Life in Three Divine Persons by knowledge and love? How can it be maintained that Christ is for others the source of the Divine Life, and yet is Himself deprived of it? Nothing can be a principle of perfection in a given order, unless it be itself perfect in that order. Of course, we know that Christ, in His Humanity, is simply an intermediary between God and man, a channel for the Life which, coming from God, is diffused by Him into our souls. Nevertheless, Christ is a perfect man. Therefore, His mediation must be exercised in a human way, that is to say, by the play of intelligence and will. When God makes use of a creature to realize His designs, He demands its active cooperation. He, on His side, takes account of the nature of this activity, so that if the creature is free, He may allow it a certain autonomy in fulfilling its rôle. If we bear in mind that Christ, by the Hypostatic Union, dominates the universe and that all things converge on Him as on the apex of creation, we can readily understand that Christ depends on God as on the first Uncreated Principle of Supernatural Life. Since Christ Himself is the first created, and therefore dependent, principle of that same Life, He can, in virtue of this prerogative, transmit that Life to men.

Nay more, if we envisage Christ in Himself, even leaving out of account His predestined vocation, we cannot see how it would be possible for God to refuse Him the fulness of Supernatural Life. This Man is really and truly the Only Son of God, having thus inalienable rights to share the Life of His Father, a right to know Him, to understand the bonds of personal filiation which unite them, and a right to grasp by His human faculties the relations which draw Him into the intimacy of the Three Divine Persons. God was in no way obliged to unite Himself to our nature, but from the moment that, by a special favour, He condescended to do so, He was obliged to confer on the human nature of Christ a perfection of life in harmony with the life of His Divine Nature. To act otherwise would have meant a lowering of the dignity of the Man-God, and would have been unworthy of Uncreated wisdom.

Does this mean that the Hypostatic Union was of itself sufficient to elevate the human nature to this participation in the Divine Nature in the order of knowledge and love? Certain theologians have thought so, and have maintained that the grace of union took the place of sanctifying grace completely and entirely, and was of itself sufficient to explain all the effects of the Supernatural Life in the Man-God. The Church has not made any solemn pronouncement concerning this point of doctrine. But the majority of her Doctors are unanimous in holding that without sanctifying grace, it would have been impossible for the human faculties of Christ to attain to God as He is in Himself, and that, therefore, sanctifying grace was a necessary and immediate consequence of the grace of union. If the reader recalls what we have already said about the nature of the Hypostatic Union, he will have no difficulty in accepting this opinion of St. Thomas, which is also the common opinion of theologians.

By the Incarnation, the Word subsists in human nature, and unites it to the Divine Nature in the unity of His Personality. But He does not make any change in the essential elements of the human nature. Subsistence is defined from the point of view of being; it gives to a nature unity of existence; it does not give a nature unity of essence. Thanks to the Hypostatic Union, the human nature of Christ depends on the subsistence and existence of the Word, but it is unchanged in regard to its essence, and in what concerns the properties flowing from that essence. The human faculties of Christ, and in particular His intellect and will, keep their natural mode of acting and remain ordained to their proper object. Unquestionably, action belongs to the *person*, who is the responsible subject of it, but the *suppositum* is the principle of action only in virtue of the faculties emanating from the nature. Subsistence is the condition of action, because it is the principle of unity in the being, and action is dependent on and proportioned to being. But subsistence is not the source of action. The source of action must be sought for in the nature or essence which places the being amongst the members of a certain species. As we have already remarked, metaphysical personality does not, strictly speaking, affect our psychological life: it does not form part of the immediate data of consciousness. We know of its existence by reasoning, just as we know of the existence of every invisible reality beyond the field of inner perception. And the knowledge conveyed to us by this inference gives us information about our metaphysical personality, merely as "a principle of subsistence and unity in being." "If by a supernatural operation," writes Lachelier, "the Ego (substance) of another man were to take the place of our own, it would be absolutely impossible for us to become aware of the fact."[1]

However strange it may appear at first sight, it is thus evident that, if Christ were dependent on His human faculties alone, it would be impossible for Him to become aware of His Divine Personality. The Word, subsisting in the human nature of Our Lord, was for it exclusively a principle of unity in being. The subsistence communicated by the Second Person of the Blessed Trinity was that of the Divine Being Itself, but in thus making the human nature participate in the unity of the Divine Subsistence, the Divine Personality merely took the place of the created

---

[1] *Des fondements de l'induction,* 2nd. Edition, p. 116.

personality and in no way revealed its own uncreated transcendence. The only psychological effect resulting from the Hypostatic Union is the perfect moral rectitude of Christ. This result is, however, only indirect. God, personally united to a human nature, is obliged to preserve that nature from every fault, by a special efficacious assistance. There is no question here of Christ's being made conscious of the fact of the Incarnation. Our Lord, experiencing His absolute impeccability, could have known of a special benevolence on the part of God towards Himself, and of a very high moral union of His soul with God, but not of the Hypostatic Union or of the mystery of grace it implied.

But how could we imagine Christ being unaware of His eminent dignity as the only Son of God? We have seen that His priestly rôle in its entirety is founded on that dignity, and we know that the priest is no inert instrument in the hands of God. He is the conscious minister of the divine generosity and can act only on condition of being aware of the place he occupies between God and man. If He were not conscious of His dignity, Christ would not only be deprived of a perfection demanded by His character of God made man, but He would not even be capable of filling His rôle as Sovereign High-Priest and Mediator of the human race. Such a supposition cannot be reconciled with the Gospel narrative, which shows us clearly that Jesus was perfectly aware of His Divine Sonship and fully enlightened with regard to the mission for which He came on earth: "Father, I have glorified Thee on the earth: I have finished the work which Thou gavest me to do: And now glorify Thou Me, O Father, with Thyself, with the glory which I had, before the world was, with Thee."[1] In addition, the teaching of the Church obliges us to admit this supernatural perfection of the human soul of Christ, and we must only confess with St. John "(His glory was) the glory as it were of the only begotten of the Father, full of grace and of truth."[2]

The Relations between the Hypostatic Union and the Sanctifying Grace of Christ.

It is now easy to perceive the relation between the Hypostatic Union and the treasure of sanctifying grace in Christ's soul. There is not a physical link such as is to be found between the essential property of a being and its nature. If we consider the Incarnation in Itself, abstracting from its moral significance and the Divine Intention which brought it to pass, there is nothing to prevent us from conceiving the possibility of a human nature personally united to the Word, but not endowed with sanctifying grace. But if we consider those same realities from the standpoint of Eternal Wisdom, which arranges everything in order and proportion, and which does not deprive any creature of the gifts necessary for the accomplishment of its destined work, it seems

---

[1] *St. John*, XVII, 4-5.
[2] *St. John*, I, 14.

impossible to conceive Christ without that elevation to the supernatural order which grace alone can confer. There is involved a moral necessity of which Divine Wisdom must take account. Sanctifying grace is a consequence of the Hypostatic Union in the sense that Christ has a strict right to it because He is the Only Son of God. Never will God have a stronger and more pressing reason for according this grace to a man, because no creature will ever attain the supreme perfection of Christ. The angels themselves are sanctified only by the divine favour.

The Infinity of Christ's Grace.

We must remember that of all the beings raised to the supernatural order, Christ is the one who possesses the Divine Life of Grace in the most eminent degree. "He is full of grace and of truth," and this fulness is absolute; it will not and it cannot be surpassed. It is in this sense that we speak in theology of the infinity of Christ's grace; a relative infinity, of course, since we are treating of a created reality, which of necessity is limited. But at the same time, it is an infinity that reaches the supreme degree of plenitude marked out for it in God's eternal designs. We may consider this plenitude of the Inner Life of the Blessed Trinity in Christ's human soul either from the point of view of its intensive perfection or from that of its extensive perfection. In the former case, one might argue at length about the question whether God, by His absolute power, could produce a degree of grace higher than Christ's. The intensity of grace is measured by the power it gives the intelligence to penetrate the secrets of the Divine Life, and by the power it bestows on the will to love the Blessed Trinity. It would seem to be clear that between the full comprehension of the Divine Essence, reserved to God alone, and the intuitive but not exhaustive knowledge which the Beatific Vision confers on a creature, there is room for an indefinite number of degrees of beatitude. Beyond that of Christ, others higher still can at least be imagined. Yet, though this is so, it still remains certain that Christ, being by the fact of the Hypostatic Union the first of all creatures, will never be surpassed or even equalled by anyone else, in the order of grace. "But thou hast ordered all things in measure, and number, and weight," says St. Thomas, quoting from the Book of Wisdom, IX, 21. Hence God has measured out to Christ grace proportionate to His dignity as Only Son, so that the fulness of this grace is, in point of fact, the greatest and the most complete that God, in His wisdom, can produce.

The grace of Christ, infinite in intensity, is also infinite in its extent. By that we mean that Christ possesses, in the most perfect way, every form of divine activity of which grace can be the source in the souls of the just. One must especially examine this perfection of His, in order to understand all the supernatural richness bestowed on Our Lord's human nature by sanctifying grace.

The Virtues of Christ.

Because sanctifying grace gives us a share in the Divine Nature, it implants in our souls certain permanent dispositions which enable us to act in the way that belongs to the strictly super-natural order, the order of God's Inner Life. These dispositions are called infused virtues. They include not only the theological virtues of faith, hope and charity, which make it possible for us to attain to God as He is in Himself, but also the cardinal virtues of prudence, justice, fortitude and temperance, corresponding to the natural *habitus* acquired by a moral life. The infused moral virtues enable us to act on the level of our higher life of grace. The perfection of these virtues depends directly on that of their principle, so they are found in Christ with the same plenitude of perfection as sanctifying grace. In our case, on the contrary, grace remains imperfect here below and blossoms into maturity only in heaven. Hence, in our supernatural virtues, we can notice certain imperfections belonging either to our condition as travellers to our eternal home, or to our fallen state which entails such a painful struggle on our part. The Beatific Vision is not ours as yet. Consequently we reach God as He is in Himself only in the obscurity of faith, and our love can cleave to Him, only in the hope of one day possessing Him without fear of loss. When that day shall have dawned, faith and hope will disappear, to give place to the light of vision and to the joy of eternal possession. But in Christ, the fulness of grace is incompatible with virtues such as faith and hope, which are marked by a certain incompleteness. Christ, therefore, must see God face to face in the Beatific Vision, from the very moment He receives grace. Now, since grace comes to Him simultaneously with the Hypostatic Union, of which it is the immediate consequence, He enjoys the Vision of God from the very first moment of His conception in the womb of the Blessed Virgin Mary. This conclusion is not a defined dogma of faith, but the Church has clearly manifested its mind on the matter by forbidding the opposite doctrine to be taught to the faithful.[1]

Similar observations might be made about certain moral virtues or certain virtuous dispositions, such as (chastity) and penance, which presuppose that the soul having known sin or not yet arrived at complete moral equilibrium, has to struggle against the revolt of the passions and to make vigorous efforts to keep them in check. In Christ, even the tendency to evil does not exist.

The Gifts and Charismata of Christ.

From Divine Grace in the soul there emanate also the Gifts of the Holy Ghost. These Gifts are supernatural dispositions which make us receptive of divine impulses urging us to a life of greater light and love. Wherever the Gifts come into action, the initiative

---

[1] Decree of the Sacred Congregation of the Holy Office, July 1st., 1918.

in directing one's life belongs more fully to the Holy Ghost, so that the soul is drawn on to a degree of perfection unattainable by the ordinary infused virtues. This life under the influence of the Gifts is, of course, present in its perfection in Christ. Do we not see Him, at the beginning of His public life "driven by the Spirit into the desert"?[1] And is it not Jesus Himself, Who, in the synagogue of Nazareth, applies to Himself those words of Isaias: "The Spirit of the Lord is upon me"?[2] Of course, when we are considering the action of the Gifts in all their perfection in Christ, we must not forget that His complete dependence on the inspirations of the Holy Spirit in no way interferes with the autonomy of His human activity.

Besides the favours and graces of which we have spoken, it sometimes pleases God to grant to certain men, particularly to His saints, gifts which are called charismata. By these charismata God diffuses His blessings upon the world so as to draw it to Himself. Such, for example, are the gifts of prophecy or of miracles. The charismata do not follow necessarily and inevitably from grace, for their object is primarily social. God sometimes grants them to sinners in view of the common good. Yet since saints hold the first place amongst those whom God destines to exercise a profound supernatural influence on the world and are His specially chosen instruments, it is to them that these extraordinary graces are most frequently given, to enable them to carry out their apostolic mission. These graces are passing. They depend entirely on the good pleasure of God, who manifests His power as He wills, in view of His Divine Designs. The recipient does not receive them all at the same time. "And the manifestation of the Spirit is given to every man unto profit. To one indeed, by the Spirit, is given the word of wisdom: and to another, the word of knowledge, according to the same Spirit. To another faith in the same Spirit: to another the grace of healing in one Spirit. To another the working of miracles: to another, prophecy: to another, the discerning of spirits: to another diverse kinds of tongues: to another, interpretation of speeches. But all these things, one and the same Spirit worketh, dividing to everyone according as he will."[3]

These gifts or charismata are evidently to be found in Christ, since He is the Holy One *par excellence*, and His mission is to all men. From this point of view also grace in Him possesses a plenitude of extension, which none other can equal. None of the charismata of the saints can be wanting to Christ. Even if the order established by Divine Providence did not demand that He should use them, still they ought to be at His disposal, if He is to be equal to the task of redemption and salvation. To understand

[1] *St. Luke*, IV, 1.
[2] *St. Luke*, IV, 18.
[3] *I. Cor.*, XII, 7-11.

the point thoroughly, we must penetrate more deeply into the supernatural psychology of Christ, and reviewing the whole array of His gifts, we must subject to a closer scrutiny the perfections with which Divine Grace adorns His intelligence and His will.

The Beatific Vision in Christ.

Christ, as we have said, possesses the Beatific Vision in a manner superior to that of any of the blessed. The perfection of His vision of God, however, does not make Him humanly equal to God in the sense of giving His intelligence an adequate comprehension of the Godhead. Accordingly, Christ does not know in God all the infinity of beings which it would be possible for Him to create and which would be, as it were, the complete expression of His power. But every actual work of creation, everything brought into being by the Divine Wisdom throughout the ages, both in regard to its nature and its place in the Divine Plan, is seen by Christ in God as in the ideal and perfect model. It is commonly admitted that the glorified soul sees in the Divine Essence everything which concerns it and which contributes to its glory. Now all things converge on Christ, all things are ordained to Him as to the apex of creation. There is therefore no created reality, natural or supernatural, that can escape His knowledge. In God He perceives all things, as well as their relation to Himself, and His relation to God. In this respect His vision is perfect and complete, surpassing in vastness as in depth, that of angels and of men.

Christ's Infused Knowledge.

Despite the eminent perfection which the vision of God confers on the human intellect, it still remains possible for it to exercise other acts more in keeping with its finite and created nature. The vision of God is really an act of a created intelligence akin to the uncreated act by which God knows Himself. By deifying our intelligence, the vision of God elevates it to such heights that the life which results is, in a certain way, out of proportion to its natural mode of action. It is as if an inhabitant of our planet were transported by Divine Power through ethereal space and allowed to contemplate the silent harmony of the spheres. When the mind has grasped its object, it feels the need to express this to itself and then to inform other intelligences of it. Now the object of the Beatific Vision is inexpressible in its transcendent unity. Only God—because He alone knows Himself perfectly—can give utterance to a Word, which is the perfect expression of His Substance. The Beatific Vision lays hold of the created intelligence and ravishes it in God, but it excludes any possibility of the intellect's expressing that Vision to itself. It is fitting, then, that besides this Vision there should have been in Christ other kinds of knowledge, inferior in themselves, but better adapted to the human mind and subject to the working of the human will. Christ, during His mortal life, was destined to communicate to the world the knowledge of those supernatural realities that illumined the summits of His soul. He had to live a human life, to enter into relations with men, and exercise in human fashion all His faculties of knowing. Hence His mind needed to be specially enriched with forms of knowledge inferior to the Beatific Vision.

Amongst these we must give pride of place to that infused knowledge, thanks to which Christ knew, in a finite and created manner, and by means of ideas or *species* impressed by God on His mind, all the realities of the supernatural world. Such knowledge could not enable Him to comprehend the Divine Essence, for there is no created idea of the Uncreated. Nor did these infused ideas give Him an intuitive knowledge of the mysteries of religion in their immediate connection with the Most Holy Trinity, for that presupposes a clear knowledge of the Divine Essence. But they furnished Him with an understanding of created super- natural realities, such as sanctifying grace and its mysterious transformation of the soul, as well as the Hypostatic Union, inasmuch as it represents a created relation of the human nature with the Second Person of the Blessed Trinity. By these super- natural realities all resplendent with divine light, Christ could get in touch with the Inner Life of the Blessed Trinity, just as the saints, by the gift of wisdom, experience the Triune God through the illuminations which the Holy Ghost, living in their souls, casts on the truths of faith.

It is well, however, to note that this supernatural knowledge, thanks to its infused and habitual character, is completely under the Saviour's control. Thus, the saints, through the gifts of wisdom, understanding and knowledge, are fully subject to the movements of the Holy Spirit, but it belongs solely to Him to initiate this movement; they are illumined by lights from on high only in intermittent fashion. Christ, on the other hand, is ever illuminated by the rays of the divine sun, and its light is always at His disposal. The divine illuminations to which the Gifts of the Holy Ghost dispose us, do not bring before the mind new objects of knowledge or imply new revelations, they simply throw fresh light on the truths of faith, thus enabling us to grasp their meaning and penetrate their depth, while strengthening the certitude we have of them. But the infused knowledge of Christ, even while it illumined His intelligence, also furnished it with new objects of knowledge, in this way bearing a certain resemblance to the gift of prophecy.

This latter gift has for object all that is of its nature hidden from angels and men. Such, for example, are the truths that are super- natural in the strict sense of the term, and amongst natural realities, the future, as well as the secret thoughts and hidden designs that lie concealed in the recesses of human hearts. God reveals these things to specially chosen men called prophets; but this revelation is only a transitory lifting of the veil, absolutely dependent on the Divine Will, and in the case of any particular individual, throwing light only on a greater or lesser number of objects. Christ, on the contrary, by His infused science, had a complete and permanent knowledge of all these truths, and it was a knowledge to which He could turn at will. All that we know by faith, Christ knew by His infused knowledge. It opened to Him the past and the future and laid bare the secrets of human hearts. "Before Philip called thee," said He to Nathaniel, "when thou wast under the fig-tree, I saw thee." And Nathaniel, conscious of being as an open book before the Master, cried out: "Rabbi, Thou art the Son of God, Thou art the King of Israel."[1] Later, Simon Peter will proclaim the sincerity of his love thus: "Lord, Thou knowest all things, Thou knowest that I love Thee."[2] During the whole course of His earthly life, Christ gave unassailable proofs that He possessed perfect knowledge of events that are completely hidden from human eyes.

The gifts or charismata, then, relating to knowledge of the supernatural, are synthesized in Christ into a science of which He is completely master, a science which enables Him to bring His mind under the illuminating action of the Divine Intelligence whenever He wishes and with perfect autonomy. The ship which rides the ocean at night, sees no other light than the intermittent rays of a distant lighthouse, but in the daytime, the sun is there to assure it a free and certain passage. So the saint and the prophet, despite momentary flashes of heavenly light, remain in the obscurity of faith. Christ alone walks in the brillance of a divine noonday, because He alone possesses divine illumination as His own and can constantly call on it to guide His own conduct and that of all other men.

Yet, side by side with this infused supernatural knowledge, we must admit in Christ other kinds of knowledge which develop and perfect His intelligence. We shall only mention them in passing, because they are less directly concerned with His function as Priest. If it is a fact that the Hypostatic Union elevates Christ above all creatures, and makes the angels themselves subject to Him, it necessarily follows that He can enter into relation with the angelic intelligences and that He is not inferior to them in His manner of knowing. For St. Thomas, therefore, and the theologians of his school, Christ possessed a special knowledge enabling Him to enter into relation with created natural realities as the angels do. The Angel receives his ideas directly from God, and in them he perceives intuitively all the realities of the created world. So it must have been with Christ, and this infused science of natural things, entirely independent of His sense-faculties, had the special effect of placing Him in immediate contact with the world of immaterial spirits who are subject to His rule and government, like the rest of the universe.

---

[1] *St. John*, I, 48, 49.
[2] *St. John* XIX, 17.

Christ's Acquired Knowledge.

Lastly, Christ would not have been fully and perfectly man, if He had not been able to use His intelligence in a human manner. This involves the acquiring of universal, abstract ideas from data supplied by the senses. Such a knowledge is the fruit of experience and of reasoning and by it we can have an intellectual knowledge of all things. As this knowledge is acquired, it will mean consequently a certain progress in Christ's intelligence. Is it not written in the Gospel that "Jesus advanced in wisdom . . . before God and men"?[1] During His mortal life, Our Lord appeals unceasingly in His teachings to the sense-perceptible things about Him and to the images they evoked in His mind, in order to draw from them the parables of the kingdom of God. Jesus lived our intellectual life, as He lived that of the angels, as well as that of the blessed in heaven and that of God. If anyone feels inclined to express astonishment at such a multiplicity of forms of knowledge, let him remember that each kind fits in harmoniously with the others, because each is a stream of divine light illuminating a created intelligence. As each form of knowledge in Christ is a participation of the divine light, they all tend, each after its own fashion, to bring about the simple, ordered unity of the Divine Intelligence. We must never forget that Our Lord Jesus Christ is the Only Son of God, the term and end of all creation, and that, accordingly, we must attribute to His Humanity an intellectual perfection proportionate to that which He possesses in His Divinity, a perfection which, moreover, synthesizes all the perfections to be found in creatures.

Christ's Human Will and His Freedom of Action.

It is quite evident that in harmony with the intellectual perfection of Christ He must also enjoy a corresponding plenitude of moral excellence and strength of will. We have insisted in the preceding chapter that the Hypostatic Union did not destroy anything that was essential to the human nature of Jesus. Accordingly, we can readily understand that in Him there must be two wills, corresponding to His two natures, a Divine Will and a human will. Certain heretics known as Monothelists, while admitting the two natures, refuse to admit the existence of two wills. In their eyes, to suppose a free, independent human will in Christ would introduce a fundamental division in the Man-God, and would give Him a kind of human personality distinct from the Divine Personality of the Word. What we know already of the psychological consciousness of the Saviour makes it easy to reply to this difficulty. We believe that in Christ there exists a single metaphysical personality, a single subsistence—the subsistence of the Second Person of the Blessed Trinity. But because psychological consciousness has its starting-point in the knowledge we

---

[1] *St. Luke,* II, 52.

acquire of the phenomena of our interior life as they unfold themselves in the unity and autonomy of our Ego, it is perfectly obvious that there must be in Christ a psychological human consciousness, based on the perception of His Ego and on the awareness of His liberty. Accordingly, there is no difficulty in recognising that Christ possesses, in His human nature, a free, autonomous will, capable of rational decisions and of choosing among the different created *goods* that are presented to it.

At the same time, this human will of Christ cannot be absolutely independent of the Divine Will. It would be strange, indeed, if in one and the same being, in whom the divine element is superior to and dominates the human, the two wills could follow different paths and even clash. The human will of Christ, like any other human will, is created, and for that reason it is completely and absolutely dependent on the Divine Will. The source of its activity, too, is in God because no created will can act without being sustained and supported by God. Doubtless, God sometimes permits our wills to turn away from Him, but even in order to offend Him, we require the support of the First Cause for every element of reality in our acts. In the case of Christ, it is impossible to admit even for a moment the existence of any sin, for the fault would be imputable to the Word Himself. We must not conclude, however, that this absolute impeccability is destructive of Christ's liberty. It is a typically modern error to imagine that liberty consists in the power of choosing indifferently good or evil. Even a little reflection will suffice to bring home to us that such a power is really a sign of deficiency in a faculty of volition whose orientation is towards what is good according to reason. Moreover, it would argue a complete misunderstanding of the divine action on free will to imagine that God cannot draw it infallibly to choose what is good, without prejudice to its liberty. Such ascribing to God of human limitations finds no place in the doctrine of St. Thomas. According to him, since God is the author of our liberty, He can set all its springs in action without the slightest risk of producing any warp or strain in them. At no moment, even in our most foolish revolts, and still less in our laborious striving to attain the Supreme Good, can we escape from His sovereign dominion. The love, which attracts us to virtue and makes us holy, must be sustained by Essential Love identical with Subsistent Goodness, whose sweet and powerful aid is ever at our disposal. We are from God and we are returning to God, and in this free, conscious ascent, it is God Himself who attracts us and draws us along. It would be just as foolish to attempt to explain our liberty without God, as it would to explain the wings of a bird without the air which is their element. In a certain sense, God is the atmosphere of untrammelled aspiration, in which our activity freely moves and in which it unceasingly develops.

The radical impeccability of Christ is therefore no obstacle to

His liberty. Even if the choice between good and evil is not open to Him, it is always within His power, under the efficacious motion of God, to turn towards this or that created good which, because of its limitations, cannot fully satisfy the aspirations of the will towards the complete and unalloyed good. A particular good, on account of its incompleteness, is incapable of mastering or coercing a will that is destined for the absolute good. This suffices to explain the freedom of our actions.

But though all this be conceded, we are still obliged to admit that the plenitude of grace possessed by Christ gives rise to a new problem whose solution presents a certain difficulty. By the Beatific Vision, Christ is in perfect enjoyment of God, the Absolute Good. His will, elevated by charity to the level to which the light of glory has raised His intelligence, must of necessity cleave with all its strength to the object which satisfies its craving to love and be loved. Like the blessed in heaven, Christ is not free to refuse to love God seen and apprehended in His Essence. Accordingly, does it not follow that His will cannot love objects other than God except in the way and measure in which God loves them? In other words, is not the human will of Christ entirely determined by the Divine Will, and therefore deprived of all liberty? The problem is a serious one, for if Christ was not free, at least during His earthly life, it was not possible for Him to merit and to offer satisfaction for the human race. There is no merit except in an act that is freely done through love. Thus the whole sacerdotal rôle of Christ, in regard to the redemption of humanity, becomes impossible.

St. Thomas could not fail to put himself this question. He solves it by pointing out that Christ, during His earthly life, not only enjoyed the state of the Blessed, but also participated in the life proper to us, wayfarers and travellers on our way to our fatherland. This answer gives us to understand that Christ exercised His human faculties outside the Beatific Vision, and that for this purpose He utilized the various inferior kinds of knowledge which, as we have seen, He possessed, especially His infused supernatural science. Considering the functioning of these forms of cognition, we can say that His will could move freely towards the objects they presented to Him. These objects, no matter how lofty, were none the less finite, created realities, and therefore radically incapable of fully satisfying the human will. In particular it must be added that creatures were powerless to coerce Christ's will, for the further reason that He was in possession of the Absolute Good. Through the love of charity, Christ necessarily adhered to God apprehended in His Essence, while at the same time this love moved Him freely towards all the other realities, in which He saw a reflection of the Divine Goodness. One might even admit with certain theologians that to the infused knowledge of supernatural realities there corresponded, in Christ, a love of God, distinct from beatific love and not exercising like it an irresistible attraction on His will. The weakness of this opinion is that it easily leads one to hold that in Christ there are two distinct virtues of charity. Theologically, it is difficult to defend this thesis.

Accordingly, even when in possession of the Beatific Vision, the blessed soul which inclines necessarily towards God—the primary object of its vision—is drawn freely, it would seem, towards the secondary objects—the things seen in the Divine Essence. Is not God Himself, who necessarily loves Himself, free to will or not to will the existence of those creatures which form the objects of His eternal decrees? So Christ, in the Beatific Vision, can love and will freely what God loves and wills freely.

The liberty of Christ, defined in this way, appears as a lofty liberty of a superior kind, quite different from our halting and uncertain forms of freedom. His liberty is unlike any other except God's. This is so because His will, having attained its adequate object—an object in which it rests and remains absolutely fixed—has become more independent in regard to inferior objects. These cannot draw it to themselves by their inherent attractiveness. The love that Christ has for them is proportioned to their relation to the Infinite Good, or to put it more accurately, in strict accordance with the Divine Will which has brought them into being and marked out their place in the order of the world.

This being so we have no difficulty in understanding the superior nature of the harmony which existed between the free human will of Christ and the Divine Will. Fixed definitely in God, this human will could will only what God willed and as He willed it. Nevertheless, it maintained towards created objects an attitude of sovereign independence, and so it made its decisions exclusively for God, without the slightest deviation from the line traced out by the Father's eternal decrees. Hence follows that perfect love of Christ for His Father, which made Him seek after and accomplish the Divine Will in everything. "My meat is to do the will of Him that sent Me, that I may perfect His work."[1] With what insistence Jesus returns to this subject when talking to the Apostles and the multitude! He is, as St. Paul declares, the perfectly obedient Son, obedient even unto death. This profound rectitude of His will in regard to God's commands was brought to the pinnacle of perfection by the supernatural moral virtues with which He was endowed. For nothing was wanting to Christ that could enable Him to act conformably to the divine wishes made manifest by God's clear light from on high.

The Passions in Christ.

In Our Lord Jesus Christ, the rectitude of which we have just spoken results in a perfect mastery over the passions. The

---

[1] St. John, IV, 34.

endowment of Christ's sensitive nature was exactly the same as ours. Jesus was man in the fullest sense of the Word; and the Gospels sufficiently bring home to us that He experienced those passionate movements of anger and of fear, that we meet with in other men. A passion, of itself, is neither good nor bad. It is helpful and useful when it is at the service of reason: it is a source of weakness and sin when it is not under the control of our rational nature. In the fallen state in which we find ourselves as a result of sin, we must confess that man is not master of his passions to the extent of being always able to forestall their first movements, which thus escaping from the control of reason constitute a moral weakness. Even the saints experience this. But in Christ there could be nothing that was not fully subject to reason. When in anger He drove the traffickers from the temple, or in agony allowed sorrow to enter into His soul in Gethsemani, He lost neither the full consciousness of what was taking place, nor the sovereign autonomy of His reason and will. For that reason theologians have called the movements of the sensitive nature of Christ *propassions*, to distinguish them from our passions which are so often tarnished with disorder and sin.

The Autonomy of Christ's Human Activity.

The moral sanctity of Christ consisted, then, in the entire submission of the inferior part of His being to the superior part, and in the perfect dependence of the latter on God. At this point, however, one might ask if this dependence were such as to rob Him of all initiative in His strictly human activity. Of course, we acknowledge that this activity was free, but does it not appear that the absolute dominion of the Divine Will over it allowed only a full-time obedience, a kind of slavery accepted through love, yet one which seems appreciably to lower human dignity with its personal autonomy and power of free choice? To reason like this is to have but a feeble understanding of the relations between God and His free creatures. Apart from the fact that God is not tyrannical in His attitude towards the rational creature He draws to Himself by love, there is the further fact that He leaves it very many things between which it is free to choose. In addition, God permits that certain events in the world shall depend on man's free activity; it is precisely for this reason, as St. Thomas remarks, that certain graces are granted to us simply because the just pray for them. God does not hand over the reins of government in all things to those who love Him; but by a wonderful act of reciprocal love, He so arranges things that their desires become the object of His eternal decrees, thus concurring in the realization of His merciful designs.

It is in this light that we must consider Christ, if we wish to form an adequate idea of the nature of His activity. If God adapts the fulfilment of His plans to the desires and prayers of the saints, how much the more will He make the realization of His intentions depend on the will of Christ? Is not Christ the beloved Son in Whom the Father is well pleased? What can the Father refuse Him? If His Humanity makes Him inferior to God and subject to Him, it does not take away His rights as Son, rights which are all-powerful over the heart of His Father. He can ask for anything He wishes; His request is not, properly speaking a prayer to obtain a favour from the Father, it is rather, as St. Paul remarks,[1] a respectful and confident appeal which the Father cannot resist, for it comes from His Only-begotten Son. Thus a child can without fear ask its parents for everything it needs to develop its life; having received existence from them, it has also the right to expect the means of preserving and increasing the vigour of its existence. Jesus, accordingly, understands by divine illumination that all things have been placed in dependence on Him, and that He must guide them back to God. He knows that the acts of His human will are a part of the order of Divine Providence and that they must concur in the world's salvation. His decisions and His undertakings will never deviate from the Divine Plan, because they rightfully belong to it and form an integral part of it: far from running counter to God's designs, they further them. The human will of Christ, while in perfect harmony with the Divine Will and without ever ceasing to be submissive and obedient, acts nevertheless with full autonomy, with the autonomy of a Son whose every decision wins the approval of His Father. There can be no question of opposition between the Father and the Son.

We have already spoken of this autonomy in regard to those Gifts of the Holy Ghost which belong to the intelligence. By His infused knowledge, Christ can use them at will, unlike other men who are completely dependent on the action of God. The same must be said about the Gifts which concern practical life: Piety, Fortitude, Counsel and Fear of the Lord. Christ could, whenever He wished and as He wished, call on the divine action corresponding to these Gifts. In this respect He was perfectly free to act as He desired. Hence, after having been baptised by St. John the Baptist, we see Him led by the Spirit into the desert. In the same way, under the action of the same Holy Spirit, He was often ravished by feelings of the tenderest filial piety towards His Father.

We meet the same independence of action with regard to the charismata. Christ was always a prophet, His mind being ever illuminated by divine light. He always possessed the power to work miracles. He could call at will on the Divine Omnipotence, for it was His in virtue of His Personal Union with the Divinity. Hence in the Gospels, we see Him curing the sick and raising the dead with an ease and assurance which disconcert His enemies. He knows that the Father will never refuse Him anything.

---

[1] *Hebrews,* VII, 25.

"Father, I give Thee thanks that Thou hast heard me. And I knew that Thou hearest me always, but because of the people who stand about have I said it; that they may believe that Thou hast sent Me."[1]

The Human Perfection of Christ and His Priesthood.

It is easy now to appreciate the consequences of such a union of will between Christ and God in regard to the exercise of His Priesthood. The priest must obtain for men all the graces and blessings they need to break the bonds of sin and to live in union with God. The fulness of grace which Christ enjoys equips Him admirably for this rôle. Grace gives us the power to lay hold of God as He is in Himself; by it we can enter into the intimacy of the Blessed Trinity. It is perfect only on condition of attaining the Beatific Vision. On account of this perfection of grace which Christ has by the Beatific Vision, His human nature is transported into the bosom of the Blessed Trinity, enabling Him to know His dignity of Son of God, as well as the rights and privileges that follow from it. In God, Christ sees His Hypostatic Union: He knows who He is, and He can reveal it to the world. In God, He sees the eternal designs of the Father in His regard and the part He must take in the redemption of the human race. In God, all things are unveiled before Him, and He can exercise over them that mastery which belongs to Him in virtue of His Personal Union with the Second Person of the Blessed Trinity. All His human faculties are elevated by grace, and receive the equipment required for the supernatural mission confided to Him. In all truth Jesus becomes the source of Divine Life for souls. He can communicate this Life to them, He can raise them to that knowledge and love of God for which they were created; He can send up to God, in their name, that homage of gratitude and love which is the normal result of their sanctification.

The presence, then, of Divine Grace in the human soul of the Saviour confers on Him the proximate power to exercise all His priestly functions. Theologians consider the Hypostatic Union as the root principle of the Priesthood of Jesus, and grace as being its formal principle. This is quite correct, if properly understood. We say, in an analogous sense, that the human soul by its essence, is the root principle of our acts of understanding, while the intelligence, a faculty of the soul flowing from it as a property from a nature, is their immediate and formal principle. Similarly, the sanctifying grace of Christ springs from His Hypostatic Consecration, as a property from a nature, not that there is a physical connection between them, but simply because God's Infinite Wisdom could not allow the presence of one without the other. Just as a property enables a nature to give external expression to its specific activity, so grace confers on Christ the power to exercise

---

[1] St. John, XI, 41, 42.

in the world that priestly action which belongs to Him essentially because of His Personal Union with the Eternal Son of God. Just as the soul is truly intellectual in its essence, so Christ in virtue of the Hypostatic Union is Priest, but He still lacks the faculties which enable Him to act as Priest. He receives these faculties by the infusion of sanctifying grace.

Up to the present we have studied the gift of sanctifying grace chiefly from the point of view of the interior perfection it confers on the human nature of Christ. We must now proceed to examine the power it confers on Him of influencing souls and the precise forms in which this power manifests itself.

CHAPTER IV

CHRIST'S PRIESTLY POWER

Perfection and Power of Action.

Power to act is the natural complement of the perfection of a being: it is measured by that perfection. When a being has reached full maturity it radiates its goodness and exercises its influence on other beings less perfect than itself. It attracts them to itself and shares with them its own excellence. The older theologians made use of very simple illustrations to bring home this truth to their readers. A body that is red hot, they used to say, radiates heat and transmits it to the surrounding bodies. Now, what is true of material things is truer still in regard to spiritual beings. Anyone who is the embodiment of an ideal of truth or goodness cannot fail to exercise a corresponding influence on others. Souls are purified by contact with him and allow themselves to be drawn on towards higher aspirations of which they had scarcely thought. They soon find themselves better, or at least determined to make an effort to improve. Such is the general law of goodness, a law with which we are already acquainted, as we have touched upon it when speaking of God. Goodness naturally diffuses itself. A good man is naturally generous in the usage he makes of what is his, and his generosity, far from impoverishing him, makes him a centre of attraction for all those capable of being benefited by his influence.

By applying these principles to Christ, we shall be able to discover the full extent of His priestly power in the supernatural world of souls. Knowing His sovereign perfection, we can easily conclude that His power in regard to the supernatural life surpasses that of all others and that these latter, precisely because of the limited and relative character of their influence, necessarily depend on Him.

The Hypostatic Union and Christ's Priestly Power.

The perfection of Christ's Humanity—all that we are saying here concerns exclusively the Humanity of Our Divine Lord and not His Divinity—must be considered on a twofold level. There is in the Divine Master a fundamental perfection springing from the Hypostatic Union. This perfection raises Him to such lofty heights and unites Him so intimately to God that in Him God and Man are one and the same Person. The Sacred Humanity of Jesus receives by this transcendent union an incomparable, immeasurable dignity, unattainable by any creature. It is really the Humanity of the Son of God. The Second Person of the Blessed Trinity subsisting in it, appropriates it, makes it His own, makes it participate in a certain sense in His own being, and therefore communicates to it His own excellence which is infinite in the strict sense. And what we say of the Humanity is equally true of its acts or operations. Although these acts, considered as human acts, are physically finite, yet they are the acts of God and by this fact acquire a moral value commensurate with the dignity of the Person who performs them.

It must not be imagined that in thus speaking of moral value only, we minimize the dignity of the Man-God and of His acts. Doubtless, the moral value of an object generally evokes the idea of something extrinsic to it, namely, the attitude that a person endowed with intelligence and free-will ought to have to it. But the genuine moral value of a being is always founded on something in it which is real and physical and is not determined irrespective of these objective factors. In Christ, the moral value of His Humanity and its acts has its foundation in His consecration by the Divinity and in His substantial sanctity. Physically, Christ is as close to God as a creature can be. And it is this nearness in being that is the foundation of His moral greatness and His incomparable dignity. On the one hand, this moral dignity of Christ imposes on rational creatures the duty of adoring His Sacred Humanity, while, on the other hand, God cannot withhold from Christ as Man any of the supernatural perfections which befit Him and to which He is justly entitled.

Christ's Power of Offering Worship.

It is because of this transcendent dignity that Christ as Man is the creature that gives most glory to God. The acts of Christ, being the acts of the Son of God Himself, cannot but be supremely pleasing to God. "This is My beloved Son, in Whom I am well pleased."[1] This sentence of the Father expresses perfectly the dignity of His Son's Humanity in His eyes. Thus, as a result of the Hypostatic Union, Christ is enabled to offer perfect worship to His Father, to give Him a homage which cannot fail to be agreeable, and which surpasses in value all the praise and adoration that all other creatures could ever send up to God.

Nay more, since by His substantial sanctity Christ is the highest of creatures, all others are meant to return to God through Him and by Him. Because of this, He is in some measure responsible for all inferior creatures, more especially for rational creatures. He has not only the right, but the duty, to offer homage to God in the name of the whole created universe, for it is by Him that this homage must be offered if it is to find adequate expression. It would betray a very weak understanding of the providential order of the world to imagine that Christ was made Head of humanity and of the universe simply by a divine decree, and that that Headship connotes a relation to God and to creatures that is merely notional. God's gifts are positive and real. When God looks with complacency on a creature, His love is

---
[1] *St. Matthew*, III, 17; XVII, 5.

before all else an active love, and it produces in that creature whatever is intended to be an object of divine predilection. God, having willed that Christ should be the Head of all creatures, constituted Him such by the Hypostatic Union, and it is this Union which places Him at the summit of the entire universe.

Accordingly, if the Sacred Humanity of Christ and His human actions have an incomparable value, we must expect this value to have a social character. Every created thing will derive some advantage from it, were it only a certain participation in that perfect homage which ascends from Christ to His Father.

Christ's Power of Offering Satisfaction.

We must never forget that the determining motive of the Incarnation was the redemption of man. To restore the order destroyed by Adam's sin the Word was made Flesh. And if it is His duty to offer homage to God in the name of creation, it is a more pressing duty still to make sure that the act of homage offered shall be capable of re-establishing the order overthrown by the Fall. Christ is man, and as man, He forms part of that sinful humanity which has violated the rights of God and offered Him the insult of refusing the homage of its obedience and its love. Therefore Christ's first duty is to repair the outrage offered to the rights of God and, as the Holy One and the Just *par excellence,* to address to God, in the name of the whole human race, a homage perfect enough to compensate for the insult to His Majesty. That is possible, for however grave the fault committed, it cannot outweigh the dignity and grandeur of an act of worship offered by the God-Man. Through Christ, the glory of God is vindicated and the violated order is restored. And, even if no man were to benefit by the salvation brought by Jesus, the work of Christ would not be thereby rendered vain, for it would have sent up to God the homage of a pure and innocent human nature, surpassing in value all the acts of injustice and disorder perpetrated in the world.

Christ's homage to God, then, is not merely an act of perfect worship, but also a super-eminent satisfaction for the insult offered to Him by sinful man. It inclines the Divine Mercy to grant pardon to man, and to remit all the punishment due to sin. It is the payment of a debt. The offence caused by sin had made man God's debtor; proportionate reparation was demanded. But, because every offence is measured by the dignity of the person offended, it was not in man's power to repair in full the infinite outrage of sin. Only the Man-God, by reason of the infinite value of His acts, could give complete and entire satisfaction to the Divine Justice. That was Christ's task on earth. The Hypostatic Union not only gave Him the power to offer to God, in the name of all creation, a worship really worthy of the Divine Majesty; it also conferred on Him a limitless power of satisfying for the sins of men.

Christ's Power of Meriting Supernatural Life for Men.

To the power of satisfying Divine Justice must be added that of meriting Supernatural Life for men. While the satisfaction of Christ is destined to make reparation for the outrage offered to the rights of God, His power of meriting is directed to the acquisition of that Supernatural Life which will enable man to attain his final end. Sanctifying grace, all the supernatural aids necessary for us to live for and with God, the Beatific Vision—such are the blessings which Christ merits for us. As a matter of fact, in the present instance, merit and satisfaction are but two aspects of one and the same action. If the satisfaction of Christ repairs the outrage offered to God and enables man to obtain pardon and escape punishment, this is conceivable only because Supernatural Life has thereby been restored to the human race. For seeing that the chief punishment of sin is eternal separation from God, forgiveness is complete only on condition of recovering the divine friendship forfeited by sin, and of becoming capable, by grace, of one day enjoying the vision and possession of God. Christ, therefore, both satisfies for sinful man and merits for him; and His power of meriting, based as it is on the infinite value of His human acts, cannot but be just as efficacious as His power of offering satisfaction. There is no supernatural favour, however lofty, that Christ cannot merit for us, because the highest grace is ever inferior, in value and dignity, to the slightest act of love coming from the Heart of the God-Man.

To sum up then, the substantial consecration conferred on the Sacred Humanity of Christ by the Hypostatic Union, gives to His every act a personal moral dignity of infinite value. By it, Christ is constituted the Head of all creatures, but more especially the Head of sinful humanity. Because He is God and Man, Christ is able to offer to God, in the name of all creation, that perfect homage which is His due. Thanks to this consecration also, the homage He offers is a complete, nay a superabundant, satisfaction for the sins of men, and obtains the restoration of all the supernatural favours forfeited by the fall of the first Adam. All this brings home to us that we are in the presence of a sacerdotal power of transcendent dignity.

Sanctifying Grace and the Sacerdotal Power of Christ.

At the same time, this sacerdotal power, notwithstanding its eminence, is in itself only basic and fundamental. For its perfect functioning it requires other powers of action, more direct and more immediate. These of course do not increase its absolute dignity, but they do modify it and adapt it to the effects it is intended to produce. We meet here again, in dealing with the priestly power of Christ, the very same problem which we have already encountered in treating of His perfection. Christ, we then said, is perfect by reason of His consecration or substantial holiness, a holiness that is altogether incomparable. But, as this holiness is one of the order of being and not of the order of operation, it requires in addition the accidental sanctity bestowed by sanctifying grace. Sanctifying grace alone can raise the activity of Christ to the supernatural level, and thus bring it into perfect harmony with the super-eminent dignity of the Person responsible for it. The operations of Christ continue nevertheless to receive their interior consecration from the Second Person of the Blessed Trinity whose actions they are. They are thus endowed with absolute divine value; but by grace they are raised to the supernatural level, and can have for proper object God as He is in Himself, in the ineffable mystery of the Blessed Trinity.

Now, what we demand for the holiness and perfection of Christ's Humanity, is also required for His priestly power. The Hypostatic Union bestows on Christ a sovereign power, in the sense that it confers on His activity an infinite moral value, a value of homage, of reparation and of salvation to which no limits can be assigned. In using this power, it is fitting that Christ should be conscious of possessing it. He must be aware of the character of His action, for He must direct the power He enjoys and adapt it to the effects He desires to produce. Christ is Man; He must accordingly act in a human fashion, bringing into play His faculties of intelligence and will. It is impossible to conceive Him saving men without knowing what He was doing, anymore than one can imagine His being united to the Second Person of the Blessed Trinity without being aware of the fact. Besides, if the human activity of Christ possesses an infinite value in the eyes of God, still as long as it is not elevated by sanctifying grace, it can be directed only to natural, not to supernatural objects, He can get into relation with God only by the natural light of reason. But it is to God as known by revelation that Christ must offer homage in the name of fallen humanity; it is to the Blessed Trinity that He must present His sovereign intercession, in order that sinful man may be pardoned and receive back Supernatural Life. Accordingly, just as sanctifying grace, with all its accompanying gifts, completes the natural perfection of Christ, so does it also perfect His priestly power, by effectively constituting Him Head of the human race in the supernatural order and enabling Him to be the source of that Life for the world.

The head lives with the same life as the other members, and it is because it has this life in its fulness that the head can transmit it to the whole body by means of the nerves and muscles. This analogy, so dear to St. Paul, can be applied with all its wealth of meaning to Christ. Christ is the Head of the human race, and therefore has that fulness of Supernatural Life which He is destined to communicate to the rest of mankind. But Supernatural Life is sanctifying grace and its full development supposes the perfect possession of God in the Beatific Vision. And it is this grace, in its fulness, that we must attribute to Christ. "And we saw His glory, full of grace and truth; and of His fulness we have all received."[1]

The Supernatural Character of Christ's Priestly Power.

Let us examine the powers conferred on Christ by the Hypostatic Union. We shall then see how sanctifying grace confers on them the plenitude of perfection required for their application to action.

First, there is the power of offering homage. The homage of the Man-God is of infinite value; but sanctifying grace is necessary in order that this homage may attain its proper object—the adorable Trinity. Jesus, full of grace from the first moment of His existence, knows and sees God in His Essence; to Him He can consciously direct His adoration and His prayers, not only in His own name, but in the name of His human brethren, because the worship which man owes to God is worship animated with Supernatural Life. It is sanctifying grace which enables Christ to offer homage animated with that Life. Christ's homage is of infinite dignity, because it proceeds from a human being personally united to the Second Person of the Blessed Trinity; grace enables Him to vivify it with supernatural love of the object of all worship—God in Three Divine Persons. The grace of union and sanctifying grace are linked together in Christ, so that He may inaugurate for fallen man perfect worship of the Blessed Trinity.

The same observations apply to Christ's power of satisfaction. Strictly speaking one could conceive Christ offering real satisfaction for sinful man by acts directed to God as known by the natural light of reason. The personal value of these acts would doubtless compensate for the infinite malice of the offence. But who does not see that such a satisfaction would be lacking in certain qualities indispensable for full perfection? To offer satisfaction is to restore to a person that of which he has been wrongfully deprived. Sin has deprived God of the supernatural love of a free creature; this same supernatural love must therefore be restored. If justice is to be fully satisfied, goods of the same quality as those of which he had been deprived must be given back to the injured person. Otherwise, even if there is material equality between the reparation and the injury inflicted, the expiation will always lack a certain proportion and a certain fitness which the creditor has a right to demand. The true satisfaction which Christ owes to God in man's name is, therefore, a homage of supernatural charity and love. All His sufferings, accepted to expiate man's fall, have full value, only because they are consented to and willingly endured with all the supernatural love of His Sacred Heart.

In sin, there are two aspects to be considered. There is firstly the turning away from God, and this can be repaired only by a loving return of the will to God. There is secondly the disordered

---

[1] *St. John*, I, 14-16.

attachment to created things, And this has to be expiated by the willing endurance of some suffering proportionate to the fault. This latter aspect is, however, secondary. only the first is essential, and in certain cases it can even make up for the absence of the second. Christ need not have suffered. The intensity of His love for His Father was amply sufficient to appease the Divine wrath. If He voluntarily submitted to the torments of the Cross, it was, as St. Thomas remarks, in order to offer satisfaction in a properly human fashion as well as to induce us to follow in His footsteps in the path of expiation. When we want to express our love of God and our sorrow for our sins, we have no other means of so doing than detaching ourselves from and voluntarily depriving ourselves of the pleasures illicitly desired. Suffering is an expression of ardent love and it is by the path of suffering and self-sacrifice that we can retrace our steps and return to God. Our Lord Jesus Christ knew that well: and therefore He led the way up the hill of Calvary, that we might follow. Yet it was His love which, first and before all, gave full and entire satisfaction to God; the Cross only added a marvellous superabundance, capable of bringing home to us the enormity of sin, and spurring us on to repentance. And, since grace alone is the source of the love of charity, it was therefore indispensable for Christ to possess sanctifying grace, if He was to give complete satisfaction to the Divine Justice.

It was necessary, too, if Christ was to be capable of meriting for us. Merit supposes a certain proportion between the action performed and the recompense to which it gives right, a proportion that is calculated not only according to the personal worth of the author, but also according to the quality and the nature of the action. However lofty may be the dignity of the person performing a purely natural action, there still remains a real disproportion between this action considered in itself, and a supernatural reward, It is certain that Christ, by acts of merely natural love of God, could have won salvation for the whole human race, for such acts would have had their infinite personal value, even though in themselves they would not have been adapted to the supernatural character of the reward. For the merit of Christ to be perfect from every point of view, it had to be the fruit of activity on the supernatural plane. For the reasons just given, the law of merit, which allows no act to be meritorious of eternal life without charity, applies to Christ as well as to all others.

Christ's Grace of Headship.

The truth whose gradual unfolding occupied us in the last chapter now stands forth in all its clarity. Christ is consecrated Priest by the Hypostatic Union, but in the exercise of His Priesthood, He must possess those supernatural faculties that are requisite for the harmonious discharge of His priestly function in relation to God and in regard to man. If He is to render God the homage that is His due, or to satisfy God's justice, or to obtain divine forgiveness for the world, He must be endowed with sanctifying grace. The Hypostatic Union is the root or ultimate principle of His power and of His sacerdotal perfection, as sanctifying grace is their formal and immediate or proximate principle.

Grace is a necessary consequence of the Hypostatic Union and is demanded by it. It is derived from that Union as a property from a nature.[1] It is, so to speak, the normal development of the Hypostatic Union, its fitting and necessary prolongation. And if grace ennobles the Humanity of Christ by elevating it to the supernatural level, grace in its turn shares in the substantial consecration this same Humanity receives from its union with the Divinity. As the grace of the God-Man, who is destined to be the Supernatural Head of the human race, it has a transcendent value and is inexhaustible.

Because the Hypostatic Union raises Christ above all creatures and ordains them all to Him, the grace which is bestowed on His Humanity is necessarily a grace of Headship in the supernatural order. How could it be otherwise? The Hypostatic Union demands for Christ a grace that will be in harmony with His dignity of Word Incarnate, and that will enable Him to act as befits His rank. Accordingly, the grace which is due to the Sacred Humanity must be capable of sanctifying not merely the soul of Christ, but of exercising its influence on every being that is called to share in the Divine Life, in such wise that all may gravitate towards Him as towards their centre of vital attraction.

Of course the motive of the Incarnation exercises an influence on the field of action of this grace of Headship. The Word became Man to restore guilty humanity to God's friendship, and it is above all to this humanity that Christ will communicate sanctity and salvation. It is on behalf of the human race that He will offer to God the homage of His adoration and His love. Nevertheless, —according to St. Thomas, the grace of Christ has a rôle to fulfil even in regard to the Angels. It controls their holiness, for it is the measure of their grace. And besides, the angels, like men, are subject to Christ in the worship of supreme adoration which they offer to the Infinite Majesty.

Accordingly, it is because of the Hypostatic Union that the grace of Christ is a grace of Headship. But this grace, in its turn, enables the Man-God to fulfil all the functions that are incumbent on Him in virtue of His union with the Word. Such is the admirable harmony of which we must never lose sight, either when studying the Humanity of Jesus, or when striving to penetrate into the mystery of His Priesthood.

It is clear, then, from all that we have been saying that the Priesthood of Christ is intimately linked up with His grace of Headship. As we shall see further on, the Priesthood does not

---

[1] Cf. Chapter III for more detailed explanation.

exhaust all the riches of the grace of Headship, but it does lay claim to some of its choicest treasures. For example, it is the prerogative of Christ, the Head of humanity, to pray and adore in its name; it is for Him to act as an advocate with God the Father and to pay our debts; it is His privilege to communicate supernatural Life to the world and to lead it back to God. In virtue of the Priesthood of Christ we are closely united with our Mystical Head. In Him and by Him we expiate our faults; in Him and by Him we live with the Supernatural Life of Grace; in Him and by Him we render to God the worship which is His due. Christ is really the Head of the Mystical Body and we are His Members; from Him the Divine Life of grace comes to us to revivify our souls, to free them from evil, and to deliver them up to God as victims of agreeable odour.

At first sight this outpouring of Divine Life seems to be simply an image destined to express that only a moral union exists between Christ and us. By the power of His Priesthood, Christ is our sole official Advocate with the Father, but the graces of pardon and of life which we need descend into our souls directly from the Father. We must, however, push our investigations further, and following in the footsteps of the Angelic Doctor, show that a still more real and more vital union exists between Christ and His Members. For if, as we hold, Christ is God's active, conscious instrument of pouring grace into our souls, His action will not be merely one of advocacy. It will imply a real communication of Divine Life passing from God through Christ to us. A real vital current will be set up between Christ and us, intensifying the power of His Priesthood and realizing in a certain physical manner that unity that Christ prayed for at the Last Supper: "That they may be one, as we also are one: I in them, and thou in me."[1]

The Sacred Humanity, Conjoint Instrument of the Word.

To express the mysterious relations between the divine and human natures in Christ, St. Thomas frequently has recourse to the idea that the Humanity of Christ is the conjoint instrument of the Word, as the human body is the instrument of the soul. This analogy tends to show the intimate and personal union of the Humanity with the Word, and its dependence on Him. As our souls appropriate and govern the operations of our bodies, so the Word makes His own the activities of the Sacred Humanity and utilizes them for His purposes. We have already insisted sufficiently on the corrections and limitations that are indispensable when a comparison such as this is employed, so that it is not necessary to repeat them here. It will be enough to recall that the Sacred Humanity of Christ is a perfect human nature

---

[1] St. John, XVII, 22.

endowed with intelligence and free-will and therefore having
its own deliberations and decisions. Accordingly, when we speak
of it as the instrument of the Word, it is a question of an instrument in the ontological order, and not in the psychological order.
The Hypostatic Union deprives the Sacred Humanity of its
autonomy in the order of being, but because this union does not
destroy either the will or its liberty, it does not deprive it of its
autonomy in any department of human activity.

Nevertheless, Christ is a being at once human and divine,
capable of both divine and human operations. When He acts as
man His actions are performed with the aid of God's efficacious
grace, and the Divinity assures them moral indefectibility. In this
respect it can be asserted without fear of error that Christ, in His
human actions, is the instrument of the Word of God. Indeed,
St. Thomas does not hesitate to speak of every man as the
instrument of God when he performs good acts under the impulse
of grace. In such expressions the word 'instrument' is used in a
broad sense, and this way of speaking only serves to give some
idea of the superiority of the Divine Action over the activity of
the creature. In reality, when we act under the influence of
efficacious grace, we are principal, though secondary causes, of
our acts of virtue. Christ, too in His human life supernaturalized
by grace, remains principal cause of His actions.

But because Christ was God, He could also act divinely and
produce effects to be attributed exclusively to His divine nature,
as to their sole principal cause. Such, for example, were the
miracles worked during His sojourn on this earth. Such, too, was
the grace communicated by Him to souls. What share has His
Sacred Humanity in these works that are properly divine? Can
we assign to it a rôle of efficiency in our sanctification to the extent
of making it a genuine instrument of grace in the hands of God?
Is Christ in His Humanity, a physical efficient cause of Supernatural Life in the world? One can see how interesting the
problem is, and how by its nature it seems destined to knit
closer the bonds of intimate dependence which unite us to Christ,
and to enhance the power of His Priesthood.

A priori, it seems logical enough to admit the instrumental
efficiency of our Saviour's Humanity. Christ is one Person and,
corresponding to His twofold nature He has a twofold power of
action—divine and human. But if He cannot act humanly without the intervention of His Divinity, is it not also fitting that when
He acts divinely, His Humanity should have a part in the effect
produced? The Church has not given an official decision on this
point and one is free not to accept this doctrine. Yet there is no
denying that the Thomistic teaching on the point agrees wonderfully well with several texts of Scripture, the Fathers and even the
Councils. We read in the Acts of the Council of Ephesus (Canon
XI) that "The flesh of Christ is vivifying, because it is the very
flesh of the Word, who can vivify all things." And St. Cyril of

Alexandria writes in his 'Anathemas,'[1] that: "It is because the Word, engendered by the Father, is Life Itself, that He has made His flesh vivifying." "I live; now not I," says St. Paul, "but Christ liveth in me."[2] We know with what realism Jesus Himself described the intimate union between Himself and the faithful: "I am the vine: you the branches: he that abideth in Me, and I in him, the same beareth much fruit: for without Me you can do nothing."[3]

The whole difficulty, then, resolves itself into the question whether we can translate these truths of faith in terms which authorize us to conceive the Humanity of Christ as a true instrument of the divine work of our sanctification. To prove this, we shall appeal to certain philosophical notions which are commonly regarded as applicable to the realities of the natural order. It is very obvious that when we transfer these ideas to the domain of the supernatural, we shall have to strip them of whatever is too material and too imperfect. In penetrating the mysteries of Revelation, it is the rôle of theology to have recourse to rational notions and concepts, and to apply them to divine things by analogy. If we admit that God uses created instruments in His works, it is evident that He will do so in a divine, and not in a human way. We make no pretence of sounding the depths of the mystery. We simply wish to throw light on it, while taking care to avoid that anthropomorphism which the imagination often finds it difficult to lay aside.

The Nature of Instrumental Causality.

Every instrument has a twofold activity: one which is proper to it, and another which is communicated to it by the principal cause. The chisel cuts the marble: that is its proper operation, which it has in virtue of its own form. The chisel, guided by the artist's hand serves to make a statue: that is its instrumental activity. In the latter case, as St. Thomas observes, "the instrumental cause does not act in virtue of its own form, but in virtue of the impulse which it receives from the principal agent."[4]

This communicated motion however, may be twofold. It may be a mere local motion, as for instance, when I stir the water in a basin with a stick. Or it may be a motion by which the instrument co-operates in a work executed by the principal agent, a work on which the latter leaves the impress of its own superiority. This is the case in a work of art. When a person takes up an inert instrument, in order to use it, he must first of all communicate activity or movement to it. That however, is not enough. If the instrument is to be really such, this communicated activity must be raised to the point of producing something of which it was

---

[1] *Anath.*, II.
[2] *Galatians,* II, 20.
[3] *St. John,* XV, 5.
[4] IIIaP., Q.62, a. 1.

F

itself incapable. Properly speaking one does not play a piano by touching the keys at random: to play a musical instrument one must use it to give expression to a piece of music.

There is, then, in an instrument, a twofold passive potentiality one for local motion, the other for the execution of the work the principal agent has in view. It is only in the latter case that instrumental causality is realized. The use which the agent makes of his instrument in this case constitutes it an instrumental cause in act, and causes all the force and active power of the principal agent to pass, so to speak, into the instrument. "This use," writes Cajetan, "is, as it were, a penetration of the artist's genius into the instrument."[1]

A study of the relations between the special action of the instrument and the special action of the agent who uses it will enable us to probe deeper into the nature of instrumental causality. For St. Thomas it would be a waste of time to employ an instrument if it had not its own special form of activity; the instrument has its *raison d'être* precisely because it canalizes the activity of the principal cause towards a particular effect. The chisel of Michael Angelo cuts the marble, and because that is precisely what it is for, Michael Angelo can produce a masterpiece. Therefore, it is owing to its own special activity that the instrument can share in the effect of the principal cause. Of course, as we have pointed out, the instrument does not always exercise its activity of itself; if by nature it is inert, it has to be put in motion by the principal cause. That, however, is a purely accidental circumstance. There can also be living instruments whose natural movement and activity the agent utilizes to accomplish his work.

What is the part played by the instrument's activity in relation to that of the principal cause? How are the two activities linked together? When the principal cause takes hold of the instrument, the latter, in the very motion it receives, restricts and determines to its own *form* the force which passes through it. Consequently, it impresses its particular mark on the final result. The principal cause is obliged, in its action, to yield to the exigencies of the instrument, to adapt itself to it, to let itself be determined and influenced by it; and this determining influence is necessarily found in the effect. It is the rôle of the instrument thus to impose itself on the principal cause, and to canalize its action. But, on the other hand, the principal cause, within the limits in some way determined for it by the instrument, dominates the latter in its turn, elevates its activity, and adapts it to the production of the work that is beyond its unaided powers. Instrumental causality is, then, the harmonious co-operation of two activities, of which one, that of the instrument, imposes a certain order and certain limits in action, and the other, that of the principal cause, brings about in this order an effect beyond the natural powers of the instrument.

---

[1] *Comment. in III P.,* Q.62, a. 1.

It must be added that the force or energy which is communicated to the instrument by the principal cause is in the latter only in a passing way. As soon as the cause which moves it ceases to act, the instrument loses its operative power. The latter, therefore, is not inherent in it. While the instrument is being utilized, the whole tendency of the energy temporarily received is towards producing the desired result. That is why it is often called intentional or tendential power.

It is not surprising that this concept of instrumental causality gives rise to certain difficulties, when it is applied to the realities of the supernatural order. Between creatures and God there is all the distance between the finite and the infinite, and the same applies to the gulf separating created and uncreated activity. We must therefore try to find out how an instrument acts in the hands of God.

The created agent acts on beings from the outside. He gets into immediate contact only with the accidental forms or exterior modalities of things. Hence these forms determine the scope of what he can achieve. Sculpture, painting, music, to speak only of the fine arts, demand special instruments. Of course, it often happens that the genius of the artist is so outstanding that it is not hampered by the mediocrity of his instruments. The greater his artistic power, the greater, too, will be his mastery over them and his independence of them. He can communicate his genius to the meanest objects and make them express the lofty ideal he has visualized. But at the same time his instruments inevitably impose certain limitations on him. The chisel of the most gifted master is powerless to make marble give forth music: other objects, capable of adaptation to the laws of harmony, are required for that.

With God, on the other hand, the case is different. God does not act on things exclusively from without, as creatures do. He penetrates to their very depths. As the Author and Preserver of their being, he acts on them, so to say, from within. The created agent has power only over the exterior properties of things, and these properties define the limits beyond which they cannot serve as instruments. But God has complete mastery over the very being of creatures, and if He uses them as instruments, they can place no limits to His action from the point of view of their exterior forms, but solely from the point of view of their being. Now what limits can being oppose to His action save those of contradiction? Accordingly, when God uses any created object as an instrument, He can use it for anything that is not contradictory. What does this mean?

We must here recall to mind that when the instrument receives the influence of the principal cause, it combines this influence in a certain way with its own activity, in order to produce the effect. The instrument, then, assimilates the action of the principal cause and makes it, so to say, its own, for it is really the cause of the whole work, and of everything in the work that surpasses its natural powers. Now, if this be so, it seems impossible that the Divine Action, in utilizing the created activity of the instrument, can elevate it to the point of making it an uncreated activity. Even in the hands of God, every instrument, since it is a real cause, must act after the manner of a created cause. Every work, therefore, which by its very nature, excludes the intervention of a created cause, cannot be produced by God with the aid of an instrument. This is the case with creation. Creation is a work involving the absolute power of God. It presupposes no subject, no matter, from which creatures can be drawn and brought forth. Creation means the production of something from nothing. Now no created agent of any kind whatsoever, can exercise its active power except it find itself in the presence of something passive, a portion of matter on which it can exert its power and energy. Even when an instrument is under the influence of Divine Causality, it remains a creature, and is therefore subject to the conditions which govern the exercise of all created activity. Accordingly, it requires a subject on which to act, it cannot bring anything into existence from nothing. When God deigns to employ any created thing as an instrument, when He consents to make it the channel of His own power, He must adapt His power to the exigencies of the creature. The instrument in receiving the Divine Influence, subjects it to the limitations of its own being, thus taking from it the possibility of creating in the strict sense of the term and restricting it to the production, in a given matter, of transformations and changes more or less profound. We find here even in regard to God, the general law according to which an instrument imposes a certain limitation on an agent and restricts his activity. Of course, we must bear in mind God's infinite dignity and understand the law analogously. We must hasten to add, therefore, that once this reservation has been made, there is nothing which God cannot produce with any created instrument whatever. God acts on the being of the instrument, and not on its external form. It is as *being*, and not because it is *such a being*, that God deigns to make use of it. In this respect, there is a proportion between the instrument elevated by Divine Power and everything that can be produced in the order of being. If the artist can elevate his instrument and make it capable of effects that bear the stamp of his intelligence and his genius, how much more readily can the Divine Omnipotence utilize things and make use of them to produce works that surpass the power of every creature. Thus there are no effects, even supernatural, which cannot be brought about by created instruments in the hands of God.

At the same time, we must not forget the primary condition imposed on every instrument in order that it may concur in the work of a principal cause; it must be capable of some particular form of activity. This condition holds good, even when the principal cause is divine, except that God is concerned with the being of this activity, and not with its limitations. It does not matter whether the activity be material or spiritual. From the moment that it is being, and in as much as it is, it is apt under the divine impulsion to be employed in the whole domain of what is. With a few drops of water God can produce sanctifying grace in the soul and purify it of its faults. All that is required is that the water be employed according to the mode of activity that is proper to it, namely, in washing and cleansing bodies. In the same way, because of God's being present everywhere, one cannot see how distance can limit the range of the Divine Power. God is intimately present to the instrument He uses, and to the subject on which He exerts His all-powerful energy. It is He who acts as the link between them, and unites them by His universal activity. There is even no necessity for the instrument to exteriorize its activity when acting on things outside itself: immanent acts, such as acts of intelligence and will, in God's all-powerful hands, can be intermediaries and agents for the transmission of His Power. The Divine Operation, which is essentially immanent and virtually transitive, can communicate to our spiritual faculties that which is proper to itself—the power to act on exterior objects, and to produce in the world the effects of His infinite Goodness. To the person who is acquainted with the mystery of the Divine Transcendence, such conclusions must appear normal. We cannot apply our ideas derived from creatures to God univocally, and it is only by keeping constantly before our minds the lofty exigencies of God's Being that we can hope to form some faint idea of the reality. We repeat: if God uses an instrument, it cannot be in the way human beings do so. The divine mode of action is far beyond our weak conceptions, but at least we can try to set down the principal points which safeguard the greatness of God and manifest His Transcendence.

The Instrumental Causality of Christ's Humanity.

It will be easy for us now to apply this explanation of instrumental causality to Our Lord's Humanity. Indefectibly united to the Word, become, as the older theologians say, the organ of the Divinity, how can we refuse to admit that this Humanity is the most appropriate instrument of the Divine Omnipotence? What can hinder God from utilizing this marvellous conjoint instrument to transmit to the world the benefits of His Mercy? It is a living instrument and one which by acts of intellect and will impregnated with Divine Light and Divine Sweetness, can put itself at God's disposal and thus serve to transmit to the world the power of the Most High for healing bodies and transforming souls. It is at the same time a permanent instrument that understands that a divine force is ever ready to use it, and that it has but to express a desire in order to have all that force at its disposal. When Jesus walked the roads of Galilee or Judaea, and addressed to the paralytics or the blind the healing command : "Arise and walk; open your eyes and see," these few syllables that passed through the air and struck the ear, bore with them the power of God. They were really capable of effecting what they signified, because God worked through and by means of them. Thus the human soul makes the vocal chords vibrate and, producing words, animates them with all the force of its intelligence and will. When Jesus said to the fallen woman: "Thy sins are forgiven thee"; when His look of sorrowing reproach fell on Peter after his denial, there was in that word and in that look far more than the expression of the tenderness and mercy of a human soul. There was God Himself, passing through with irresistible power, and penetrating to the most intimate recesses of those sinful consciences to draw them back to Himself.

That is what a human action of Christ's means:—an action through which the Omnipotence of God passes, an action which transforms souls by purifying and sanctifying them. Down the centuries, Christ has been accomplishing the work of moral regeneration in our regard. We are united to Christ in heaven, and through Him, through His now immortal and glorious Humanity, passes the Divine Virtue which vivifies our souls. It is useless to urge the objection of distance. Christ is in God, we also are in God, and by God the distance between Christ and us is bridged. Is not the soul in the whole body, and does it not form the connecting-link between the head and the most remote members? God, the Life of our life, unites us to Christ as members to their head; from God to Christ, and from Christ to us, there is that intimate penetration which binds together soul and body, head and members.

Thus our salvation is not only dependent on the merits and satisfactions of Christ; it is not alone by His all-powerful intercession that He save us; the acts of intellect and will by which He intercedes for us with the Father, His Sacred Humanity—Body and Soul—which He offers to God in reparation and expiation, are also real instruments at God's disposal for the transmission of the Supernatural Life of Grace to our souls. The Saviour's Humanity is full of grace, and of its plenitude we receive in abundance, "grace for grace," as St. John says; for "grace and truth came by Jesus Christ."[1] Christ is the first in the supernatural order of grace, and by that very fact He becomes the universal cause of the Divine Life for all those who in any way participate in it. Of course, we do not mean to convey that Christ, by His grace, is the first and principal cause of ours. Grace is a participation of the Divine Nature; it belongs to God alone to be its first principal and proper cause. But the grace of Christ, or rather the Humanity of Christ, sanctified by grace, is, in the hands of God, the efficient and universal instrument of our sanctification.

---

[1] *St. John*, I, 16-17.

This grace gives Christ a marvellous perfection in the exercise of His instrumental causality. If He were merely an inert material instrument, as for example the water used in Baptism, there would be no necessity for Him to possess grace Himself. We know that God can make use of any creature He chooses, to produce supernatural effects in our souls; the sacraments are proof enough of that. But Christ, in His Humanity, is a living, intelligent, free instrument, capable of free and conscious action. He is also the depository of God's gifts, with full control over their distribution. Finally, He can call at will on the Divine Power in order to communicate its beneficent effects to the world. As God's instrument in the work of salvation, He can act in regard to it almost like a principal cause. We can never repeat too often that the perfect harmony which exists between the Divine Will and the human will in Christ allows the human will to take the initiative, even of works that are properly divine, and to provoke, in a certain sense, the intervention of God in the sanctification of our souls.

But if Christ, in producing grace, acts as a proper and principal cause would act, He must possess in some way a corresponding perfection. Now, a proper cause has always in its fulness what it produces in others. Christ, then, must have superabundantly the grace He has the mission to give to others. This argument, so dear to St. Thomas, and on which he often insists, recalls what we have already said: if Christ is to fulfil the rôle assigned to Him by God and to which He is destined by the Hypostatic Union—the rôle of Sanctifier and Saviour—He must possess sanctifying grace in its plenitude. It is this grace which enables Him to satisfy and to merit according to all the exigencies demanded by the Fall. It is this grace which will make Him a living instrument, perfectly united to the work in hand, and which will raise Him to the dignity of being the efficient, universal cause of our salvation. Because of this plenitude of grace, Christ can accomplish the work of our salvation, which He has taken in hand, with supreme facility: supernatural light floods His intelligence, and unfolds to Him the needs of a sin-sick world; His will is on fire with an ardent charity that makes Him stoop down mercifully to us wretched sinners and pour into our souls those treasures of Divine Life which He draws in abundance from the infinite riches of God.

Another reason will bring home to us still more clearly the wonderful power of Christ in the work of our sanctification and will make more manifest the need for Him to possess sanctifying grace in His own soul. Ordinarily, when we make use of an instrument, it imposes its limitation on us, as we have seen, and stamps the work done with its seal. But God is more independent with regard to the instruments He employs. He uses them as created entities, whose whole being is dependent on Him, and He is not hampered by their limitations. It follows that these instru-

ments need not, at least in principle, impress any special mark on
the effect produced. Nevertheless, if God deigns to use a certain
creature for the realization of His designs, if He choose one rather
than another, it is not without a reason. And by divine permission,
it may happen that the creature thus chosen may leave its mark,
and, as it were, its image, on the work accomplished. For example,
the sacraments, by their rites, signify certain determined graces,
and they effect what they signify. Thus, as instruments of God,
they leave their special mark on the soul they sanctify. This holds
also, and with greater force, for the Humanity of Christ. A divine
instrument for the production of grace in us, and itself full of
holiness, it is to its own image and likeness that it produces
holiness in us. The grace which comes to us from Christ is different
from that which would come directly to us from God, without an
intermediary. It is, properly speaking, a *Christian* grace, con-
figuring us to the image of the Saviour. And all the supernatural aids communicated to us by Christ have no other end in
view than to develop unceasingly this resemblance in our souls.
We are really other Christs, rendered conformable to Him. It is
because the Father recognizes in us the image of His only-begotten
Son that He accepts our homage, and makes us partakers of the
heavenly kingdom.

The Instrumental Causality of Christ and His Priesthood.
    This Thomistic presentation of instrumental causality enriches
considerably the doctrine of the Priesthood of Christ. By His
Priesthood, Christ has the charge of communicating to us the
gifts of God. Now this communication is rendered far more real
and impressive by the fact that the Humanity of Christ is the
channel through which passes the Divine Life that floods our
souls. We are no longer united to Christ in a merely moral solidarity, but we form with Him one organic whole. This is clearly the
thought of St. Paul, when he writes: "We grow up in Him, who is
the head, Christ: from Whom the whole body, being compacted
and fitly joined together by what every joint supplieth, according
to the operation in the measure of every part, maketh increase of
the body unto the edifying of itself in charity."[1] It is this truth, at
once so lofty and so fruitful, that we must keep before our minds as
we advance in our study. It is of primary importance. From this
on let us bear well in mind that in virtue of the intimate bond
which unites us with Christ, His homage and His worship are
ours; we have the right to call our own His satisfactions and His
merits, and He is the source of our regeneration and of our

---

[1] *Ephesians*, IV, 15. In *The Westminster Version* we read: "Rather we shall
hold the truth in charity, and grow in all things into Him who is the head,
Christ. From Him the whole body, welded and compacted together by means of
every joint of the system, part working in harmony with part—from Him the
body deriveth increase, unto the building up of itself in charity."

grace. His mediation sets up between Him and us a continuous current of life, moving from God to us and from us to God, but passing through Him. "Who needeth not daily as the other priests to offer sacrifice first for His own sins, and then for the people's, for this He did once, in offering Himself. For the law maketh men priests who have infirmity: but the Word of the oath, which was since the law, the Son who is perfected for evermore. . . .

"We have such an high-priest, who is set on the right hand of the throne of majesty in the heavens, a minister of the holies, and of the true tabernacle. . . .

But now He hath obtained a better ministry, by how much also he is a mediator of a better testament, which is established on better promises."[1]

Such is the priestly power of Christ. It now remains for us to supplement the concept we have acquired of it by a study of its relations to that other prerogative of the Saviour's Humanity—His Kingship.

---

[1] *Hebrews*, VII, 27-28: VIII, 1-2: 6. In *The Westminster Version* we read: "Who hath not need daily, like the high priests, to offer sacrifice first of all for His own sins, and then for those of the people: for the latter He did once for all when he offered himself. For the Law setteth up as high priests men who are weak, but the word of the oath which followed the Law setteth up One Who is a Son, for ever perfect. Now to crown what we have said: such a High Priest we have, Who 'hath taken His seat at the right hand' of the throne of Majesty in heaven as priestly servant of the sanctuary and of the true tabernacle which the Lord, and not man 'hath set up'. . . . But now he hath attained to a ministry so much the more excellent, as the testament is better whereof He is Mediator, which hath been enacted on the basis of more important promises."

CHAPTER V

THE PRIESTHOOD AND THE KINGSHIP OF CHRIST

Christ's Grace of Headship and His Kingship.

In order to illustrate the action of Christ on man through His grace of Headship, St. Thomas uses the comparison of the head of the physical body in regard to the other members. "The head," he writes, "exerts a twofold influence over the members; firstly it has an *interior* influence, because the head transmits to the other members the power of moving and feeling; secondly it exerts an *exterior* influence of government, because by the sense of sight and the other senses which reside in it, the head directs a man in his exterior actions."[1] And St. Thomas goes on to say that Christ, being the Head of His Mystical Body the Church, has a twofold influence over souls: an *interior* influence of supernatural life, because His Humanity united to His Divinity has the power of justifying; an *exterior* influence, by His government of His subjects.

In the first influence we recognize that priestly power of which we have been treating in the last chapter. The second constitutes the Kingship of Christ, properly so called. We shall now proceed to study this Kingship with a view to appreciating how it enriches the Priesthood of Christ and is ordained to it. Here we shall have the guidance not only of St. Thomas, but also and principally, of the official teaching of the Church, as solemnly set forth in the Encyclical of Pope Pius XI on the Kingship of Christ.[2]

The Idea of Kingship.

Since we are to treat of Kingship, our first step must be to get a clear idea of it. St. Thomas gives it to us with rare felicity, in the first chapter of his work, *De Regimine Principum*, and we have but to follow him with docility. He points out that among the realities that are ordained to an end, there are some that can reach their end in different ways and by a multiplicity of routes. For that reason they require special direction and a guide. The ship, at the mercy of contrary winds, would never make the harbour if the pilot did not guide it through the reefs with decision and prudence. For every man there is a common end towards which he must direct his life, but this orientation will assume different forms, according to temperament and circumstances. Man must needs utilize all his powers of reasoning and all his prudence in order to govern his life properly: he is his own guide.

The need of government and guidance that is indispensable in individual conduct is to be found *a fortiori* in the constitution and development of social groups, where there is much greater

---

[1] IIIa P., Q.8, a. 6.
[2] Encyclical *Quas Primas*, in *Acta Apost. Sedis*, 28th Dec., 1925, p. 600.

scope for what is accidental, contingent and free. No society is possible unless there is a head to organize and direct it in the pursuit of the end it has in view. The head may, in the concrete, be a group of many men on whom authority has devolved, but it may also be a single individual, and in this case the individual is called a king. "By definition, the king is sole ruler and guide, whose function it is to seek the common good of the multitude, and not his own advantage."[1]

The king must bring about unity in the group he commands. The different individuals who compose the group have particular personal interests. Furthermore, they are not of equal worth as men. The king's duty is to establish order among them, to unify them in a harmonious combination, to organize their efforts in the pursuit of the end to be attained—the common good of all which will also ultimately redound to the happiness of each.

In order to realize this programme the king must first of all form a clear concept of the common end of the society he directs. He must make this his own by thought and reflection, and become its living personification. He must then consider the practical means by which the end will be attained, and having chosen from among these means, make them known to his subjects. His principal rôle is to command. There can be no question of merely offering advice, to be freely accepted or rejected by his subjects. We are quite well aware that, in the conduct of private life, the mere fact of taking good advice does not of itself lead to the performance of a virtuous act. A man must prescribe it to himself by an act of his intellect. Accordingly, no society will efficaciously pursue an end, unless it imposes on itself, by an act of the intellect, expressed in the form of a precept or law, the means and acts that lead to the end. But the intelligence of a group is the head or king. It is for him to order and to legislate so that the common good aimed at may be attained.

Other consequences, which we need mention here only in passing, follow immediately from the king's legislative power. Having laid down laws, it devolves on him to apply them in the concrete to the individuals whom they bind, and to see that they are observed. It is his business also to determine sanctions for these laws, so that they may have the constraining force which rightly belongs to them. Finally it is for him to judge and condemn the members of the group, if they fail in their duty and try to evade the laws. "Judicial power," says St. Thomas, "is a consequence of royal dignity."[2]

Of course, the king can delegate and communicate these different powers to others; but these are only his ministers, with no authority save that which they have received, and which they keep in complete and permanent dependence on their head.

---

[1] *De Regim. Princ.*, cap. I.
[2] IIIa P., Q. 59, a. 4, ad. I.

These few general notions concerning the nature of kingship in general will help us to form an idea of the Kingship of Christ.

The Teaching of the Church.

First of all, it is well to remark that there is not a shadow of doubt about the reality of Christ's Kingship. That Christ is King is a truth proclaimed by Scripture and Tradition, affirmed by Our Lord Himself, and taught officially by the Church as a doctrine to be believed by all the faithful. This is not the place to discuss all the texts. It will be enough for us to mention, in accordance with the Encyclical Letter, *Quas Primas,* the chief points they contain, and which will constitute the subject matter of this chapter.

The first and principal characteristic of Christ's kingly Power as made known to us by faith, is undoubtedly its universality. The Kingship of Christ is universal both in comprehension and in extension. By universality of comprehension we mean that Christ possesses all the prerogatives and all the functions which characterize royal power. He is legislator, and the precepts He gives to the world are His own: "If you keep My Commandments."[1] He is Judge: "For neither doth the Father judge any man: but He hath given all judgement to the Son."[2] This judicial power confers on Him the right of rewarding and punishing the faithful, of passing and executing sentence Himself. Jesus bears formal witness to this by the way He describes the last judgement to His Apostles.[3]

The royal power of Christ is also universal in extension. It extends to all creatures and to all the orders and societies to which they belong, whether the order be supernatural or natural, whether the society be civil or spiritual: "He however, would be guilty of shameful error," writes Pope Pius XI, "who would deny to Christ as man authority over civil affairs, no matter what their nature, since by virtue of the absolute dominion over all creatures He holds from the Father, all things are in His power."[4]

In addition, it must be carefully borne in mind that this universal kingly power belongs to Christ, not only because He is God, and therefore Ruler of all things, but precisely inasmuch as He is man, and in virtue of the power which has been given to Him by God: "Angels and men must not only adore Christ as God, but they must obey and be subject to His authority as man, for in virtue of the Hypostatic Union, Christ has power over all creatures."[5] It is to the elaboration of this doctrine of the Church that we must now apply ourselves.

---

[1] *St. John,* XIV, 15: XV, 10.
[2] *St. John,* V, 22.
[3] *St. Matthew,* XXV, 31.
[4] Encyclical Letter, *Quas Primas.*
[5] *Ibid.*

The Hypostatic Union and The Kingship of Christ.

The words we have just quoted from the Encyclical Letter, *Quas Primas,* show us that if we wish to discover the real foundation of the Kingship of Christ, we must look for it—as in the case of His Priesthood—in the Hypostatic Union, for it alone can furnish the ultimate explanation of this new prerogative. Substantial union with the Person of the Word of God raises the Humanity of Christ to a level surpassing that of all other creatures. Our Lord's Humanity thus acquires an incomparable degree of dignity, and by that very fact, a right to absolute pre-eminence also. In that indisputable doctrine there is to be found the obvious foundation for the universal royalty of Christ.

However, to proceed in an ordered fashion in so complex a matter, we must begin by making a distinction between the spiritual and the temporal Kingship of Christ, that is, between His primacy in the order of grace and His primacy in the order of nature. Of these two the first is the principal one.

Christ's Spiritual Kingship.

The life of grace directs us to our final end, that is, to the possession of God in the Beatific Vision. Accordingly, it transcends those secondary ends which are marked out for us by our nature as men. It has, therefore, a right to the place of honour in our scheme of existence. If Christ is Head and King in this domain, His primacy in it is endowed with a special importance surpassing any other that may be His. It is to this, then, that we shall first devote attention. Besides it has a more direct connection with His Priesthood, which also belongs to the supernatural order.

The Hypostatic Union is sufficient of itself to place the Humanity of Christ at the summit of creation, giving it absolute pre-eminence there. Yet if this pre-eminence is to constitute an effective royalty in an order like that of grace, it seems absolutely essential for Christ to be in perfect possession of grace. The King, as we have already said, is the living personification of the end towards which his subjects tend. He must possess that end himself, and he must live it by his highest faculties, for he is set as a light to the community. In the present case the common end is the flowering of the life of grace in the Beatific Vision. Accordingly, Christ can be really King in the spiritual order only on condition of possessing the fulness of this blessed life.

The Hypostatic Union of itself demands full participation in Supernatural Life. The fact of the Sacred Humanity being united to the Person of the Word does not change the human nature either in itself or in its operations. Harmony, however, would be wanting if the Humanity, which is thus united personally to God in its substance, were not equally united to Him in its operations, and that in the most perfect way. Son of God by nature, Christ, as man, has a strict right to His heavenly inheritance. Never could God have a greater or more pressing reason for raising a soul to Himself by the life of grace than in the case of Christ. The plenitude of grace demanded by the Hypostatic Union surpasses all the treasures of Supernatural Life which God could pour into other souls, and therefore constitutes Christ as the Head in the order of grace. It makes Him Head of all those creatures who compose that order, and who share in the Divine Life.

Saint Thomas rightly remarks[1] that every perfect principle of action is diffusive of its influence, and that if the power by which it acts is its own, it is the fontal source of its exterior manifestations. This is precisely the case with the Head or King. Accordingly, since Christ possesses Supernatural Life as His own —as a perfection demanded by His nature—and since He has it in its fulness, it is but normal that He should distribute it with discrimination and authority, and that He should thus enjoy real spiritual royalty. His grace is that of one who is Head and King.

Therefore, before continuing our inquiry, we can set down as definitely established that the primary source of Christ's spiritual Kingship is, unquestionably, the Hypostatic Union, but that the fulness of His habitual grace is its immediate and proximate foundation.

The Exercise of Christ's Spiritual Kingship.

It now remains for us to see how Christ exercises His Kingship in the concrete. To do so, we must rise in thought above the grace of Union and the grace of Headship, and concentrate our attention on the determining motive of the Incarnation.

All that refers to Christ and to His different prerogatives, all that concerns the development of His action on the world, can be explained only in the light of God's purpose or of what we have called the sacerdotal vocation of Christ. It is this vocation which not only explains the Hypostatic Union itself, but the particular mode of its realization, for it is quite evident that the Son of God could have become Incarnate and have lived on earth in an entirely different providential order of things. In all this, of course, we are accepting the Thomistic opinion regarding the motive of the Incarnation, and rejecting the view held by the Scotists. We are in the field of theological science, and we must accordingly aim at giving scientific unity to the data which Faith supplies concerning the Incarnation, in view of getting a deeper insight into God's loving designs in our regard. The perfect harmony between the conclusions we shall reach and the Church's teaching will justify and corroborate our way of looking at things.

The essential mission of Christ, the formal reason and determining motive of the Incarnation, is to save men, to draw them from sin, to restore them to the lost life of grace, and to lead them back to God that they may participate in eternal happiness. This mission is a strictly spiritual one, and this again contributes to

---

[1] IIIa P., Q.8, a. 5.

make the spiritual Kingship of Christ more important than the temporal. Christ, first and foremost, came to rule men spiritually and to lead them to eternal life. "This Kingdom," we read in the Encyclical *Quas Primas* of Pius XI, "is principally spiritual and chiefly concerned with things spiritual. This is quite plain from the extracts from Scripture above quoted, and Christ's own line of action confirms this view."

Another equally important consequence of Christ's redemptive mission is that it influences His social activity by directing it in an especial manner towards men. It cannot be doubted that the angels form part of the spiritual Kingdom of Jesus: the fulness of His grace is the measure of theirs: they receive abundant supernatural lights from Him, and finally they are at His service in the work of our salvation. But men belong to Him much more intimately; they are the chief part of His Kingdom; and it is especially in regard to them that we must see how Christ rules.

From what has just been said, it is easy to see that the spiritual Kingship of Christ, is, in the last resort, simply a function of His grace of Headship. That function does not, however, exhaust its possibilities. By this same grace, though under another title— that of Priest—Christ communicates Supernatural Life to the world. It is very important to distinguish accurately between these two aspects of the grace of Headship, because by accurately delineating the contents and limits of each of these two functions of Christ Our Saviour, we can get a more appropriate idea of the second—His Kingship.

Christ's Kingship and His Priesthood.

In the ordinary course of human events, it belongs to the King, through the many powers vested in his person, to conduct the body of his subjects to their end, in a manner at once visible and social. But it is not his function to bestow on them the vital power and the physical aptitudes they require if they are to follow him. His government presupposes the existence of these gifts. It favours their development by putting them at the service of the ideal to be attained, but it does not create them. The rôle of the head is to guide; the function of the king is to rule, but not strictly speaking to transmit life to his subjects.

Christ's mission, however, does not merely make Him a guide of souls in their progress in the life of grace: it makes Him the very source of this life. He is charged with communicating to men the grace He possesses in His Humanity, and in doing so He resembles a universal cause whose fruitful influence diffuses itself over all the beings dependent on it. We do not, of course, mean to convey that the grace of Christ is the physical, efficient and principal cause of the grace of other men. It has, however a universal influence in two ways, firstly, inasmuch as the Sacred Humanity is the inexhaustible source of merit and satisfaction for the whole world, and secondly, because it is constituted the perfect instrument of God for the transmission of the Divine Life of Grace.

The rôle of sanctification which Christ has in virtue of His grace of Headship belongs, as we have said, rather to His Priesthood than to His Kingship. It is the priest's function to act as intermediary between God and men; to transmit to God the petitions of men, to offer Him their sacrifices, and in return to dispense gifts and benefits to men on God's behalf. When Christ merits and satisfies for us by offering up His sufferings and death, He acts as Priest, not as King; when through His Humanity, God's instrument, He communicates the graces of pardon and regeneration; when He imparts the truth that saves and transforms souls, He is again acting as Priest, not as King. Further, every duty that makes Christ the indispensable Mediator between God and men belongs necessarily to His Priesthood.

We must not forget, however, that Christ is not priest as ordinary men are priests. St. Paul says that every priest must offer for His own sins as well as for those of the people.[1] Our Lord Jesus Christ does not come under this rule; He has neither to expiate for Himself nor solicit the Divine Mercy in His own regard. On the contrary, because of His personal union with the Divinity, His offerings and satisfactions are of such value that they have a right to be accepted in strict justice. That alone is sufficient to make it possible for Christ to enjoy real authority in applying His sacrifice to the world. His Humanity is not a mere lifeless, passive instrument of sanctification in the hands of the Word. It is fully conscious of its acts, and it remains free, even when acting in full accord with the Divine Will, it puts itself under His all-powerful influence in order to produce grace in us. Christ's perfect knowledge of supernatural things and of the mysteries of predestination allows Him complete freedom of action in the work of our salvation.

Accordingly, both as meritorious and as instrumental cause of the Divine Life of our souls, the grace of Headship makes Christ the conscious willing agent of our sanctification. Thus, freely and with a full understanding of God's eternal designs on the world, He co-operates in the work of the redemption. One obvious consequence follows. Remaining completely master of His actions, knowing perfectly how to ordain them to the salvation of men in conformity with God's will, and understanding that human beings can be sanctified and saved only on condition of being closely united to Him, and of forming with Him one Mystical Body, Christ has the function of organizing the enterprise of our salvation, drawing men to Himself, grouping His faithful ones around Him, ruling and governing them. In all this, Christ acts as Head, and not merely as Mediator, for this is part of His office as King and spiritual Ruler. Christ's spiritual Kingship is called for by the grace of the Hypostatic Union, but

---

[1] Cf. *Epistle to the Hebrews*, V, 3.

in the grace of Headship, which is ordained to the redemption of the human race, it attains its realization and finds its concrete expression.

It is quite certain that Christ's Kingship is intimately bound up with His Priesthood, and that in His actions it is not always easy to distinguish those which belong to one and those which belong to the other of these two prerogatives. The task is all the more difficult because sometimes an action can be referred to both. We have just seen a case in point in regard to the bestowal of grace on men, for here Christ is not just an intermediary—He enjoys real autonomy. Nevertheless the functions of Priest and King are different and must be distinguished. To merit grace, to produce it as an instrument, are essentially sacerdotal actions, because their immediate effect is to unite men to God, and God must always be the principal cause of this union. But to establish order in the sanctification of souls, to initiate holiness at will, to dispose of the gifts of God by distributing them intelligently— all this supposes a hierarchical power quite different from, though not exclusive of, priestly power.

To Christ the King, therefore, it belongs to fix a just proportion in the distribution of His gifts to the faithful, giving grace to each one according to His good pleasure. So, under His influence, as St. Paul says, "the whole body, being compacted and fitly joined together, by what every joint supplieth, according to the operation in the measure of every part, maketh increase of the body unto the edifying of itself in charity."[1]

To Christ the King it belongs to set before the faithful the common end to be attained, and to indicate the means for its attainment. His Priesthood, it would seem, would already require this on His part. But here it is not so much a question of promoting the development of the interior life as of guiding the visible, exterior movement of the whole Mystical Body towards the happiness of heaven. The guidance is given by an authority that commands and legislates and is not restricted to a moral exhortation drawing the soul under the influence of grace.

It is the office of Christ the King to attach sanctions to His own precepts, to recompense or punish the faithful according to their merits or demerits, to pass definitive judgement on them, and to pronounce that judgment that will cast them out among the accursed, or enrol them for ever in the ranks of the blessed of His Father.

Finally, Christ the King, by reason of the redemptive work incumbent on Him, must conquer His Kingdom, and defend His faithful subjects against the enemies who strive here below to compass their destruction. It sometimes happens in the ordinary

---

[1] *Epistle to the Ephesians*, IV, 16. "From Him the whole body, welded and compacted together by means of every joint of the system, part working in harmony with part—from Him the body deriveth its increase, unto the building up of itself in charity." (Westminster Version).

G

course of human events, either because of ill-will on the part of subjects, or on account of opposition from enemies, that the king is obliged, if he wishes to exercise his prerogatives fully, to compel his subjects to submit to his rule, and to vanquish his enemies. So it is with Christ in regard to His spiritual Kingship. King of souls, whom He is to lead to the Beatific Vision, He must first of all win them over by delivering them from sin. When they have been won over, He has to protect them unceasingly from the snares of the world and the devil, and to safeguard them from the assaults of their own passions. Victory over moral evil is the condition of His rule. His spiritual Kingship is militant and victorious, and this struggle continues so long as men remain here below, exposed to suffering and death, to corruption and sin. The fight will come to an end only in eternity with the triumph of the good and the defeat of the wicked, that is, by the complete and over-whelming victory of Christ. "Afterwards the end, when He shall have delivered up the kingdom to God and the Father, when He shall have brought to naught all principality, and power, and virtue. For He must reign *until He hath put all His enemies under His feet.*"[1]

It is true that Christ's combat against evil is, from certain points of view, closely linked with His Priesthood: for it is by sanctifying souls and uniting them to God that He withdraws them from sin and makes them part of His Kingdom. But here as in the previous case, we must distinguish two aspects of this struggle. One is negative and is concerned with the struggle against sin and the destruction of evil: this relates to Christ's Kingship. The other aspect is positive, and belongs to His Priesthood: it concerns the union of souls with God. To wage war in the name of a whole people and to lead His army to victory are both actions of the type that strictly appertain to the Ruler or King.

It is now easy to understand why the redemption constitutes a title for Christ's spiritual empire over souls. He has won these souls by shedding His Precious Blood: they are really His; by His sufferings and death, He has the right to rule over them eternally. "What reflection can give us more pleasure and joy than the thought that Christ is Our King, not only by natural, but also by acquired right, in virtue of His Redemption?"[2]

Therefore, while the Incarnation and Christ's grace of Head-ship are ordained to the redemption of men, this Redemption, in return, by exalting Christ, procures for His spiritual Kingship an incomparable glory and splendour. This is what St. Paul expressed admirably when he wrote: "For in that (God) hath subjected all things to Him, He left nothing not subject to Him. But now we see not as yet all things subject to Him. But we see Jesus, who was made a little lower than the angels, for the

---

[1] *First Epistle to the Corinthians*, XV, 24-25.
[2] Encyclical Letter, *Quas Primas*.

suffering of death, crowned with glory and honour: that through the grace of God He might taste death for all. For it became Him for whom are all things, and by whom are all things, who had brought many children into glory, to perfect the author of their salvation, by His passion."[1] St. Thomas expressed the same thought in a precise formula, when he said: "It is especially in the Passion, that the Priesthood and the Kingship of Christ receive their completion."[2]

The Extension of the Spiritual Kingship to the Temporal Order.

Christ came into this world to save men. By the fact of this mission of salvation, for which He was equipped by the grace of Headship, and more fundamentally still, by the grace of Union, He had full powers of government in the spiritual order. The supernatural order to which we have been raised by God's loving condescension does not do away with our human nature nor suppress the exigencies of that nature in the domain of temporal affairs. Though we have been endowed with the Supernatural Life of Grace, we are nevertheless meant to live our lives as human beings within the social organization demanded by our nature for the attainment of our temporal end. The pursuit of the temporal end, however, must be subordinated to our super- natural end, so that instead of impeding this latter, it may on the contrary, subserve it. It is by observing the natural conditions of existence laid down for us, and by living in contact with the lowly realities of daily life, that we must work out our salvation. Grace gives a new orientation to our efforts, by directing them to the God of revelation known and loved in Himself. The temporal order, with those in charge of it, subsists side by side with the spiritual order and its hierarchy. Authority has its proper sphere in each.

But because what is temporal is subordinate to what is spiritual, and because the final end of man, which dominates all other ends, is supernatural, we must concede to the Head or Ruler in the order of grace a right of intervention in the human order. This right will be determined by the necessity or utility of developing and preserving the Divine Life in souls. Accordingly, the spiritual Kingship of Christ comprises this power of intervention in human affairs: and, in point of fact, we find Christ using it in the Gospels when He drives the traffickers from the Temple, thus vindicating

---

[1] *Epistle to the Hebrews*, II, 8-10. *The Westminster Version* runs as follows. "How in subjecting all things to Him, he left nothing that is not subject to Him And yet, at present, we do not see all things made subject. But Him Who was made a little lower than the angels, our Jesus, we see crowned with glory because of the sufferings of death, that He, by God's grace, might taste death on behalf of all. For it behoved Him on account of Whom all things are, and through Whom all things are, when He was bringing many sons to glory, to make perfect through suffering the author of their salvation."

[2] IIIa P., Q. 35, a. 7, ad Ium.

the rights of God to fitting honour and insisting on suitable restrictions in commerce and trade.

It is of interest to note that this right of intervention in temporal matters is not an extrinsic addition to the royal dignity of Christ; it forms part of His spiritual Kingship. There is no question of commanding and legislating with a view to enabling human society to attain its end, the common good of the natural order: that is the function of the Temporal power in the strict sense. But it is question of opposing anything calculated to impede the Supernatural Life or the social order it requires, and of obtaining from kings and heads of states the freedom necessary for this. This power is one with the spiritual Kingship; it is at its service, and may even be called its instrument. "When one thing exists for another," writes St. Thomas, quoting Aristotle, "there appears to be but one thing present."[1] Accordingly the older theologians rightly designated this power as instrumental: "Christ as Man," writes Bannez, "enjoyed an instrumental power of universal sovereignty over all temporal things."[2]

It must be noted also that this right of intervention in temporal affairs, belonging, as it does, to Christ's spiritual Kingship, is attached, like it, to the grace of Headship. That is an obvious consequence, arising from the indirect and instrumental character of this power. We must also remark that if this power is limited to what is more or less closely connected with the Divine Life of souls, and with the interests of the Mystical Body, then considered from this point of view, there is no domain into which it may not enter. Not only the civil law, but also the material world, is subject to it. That is why Christ could intervene in this domain, by His miracles, in view of the expansion of His work. Needless to say, in working a miracle, the Sacred Humanity of Christ was simply God's instrument; but it belonged to Christ, as Head of the Mystical Body, to determine the manner of this miraculous intervention and to judge of its opportuneness.

Accordingly we can admit that Christ co-operated and still co-operates, really and regularly, in the unfolding of God's providential designs. If it is true that the divine government associates creatures with the realization of its designs, what can be more natural than to concede to Christ the principal part therein? We shall see that the temporal Kingship of Christ admits of this privilege; but even exclusively from the point of view of the spiritual Kingship, and to assist its exercise, it is not unreasonable to suppose that Christ can intervene in the events of this world, and that, not only in an extraordinary and miraculous way, but even in ordinary fashion, as for example, by obtaining and distributing the temporal favours needed by His Mystical Body.

---

[1] IIIa P., Q. 18, a. 2, ad 3.
[2] Bannez: *Commentary on the Summa Theol.*, IIa IIae, Q. 62.

Let us now sum up the different points in this analysis of the Kingship of Christ. The Hypostatic Union confers on Christ, in His human nature, an absolute pre-eminence over every creature, especially over those who have received the gift of Supernatural Life. This pre-eminence becomes a really effective Kingship because of the plenitude of grace accorded to Jesus, a plenitude which is called for by the Hypostatic Union. As regards the actual exercise of this Kingship, it is determined by the divine decree, which from all eternity, ordained the Incarnation for the redemption of the world. It is by saving souls from sin and leading them to God that Christ exercises His spiritual Kingship. This is the source of its militant character. This, too, is at the origin of its intimate association with the other prerogative of Jesus—His Priesthood. Lastly, this is the reason of its extension to the whole temporal domain in so far as the latter concerns the salvation of souls and the progress of the spiritual society of the Mystical Body.

Christ's Temporal Kingship.

Theologians are unanimous in admitting the sovereignty of Christ in the spiritual order. But the problem of His temporal Kingship is altogether different and, for some centuries past has given rise to a number of divergent solutions. It is not merely a question of conceding to Christ a right of intervention in temporal affairs in the name of the higher interests of His Mystical Body. Temporal kingship presupposes that he who is invested with it pursues a temporal end, and that he has directly in view the natural Common Good of the society confided to him, the temporal happiness of his people.

Of course, one cannot imagine Christ being the ruler of one particular people only. We know that His Kingship is universal; the kings and princes of the earth need have no fear of being deprived by Him of their authority. But is not Christ their sovereign and their judge? Has He not the right to govern them as a body, to dictate His laws to them, to reward or punish them according as they use or abuse their God-given power? Scripture seems to invite us to take this view since it calls Him "the prince of the kings of the earth,"[1] "the King of kings and Lord of lords."[2]

We may go even further, and because " all power has been given Him in heaven and on earth,"[3] because God has given Him dominion over the works of His hands, and "has put all things under His feet,"[4] we may ask ourselves if Christ may not claim the ownership of all things, so that He can use them according to His good pleasure in order to further His universal ends.

---

[1] *Apocalypse*, I, 5.
[2] *Apocalypse*, XIX, 16.
[3] *St. Matth.*, XXVIII, 18.
[4] *Epistle to the Hebrews*, II, 8, and foll.

The Universality of Our Lord's Temporal Kingship.

The teaching of the Church, set forth in the Encyclical Letter, *Quas Primas*, furnishes a decisive answer to those two questions. Pope Pius XI, after having declared that Christ's spiritual Kingship is one of His most important prerogatives, immediately adds: "He, however, would be guilty of shameful error who would deny to Christ as man authority over civil affairs, no matter what their nature, since by virtue of the absolute dominion over all creatures, that He holds from the Father, all things are in His power." The *right* in question therefore, is absolute and unrestricted, and confers on Christ the government and direction of all civil affairs. It even extends to all created things, for all are subject to His will.

Nevertheless, the Encyclical goes on to say that Christ, during His mortal life, refrained from intervening in matters subject to the jurisdiction of earthly governments. Spurning the ownership and the care of the goods of this world, He left the enjoyment of them to their owners, as He does to-day: during His life on earth, He refrained altogether from exercising such dominion, and despising the possession and the administration of earthly goods, He left them to their possessors then, and He does so to-day. This thought is charmingly expressed in the Hymn for the Epiphany: *Non eripit mortalia qui regna dat celestia—He does not seize earthly kingdoms Who gives heavenly kingdoms.*

It is pleasing to be able to record that this official teaching of the Church had already been formulated by St. Thomas in his theological works. At first sight it is true, there are certain texts of the Angelic Doctor which seem to convey a different impression. Thus, when dealing with the reign of Christ, in his *Commentary on the Epistle to the Hebrews*, he says: "This reign is not ordained to temporal, but to eternal things. 'My Kingdom is not of this world.' He reigns in view of leading men to eternal life."[1] Again, in the *Commentary on St. John.* he writes: "Christ reigns over the faithful, and He came into this world to gather together His faithful servants and to establish His Kingdom."[2] But these texts, to be rightly understood, must be interpreted in the light of the teaching contained in the *Summa Theologica*. In the *Summa*, it is perfectly manifest that Christ has the absolute right of temporal government over all things, but that he refrained from using it, because of his universal mission of salvation: "If we consider Christ as Man, it is evident that all human affairs are subject to his judgement."[3] "A king must of necessity have judicial power. Christ, however, though constituted King by God, did not desire, while on this earth, to act as the temporal Ruler of His earthly kingdom:"[4] St. Thomas also adds that it is in this sense of abstrac-

---

[1] Ch. I, L. 4.
[2] Ch. XVIII, L. 6.
[3] IIIa P., Q. 59, a. 4.
[4] Ibid. I.

tion from exercising His judicial power that the text, "My Kingdom is not of this world," must be understood. The commentaries on this text, and others of a like nature ought therefore to be similarly interpreted. According to he Angelic Doctor, Christ's power of government extends to all creatures: "All things are subject to Christ, because His Father has given Him power over them. But all things are not yet subject to Him as regards the exercise of this power."[1] "Christ's judicial power extends not only to the Angels but also to the government of every creature. . . . One may say that all things are ruled by His human soul, which is superior to every creature."[2] And to anyone who objects that this means conferring on Christ a providential power equal to that of God Himself, Saint Thomas replies: "Yes in as much as God has not established another like Him on earth, for the Lord Jesus Christ, God and Man, is one and the same being."[3]

Now that the broad outlines of the temporal Kingship of Our Lord have been sketched, it will be easy to set forth their theological foundations and to link them up with our study of His Priesthood.

Christ's Temporal Kingship and the Hypostatic Union.

In conformity with the teaching of the Encyclical Letter, *Quas Primas,* it is to the Hypostatic Union that we must turn if we wish to discover the ultimate foundation of the temporal Kingship of Christ: "for, in virtue of the Hypostatic Union, Christ has power over every creature."[4]

Cajetan, commenting on the first article of the Third Part of the *Summa,* rightly remarks that in a certain sense through the medium of the human nature of Christ, the whole universe is united to God in a very lofty and most intimate manner. Man is, as it were, an epitome of all creation, for in him are united material, organic and spiritual nature. In consequence, we may say that in assuming human nature God assumes the entire world, spiritual and corporeal. "He unites created nature to Himself," says St. Augustine quoted by St. Thomas," so as to form but one Person embracing these three realities: the Word, a human soul, and a body."[5]

Henceforth, by the Hypostatic Union, Christ in His human nature is raised above all creation. He is the culminating point of the universe towards which all creatures converge. St. Thomas constantly reiterates that the imperfect is for the perfect, that inferior beings in the service of those that are superior, achieve in them and by them their return to God, who is the final end of

---

[1] IIIa P., Q. 59, a. 4.
[2] IIIa P., Q. 59, a. 6.
[3] IIIa P., Q. 59, a. 6, ad. 3.
[4] Encyclical Letter, *Quas Primas.*
[5] IIIa P., Q. I, a. I.

all things. By reason of this order and hierarchy in being, it belongs to the more perfect to rule and govern the less perfect. And as Christ, by the Hypostatic Union, is at the summit of creation, He has the right to control it and to lead it to its end. This is the reasoning of the Angelic Doctor: "If, then," as St. Augustine says, "inferior beings are ruled by God through superior beings, we must hold that all things are ruled by the soul of Christ, for it is above them all."[1]

We have no difficulty, then, in seeing that Christ, in virtue of the Hypostatic Union, has been constituted in His human nature, King of the universe and of the whole temporal order, just as He is King in the spiritual order.

Christ's Temporal Kingship and His Infused Natural Knowledge.

When speaking of the spiritual Kingship of Christ, we said that while it rests on the grace of Union as upon its ultimate foundation, it needs for its actual exercise, to have a more immediate principle, namely the grace of Headship. The Ruler, when guiding his subjects to their end, must himself have a firm intellectual grasp of that end. He must be its living personification, for his commands will be really and truly such, only on condition of being the practical expression of the end envisaged. Hence, as Christ is destined to lead souls to eternal happiness, it would be altogether unseemly if He Himself did not possess that happiness in its fulness.

A similar difficulty presents itself to our minds, when we come to deal with the temporal Kingship of Christ. The Hypostatic Union, even while elevating the human nature to personal union with God, in no way changes its essential character. The divine act by which it is thus united with the Word leaves to the Humanity of Jesus its human faculties and powers. A human nature, of itself and left to its own resources, even though it be assumed into personal union with the Second Person of the Blessed Trinity, is not yet apt to exercise universal temporal Kingship. For that there is still required a knowledge of all things in the universe, of the ends proper to each and of the end common to all, as well as of the relation between the common temporal end of the world and the strictly supernatural end to which, in last analysis, all the rest is ordained. Besides, the universe contains purely spiritual natures as well as material ones. A human mind that would be proportioned to the latter would be powerless when confronted with the former.

Consequently, if Christ is to possess the proximate and immediate power to rule the whole universe, He requires a much more extensive knowledge than can be acquired by the work of His intelligence. He must have a knowledge that God alone can communicate. This knowledge must be like the infused knowledge

---

[1] IIIa P., Q. 59, a. 6, ad. 3.

of the Angels, and yet it must surpass in extent and perfection the knowledge of the highest angel, for even the most perfect of the angels is subject to Christ and is ruled by Him. Does Christ possess this perfect infused science? Unquestionably He does. And we know that it is fitting that He should have it even independently of the rôle He is called on to play in the government of the world. The Humanity of Christ, being personally united to the Word, has every right to a perfection which will make it worthy of Him who has assumed it. St. Thomas warns us that we must not deny that Christ's knowledge is absolutely complete and perfect, unless we want to leave His intelligence in a state of passive potentiality, deprived of the act in which it finds its perfection. It is certain, therefore, that Christ possesses all the powers, or if you will, all the principles and all the forms of activity which will enable Him to exercise universal temporal government. As far as this government is concerned He is fully equipped for action.

Looking at things from this standpoint, it is difficult to understand how anyone can hold—with a certain number of the older theologians—that temporal royal power is unbecoming in Christ. In order to maintain such an opinion, one would have to refuse Him certain perfections which are His by right, and which strictly though only morally, are a logical consequence of the Hypostatic Union. Such a contention upsets the harmony of the treatise on the Incarnation. In fact, the difficulty does not seem to reside here at all. It lies rather in this that the dignity and powers which Christ has in His human nature can become truly and formally royal, only if we suppose that God intends them for the temporal government of the world. So the whole question is whether, in point of fact, such a divine intention exists, and whether in decreeing the Incarnation, God deputed His Son to exercise such government. It does not seem so, if we admit that the sole determining motive of the Incarnation is the redemption of mankind by the sufferings, humiliations and death of the Word Incarnate. Most probably it was by dwelling on this incompatibility of the Redeemer's mission with the prerogative of temporal Kingship, that Billuart, Bannez, Bellarmine and others refused to admit Christ's right to govern nations, and to rule the whole world.[1]

It will be enough, however, to recall the nature of God's decree concerning the Incarnation of His Son, in order to realize that the true solution of the problem created by the temporal Kingship of Christ, is that suggested by St. Thomas and approved by the Encyclical *Quas Primas*.

---

[1] The different opinions of theologians on this subject are set forth in an excellent article by P. Lavand, O.P., in *"La Vie Spirituelle,"* March, 1926. See also P. Hugon, O.P., in *Revue Thomiste,* July, 1925, and P. Garrigou-Legrange, O.P., in *La Vie Spirituelle,* October, 1925.

The Temporal Kingship and the Motive of the Incarnation.

God wills the Incarnation for a motive which, while being in every way conducive to the attainment of His supreme ends— His own glory and that of His Son—nevertheless, brings about their realization, according to a plan and in a manner in conformity with the nature of this motive. God wills the Word to become Flesh for the salvation of the world: but He knows that the Incarnation inevitably leads to certain consequences, and that one of these consequences is precisely the conferring on Christ of a right of Universal Kingship over angels and men. God, therefore, cannot refuse to give to the Incarnate Word the title and the dignity of King which is His. In virtue of the Divine Intention, then, as well as on account of His intrinsic perfections, Christ is truly and formally King. But, because the proximate and determining end of the Incarnation is the redemption of mankind, willed by God as its formal motive, this end will wield a commanding influence over the other aspects of this mystery, both in regard to their mode of realization and their manner of functioning.

In the divine decree, the Word Incarnate must primarily save the world by a life of humility and suffering, by His Passion and Death. Before all else He is Priest, indeed High-Priest of the human race. We have already seen what this implies in the exercise of spiritual Kingship. From the same principle we shall now draw the conclusions that have a bearing on temporal Kingship. At once it becomes clear that the conditions fixed by God for the redemption of the world will run counter to the normal and ordinary functioning of Christ's temporal authority. How could Christ have saved the human race by the abasement, suffering and death of the Cross, if He had utilized His limitless power and authority over the rulers of this world? Conscious of the strictly redemptive and sacerdotal character of His mission, He knew God's will for Him, and consented fully to it. It was because He was destined to live a poor, a humble, and a suffering life that He refused to exercise any temporal authority over men. "Though constituted King by God, nevertheless, while He lived on earth, He did not accept the temporal administration of His earthly kingdom. . . . In the same way He refused to exercise judicial power over temporal affairs, for He came to lead men to heavenly things."[1] Christ did not rule over the kingdoms of the earth. He fled from the multitude, when they wished to make Him King. He refused to act as arbiter in a question of inheritance. It is just barely possible to discover here and there in the Gospel a manifestation of His power over angels and over nature, as for example, in the case of the demons whom He allowed to enter a herd of swine. In most cases the exercise of this power is ordained to the Common Good in the spiritual order.

---

[1] IIIa P., Q. 5, a. 4.

Not even after His death does Christ exercise His temporal Kingship over men, and the reason is always the same. "During His life on earth He refrained altogether from exercising such dominion and despising the possession and administration of earthly goods, He left them to their possessors then, and He does so to-day."[1] The Church, which has the charge here below of continuing His work of redemption, has not received from her Founder direct authority over men in temporal matters. Her Kingship is purely spiritual. Her mission, like that the Her Divine Master, is one of supernatural light and grace, as well as of struggle and suffering.[2] It is for earthly rulers to legislate in the temporal order, to sanction laws and to judge their subjects. Christ reserves to Himself only the right to pass the final judgement on the Last Day on their civil and temporal administration as well as on their submission to the supernatural order. Thus He will proclaim once and for all His complete dominion over them.

At the same time, as Pope Pius XI points out in the Encyclical Letter, *Quas Primas,* earthly rulers are bound to recognize and acknowledge the temporal supremacy of Christ the King. They are the more strictly bound to do this because of the greater autonomy left them by Christ in the exercise of their power. They are bound also to imitate the example given by their supreme Head by practising those virtues and loving those divine laws which should regulate their conduct. By supporting their short-lived authority by that of the Eternal Christ, they strengthen it and communicate to it a reflection of the Divine Power. Even if Christ is not the visible Ruler of States, His invisible influence is unceasing and universal even in the temporal domain. In heaven, is He not King of the Angels, and are they not at His service to carry out His orders here below? Has He not received from God dominion over the whole of created nature? "All things are ruled by the soul of Christ, which is above every creature."[3] Consequently, it is His duty to transmit to those kings who acknowledge His supremacy, the lights, graces and temporal benefits they require to govern their realms. It is His duty, also, to bless the peoples under them, and to make peace—His peace—to reign on earth. Thus we shall have the peace of Christ in the Kingdom of Christ.

At the close of this study, the harmonious unity of the Divine Plan to redeem the world in Christ clearly emerges. Christ is God, and this truth of faith is the foundation of the mystery of His being. It places Him, in His Humanity, at the summit of creation, and makes Him King of the universe. But Christ is Saviour, and His rôle as Saviour makes Him to be the Sovereign High-priest who offers up the whole human race to God as a perfect oblation. His spiritual Kingship is ordained to His Priesthood, because

---

[1] Encyclical Letter, *Quas Primas.*
[2] See Part II, Ch. IX.
[3] IIIa P., Q. 59, a. 6.

Christ rules men only in order to lead them to God. And His sacerdotal Kingship, in its turn, directs the functioning of His temporal Kingship, because man enjoys the use of natural goods here below in order to enable him to prepare for the higher life, for which he is destined by God. In every sense of the word, Christ is the keystone of the universe. God chose Him in order "to re-establish all things in Christ that are in heaven and on earth."[1] so that in Him and by Him all things thus reunited would return to God, Creator and Lord of the universe. "And when all things shall be subdued unto Him, then the Son also Himself shall be subject unto Him that put all things under Him, that God may be all in all."[2]

---

[1] *Ephesians*, I, 10.
[2] *I Cor.*, XV, 28. *The Westminster Version* has: "And when all things shall be subject to Him, then shall the Son Himself be subject to the Father who subjected all things to Him, that God may be all in all."

Chapter VI

CHRIST'S PRIESTLY ACTIVITY

Sacrifice, the Centre of Christ's Priestly Activity.

The preceding chapters have led us to consider the Priesthood of Christ in relation to the three great realities which govern and explain it. These are: the Divine Motive behind the Incarnation, the Hypostatic Union, and the grace of Headship. The Divine Intention singles out the Redemption, in which Christ is the High-Priest of humanity, as the proximate and immediate end of the Incarnation. The Hypostatic Union consecrates Christ substantially, and in every fibre of His Sacred Humanity makes Him Priest. The grace of Headship perfects His Priesthood by enabling it to exercise itself in the world with perfect efficacy. It now remains for us to see how, in the course of His earthly life, Christ effectively fulfilled the functions of Priest of God, and to see also, what special place in His priestly work must be assigned to His Passion and Death. "Every high priest is appointed to offer gifts and sacrifices,"[1] and St. Thomas says that "the principal duty of the priest is to offer sacrifice." These texts will guide us in our task. When we want to treat of the sacerdotal activity of Christ, we must concentrate our attention on His sacrificial activity. We are of course aware that the activity of Christ as Priest can be held to have a wider range; the teaching of truth, for example, is in a certain sense a priestly function, although from another point of view it can be attached to the prerogative of Kingship. The effective communication of grace and of the gifts of God is equally part of the Priesthood: it even belongs to it essentially. Still, properly speaking, all these are but preliminaries or consequences of sacrificial activity. If Christ came to reveal truth to the world, is it not that we may be able the more worthily to participate in His sacrifice, to gather its fruits, and to offer ourselves with Him in homage to the Sovereign Majesty of God? If Christ sanctifies us, is it not because, by His sacrifice, He has acquired the right to restore the Divine Life to us and to lead us to union with God for all eternity? Whatever way we consider it, therefore, sacrifice is in the centre of Christ's priestly activity, and apart from it there is no possible explanation of that activity.

What Faith Teaches.

By faith we know that Christ, on earth, offered Himself to God as a victim of sweet odour. From this point of view, His Passion and Death hold pride of place among all the events of His earthly life. In the light of Scripture and Tradition, the

---

[1] *Hebrews*, VIII, 3.

Church has always regarded Calvary as a genuine sacrifice, by which Christ saved the world and reconciled us to God. In the Old Testament the prophets announced a suffering Messiah, immolating Himself unto death for the redemption of His people. "He was offered because it was His own will," wrote Isaias . . ., "he hath delivered his soul unto death, and was reputed with the wicked; and he hath borne the sins of many, and hath prayed for the transgressors."[1] The whole Epistle to the Hebrews is simply a doctrinal exposition of the salvation wrought by Christ the Priest by the shedding of His Blood on the Cross: "But Christ, being come an high priest of the good things to come . . . neither by the blood of goats nor of calves, but by his own blood, entered once into the holies, having obtained eternal redemption. . . . And therefore he is the mediator of the new testament: that by means of his death, for the redemption of those transgressions, which were under the former testament, they that are called may receive the promise of eternal inheritance."[2] And again to the Ephesians St. Paul writes: "Christ also hath loved us, and hath delivered himself up for us, an oblation and a sacrifice to God for an odour of sweetness."[3] And St. John in his first Epistle writes: "He is himself a victim of propitiation for our sins, and not only for ours, but for those of the whole world."[4]

Tradition is so unanimous on this point that the Council of Trent did not think a special definition necessary. But in its explanation of the Eucharistic Sacrifice, and in the succeeding canons, it speaks repeatedly of "the most holy sacrifice offered by Christ on the Cross."[5] Besides, it is obvious that the Council's doctrine on the Sacrifice of the Mass would be meaningless if it were not taken for granted that Christ really and truly immolated Himself to His Father on the Cross.

For the man of faith, the Saviour's Passion holds a special place in His sacerdotal activity. The Inspired Books insist so much on this point that we even find it difficult to see exactly how the other circumstances of Our Lord's life belong to His priestly mission. It would certainly seem impossible to exclude them altogether. For did not Christ satisfy and merit for us from the first moment of His existence? Even in the womb of His mother did He not offer Himself to God as a victim for the salvation of the world? And would it be an exaggeration to say that the Blessed Virgin Mary was the altar of His first sacrifice? "Wherefore when

---

[1] *Isaias*, LIII, 7 and 12.

Translator's Note: This text of Isaias is less efficacious as a proof of Our Lord's sacrifice on Calvary than the texts of the same prophet, chapter LII, 14-15, and LIII, 10. Cf. Van Noort, *De Deo Redemptore*, p. 120.

[2] *Hebrews*, IX, 11, 12, 15.

[3] *Ephesians*, V, 2. *The Westminster Version* has: ". . . . as Christ also hath loved you and delivered Himself up for us, an offering and sacrifice of sweet savour to God."

[4] *I St. John*, V, 7.

[5] Sess. 22, Can. 4.

he cometh into the world," he saith: "Sacrifice and oblation thou wouldst not: but a body thou hast fitted to me. Holocausts for sin did not please thee. Then said I: Behold I come: that I should do thy will, O God."[1] Still, in spite of all this, faith turns our gaze to Calvary, as distinct from all the other actions of our Saviour's Life, and the sacrifice of Calvary is undoubtedly the crowning act of the priestly activity of Christ here below. What then is to be said about His other actions? Undoubtedly, this is a problem which must be faced frankly: nevertheless we prefer to leave its solution till later on, when we shall see how all the other actions of Jesus converge on the sacrifice of Calvary.

The Transcendent Character of Christ's Sacrifice.

One cannot treat adequately of sacrifice without having some idea of its nature, and of the rôle it is called on to play in the religious life of the human race. Therefore, at the outset, a brief inquiry into it is imperative. But we must be on our guard against a certain danger. In endeavouring to bring out the sacrificial character of Calvary, many authors try to show that, in the Passion and Death of Christ, the principal elements of previous religious sacrifices, especially of those of the Old Law, are to be found. This is legitimate but dangerous. One is liable to forget that the immolation of the Cross belongs to an order of its own, that it is the great and unique sacrifice instituted and willed by God, for the liberation of humanity, and, for that very reason, it is presented to us in very special guise and it is surrounded by circumstances entirely peculiar to itself. Calvary is the sacrifice of the Man-God, Who is at once Priest and Victim; and, far from having to borrow features from other sacrifices, it really predominates over them all and gives them their real value. The sacrifices of the Old Law were but the image of the sacrifice of the Cross. Now the image cannot be the measure of the reality, but is on the contrary dependent on it. Like a distant effect revealing a cause, it can help us to understand the reality, but it can in no sense define it. It is by faith that we have attained to the knowledge of Christ's sacrifice, and not by a comparison between the Passion of the Son of God and the immolation of victims in earlier forms of worship. These latter can throw some light on the mystery, but their inferior rites cannot enable us to grasp its wealth of meaning and penetrate its depths.

We are here face to face with a situation which is common to all the truths of Christian Revelation. In striving to understand these truths, rational concepts, the fruits of experience, are useful and necessary; but it would be wrong to apply them in exactly the same sense to matters of faith. We are obliged to have recourse to analogy, in order to safeguard the transcendence of the mystery. To act otherwise is to expose oneself to grievous mistakes and to

---

[1] *Hebrews*, X, 5, 6.

fall a victim to a form of materialism, which brings down what is properly divine to the merely human level. The Death of Christ on the Cross is a veritable sacrifice, but it is so in a manner altogether divine, and therefore, no merely human conception of it will ever succeed in laying bare its inner meaning. We find in it, of course, the broad outlines common to every sacrifice, but they are here incorporated into an order that infinitely surpasses the natural order. It is only in the light of principles such as these that we can avoid misunderstanding supernatural reality, when we make use of concepts derived from our experience of the world.

Sacrifice in General.

Sacrifice owes its origin to the state of subjection and dependence which man, in his helplessness, knows is his condition in regard to God.[1] Since man is a dependent being, subject by nature to a higher power, which governs him, guides him and assists him in his needs, it is right and fitting that he should give explicit recognition of his inferiority by paying homage to God, in his own human way. Now the human way of offering homage is to express the sentiments of the soul by perceptible signs. Accordingly, man will offer sensible and material things to God in order to express the entire submission of his being. He acts exactly as he does when he wishes to show honour to his master or his king. He takes some of his possessions, and offers them as a sign of fidelity and attachment.

The whole reason of sacrifice derives its origin, then, from that primitive sense of dependence on a higher power, and from the instinctive need to acknowledge that dependence by external acts. The modes of expressing dependence may vary according to time, country and race. Sentiments of affection or of interest or of fear may contribute to the richness of primitive psychology, and ideas of the divinity more or less pure will render the signification of the act of worship more or less spiritual and immaterial. Nevertheless it remains true to say that, at the root of every notion of sacrifice, lies the feeling of deep subjection to the God whom man adores, and the necessity of expressing his subjection in a sense-perceptible manner. A study of the history of the concept of sacrifice among primitive peoples would lead us to the same conclusions.[2]

Accordingly, at the origin of every exterior sacrifice, there is always postulated a sacrifice more intimate and more essential, by which man, realizing what God is and what he himself is, freely offers himself to the Sovereign Lord of all things, and subjects himself to his Creator with the whole force of his being. The exterior and visible sacrifice has no other object than to

---

[1] Cf. IIa IIae, Q. 85, a. 1.

[2] Cf. P. Schmidt—*Ethnologische Bemerkungen zu theologischen Opfertheorien,* IV and VII.

signify the interior and invisible sacrifice of the soul. It is a sign, a sacrament. For this reason Saint Thomas often recalls those words of St. Augustine: "The visible sacrifice is the sacrament or sacred sign of the invisible sacrifice."[1] "The sacrifice offered exteriorly signifies the interior spiritual sacrifice by which the soul offers itself to God."[2]

It is no surprise then to find that St. Thomas, when treating of the sacrifice of the Cross, insists on the sentiments of obedience and voluntary submission to His Father's will with which Christ immolates Himself. Sacrifice is meaningless if it does not refer to an inner state of soul: the visible gestures by which man strives to reproduce outwardly his inner attitude are devoid of value, if this inner attitude is not one of humble and complete dependence on God. As the Angelic Doctor remarks, it is not the importance of the material offering that constitutes the value of a sacrifice but the signification attached to the offering. One may pay exterior homage to the great ones of the earth, giving them gifts which surpass the material value of the offering made in a religious sacrifice. But what gives the latter its unique value is that man intends it as a homage of absolute and unreserved submission, Consequently, strictly speaking, sacrifice is due to God alone, as the one omnipotent Creator and Final End of all creatures.

The interior act by which the soul offers itself to God as to its Creator and its Final End, is an act of the virtue of religion. Thus, every manifestation of human activity, which is ordained to the accomplishment of the Divine Will, can express visibly this secret oblation of the soul, and merit the name of sacrifice. Hence the virtuous acts, by which a man freely subjects himself to God's law, can be considered as a donation of himself to Him who is the Author of nature and of the laws that govern it. However, properly speaking, these acts have a nature which is immediately determined by their object. They are acts of justice, of gratitude, of temperance before being acts of sacrifice. It is only by way of consequence, and because they are commended by religion, that they express real homage to God, the author of the moral law.

But apart from acts prescribed by the moral law, we can conceive other exterior actions which have but one aim—to symbolize submission and adoration, to express visibly the interior sacrifice of the soul and to be sign and sacrament. These actions are exclusively acts of religious worship. They constitute the true sacrifice which is the centre of all exterior and visible religion. It is in this sense alone that we shall here consider sacrifice.

The sacrifice which consists in offering to God the homage of a virtuous life is purely individual. The sacrifice with which we are here concerned belongs, on the contrary, to that public worship which man owes to God, as a member of the human race

---

[1] *De Civitate Dei*, Lib. X, cap. 5.
[2] IIa IIae, Q. 85, a. 2.

H

or of some more restricted group, family, city, tribe or nation. It belongs to the religious head of the group, that is, to the priest, to offer sacrifice in the name of all. It is for him to choose the matter of the offering and to carry out in its regard the rites required for a sacrifice. All religions have thus conceived the priest's rôle, so there is no need to stress the point.

What is of more interest to us is to know what are the particular visible things which man offers to God, and on what conditions such an offering merits the name of sacrifice. The object he has in view, as we have already pointed out, is to express the recognition of the sovereign dominion of God over all things including himself. As the inferior creatures have been put at his disposal, he can utilize them for sacrifice. The nearer they approach to him, and the more neccessary they are to his life and preservation, the better will the offering of them to God express those sentiments of submission, homage and adoration which he desires to manifest. Hence in most religious sacrifices we find man offering to God some of the things required for his sustenance. The portion offered is, no doubt, small, but it is sufficient to express the inner attitude of the soul, of which the thing offered is the sign.

How must an offering be made in order to constitute a genuine sacrifice? Saint Thomas refuses to admit that every offering is necessarily a sacrifice. The latter is unquestionably an offering, but of a special kind. In sacrifice a certain action is performed on the thing offered, which renders it sacred and makes it God's property. It is this action, this rite proper to sacrifice that we must discover. To do so, we must above all bear in mind the end to which sacrifice tends. From what has been said already it is easy to see that what man seeks in sacrifice is to effect a kind of "transference of the matter offered, to the domain of God, making it (so to speak) pass into the effective enjoyment of God."[1] Man can bring about this transference only if by a real positive action, the object is removed from ordinary use and placed at the entire disposal of God. Henceforth, the object no longer belongs to man, and he may never again use it as he wishes for his ordinary needs. It is a real abdication, by which man signifies the giving-up to God of something that is his own and thus strives to express the attitude of his soul entirely subject to its Creator. Now, nothing is more capable of signifying and effecting this abdication than a certain destructive action exercised on the object offered so that it can no longer be utilized for man's benefit. The offering of an object that is rendered unfit for man's use and benefit, in order the better to indicate the desire to renounce it and surrender it to God—such is the nature of the exterior sacrifice of worship. The wine that is spilled on the earth as a libation to the divinity, the first fruits surrendered, the

---

[1] M. Lepin, *Revue pratique d'Apologétique,* 1921, p. 474.

animals slaughtered or burned on the altar all manifest, each in its own way this primary and essential element of sacrifice.

Many theologians in striving after an exact idea of sacrifice which they can then apply without difficulty to the Blessed Eucharist, ask themselves to what extent the destruction of the matter offered is necessary for sacrifice, and they wonder if any action exercised on it suffices to signify its passage into God's exclusive dominion. We have no intention of entering into these discussions. We can say, however, without hesitation, that in the concrete, the gestures by which man expresses his abdication of dominion may assume very different forms, according to the nature of the object offered. In certain cases the destruction of the thing is reduced to a simple change in its state. We can then speak of destruction only in a wide sense: it is rather a removal from common use. The main point is that the change effected should preserve its power of signification. To do this it must be of a sense-perceptible nature. Only on that condition can it express the sentiments and the will of the offerer. Therefore, it may be remarked in passing, it is difficult to concede with M. Lepin that a simple blessing of the matter is sufficient to constitute a sacrifice.[1] For a blessing exercises only an invisible change in the thing it consecrates. Now the ritual sacrifice is essentially an exterior visible sign of interior sacrifice. It is a real effective abdication, carried out by man himself in reference to an object, in order to express this interior oblation. When the thing is merely blessed, it is God and not man, who effects the abdication. A blessing is really a prayer to God begging Him to appropriate a creature to Himself and make it the instrument of His mercy. Of course, as we shall see, sacrifice implies, on God's side, the acceptance of what is offered. But it presupposes that man has recommended the thing by suitable signs, signs which are not merely a prayer, but which effectively remove the object from human usage.

We may remark in addition that it pertains to the priest, and to him alone, to perform the visible action which transfers the matter of the sacrifice to God's exclusive dominion. It may happen as in the sacrifices of the Old Law, that the victim is slain by someone other than the priest; but then the putting to death is not a part of the sacrificial rite. It is merely a preparation for the sacrifice. To the sacrifice there will belong only the action of the priest on the slaughtered animal. This action may consist, for example. in the spilling of the blood of the victim on the altar, or in the burning of its fat.

If we now consider the ritual action by which the priest imparts to the victim its sacrificial character, it will be clear that with regard to God this gesture is one of offering. It is not even necessary to express it in words. The acknowledged dignity of the

---

[1] Cf. Article previously cited and *L' Idée du Sacrifice de la Messe d'après les théologiens*, pp. 192 and ff.

priest, the rites he performs, the circumstances that surround the sacrifice, suffice to give to his gesture the obvious meaning of an offering. This same ritual gesture, inasmuch as it is performed on the victim, bears the name of immolation: active immolation on the part of the priest; passive immolation on the side of the victim. Offering and immolation, then, are two aspects of the one sacrifice, intimately linked together in a single action—the act of the priest sacrificing the victim to God.

Accordingly, we can sum up with St. Thomas: "the term oblation is common to all things offered for the worship of God, so that if a thing be offered to be destroyed in worship of God, as though it were being made into something holy, it is both an oblation and a sacrifice. . . . If, on the other hand, it be offered with a view to its remaining entire . . . it will be an oblation and not a sacrifice."[1]

Secondary Aspects of Sacrifice.

Certain subsidiary aspects of sacrifice serve to enrich our first and essential idea of it. Human nature is very complex. When it turns to God to adore Him and offer Him homage, it quite naturally takes occasion of this opportunity to thank Him for His benefits. Is not thanksgiving to Him from Whom one has received everything very much akin to humble and deferential adoration? Besides, man realizes that, as by sacrifice he enters into relation with God and sets up social relations with Him, so if God is pleased with man's homage, He will respond by increased love and fresh benefits. To thanksgiving, therefore, is joined a sentiment of expectation, which makes the sacrifice a demand, an appeal, a prayer.

Among the elements which can add special modes to sacrifice, there is none of greater significance than the fact of sin. Sacrifice was not instituted on account of sin. Its origin lies deeper, and there would be sacrifice, even if there never had been sin. Nor is the destruction of the victim associated with sacrifice because of sin. It is inherent in sacrifice as such, for it effects that alienation of part of his goods which man makes in favour of God, in order to signify his complete and unreserved submission.

But since man has actually sinned he must expiate his fault, if he is to be restored to God's friendship; since, too, his sin involved a foolish attachment to created goods, what more appropriate mode of expiation can be found than that of depriving himself of these goods by sacrifice, and restoring them in a sense to God, from Whom he has unjustly wrested them? What more suitable way is there of doing so, after having turned away from God and offended His Divine Majesty, than to turn to Him by an act in which are to be found pre-eminently humble adoration and penance, and to signify, by the immolation of a victim, that one

---

[1] IIa IIae, Q. 86, a. 1.

submits oneself entirely to the Divine Decrees? Sacrifice for sin is found in all the religions of antiquity. Man is even prone to regard the victim which he immolates, as substituted for himself in the rigorous expiation which God expects: and, in presence of the gravity of his crime, no object, no being, even human, appears too precious, when there is question of appeasing God Whose anger he fears to have incurred.

This idea of substitution is often found in the sacrifice made by man to God. But we must be careful not to exaggerate its rôle. Since every exterior sacrifice is a sign of an interior surrender of soul, we may say that in a certain way, the visible object offered to God is substituted for man himself, or at least for all his possessions. By sacrifice man tends to deliver himself up unreservedly to God; yet, in fact, he can give, sacrifice, or immolate only a tiny fraction of his being or his goods. It is precisely this little fraction that is charged with the onus of supplying for the gift of all the rest. It is substituted for what man cannot give. In this sense it can be affirmed that substitution belongs to the essence of sacrifice, and is much more manifest in the case of sacrifice for sin.

In presence of his fault, man becomes conscious that nothing can suffice to repair it and obtain pardon. He should immolate his whole being in sacrifice. This being impossible, he prays God to accept in his stead a victim which will show his desire for reconciliation and pardon, which will in a certain fashion take upon itself his sins and so have them obliterated together with itself. One can easily see how the primitive idea of substitution will be enriched in this way. Yet all these additions are but secondary conceptions which always suppose the basic sentiment of being obliged to express exteriorly one's interior desire for self-sacrifice.

Another subsidiary aspect of sacrifice is the alliance with God contracted by it. Amongst ancient peoples, the shedding of blood held a prominent place in the conclusion of every pact or treaty. "Since for the nomads of the desert," writes Father Lagrange, O.P., "all social relations flow from blood relationship, no alliance is stable without a certain exchange of blood."[1] It is not surprising, therefore, that this idea found its way into sacrifice. The spilling of the victim's blood signifies not only that one is ready to give one's life for God, but that one intends to contract an alliance with Him by means of the blood that is shed. Moses merely applied a common idea, when he sprinkled the assembled people with blood from the altar, saying: "This is the blood of the alliance that the Lord has contracted with you."[2]

Finally, amongst the ancients, the sacrifice frequently terminates with the eating of a portion of the victim. Here again it seems that in this repast or communion, man is endeavouring to

---

[1] *Les Religions sémitiques,* p. 260.
[2] *Exodus,* XXIV, 8.

manifest in a sense-perceptible fashion the union or association which has been established between God and himself by the sacrifice. Whilst the part of the victim that is burnt appears to ascend to God, and is considered as being food and nourish- ment for Him, the other parts are eaten by man. Man thus partakes of the same repast as God, sits at the same table, so to speak, and enters into the inner circle of His familiar friends. Speaking of sacrifice amongst the Arabs, Father Lagrange, O.P., writes: "The second act of communion is to eat in presence of the god; since he does not eat, his portion is partaken of as food."[1]

The following quotation from St. Augustine sums up accurately those various aspects of sacrifice: "True sacrifice is every work performed in view of a holy intercourse with God, in order to attain that end which can make us truly happy."[2]

The Idea of Consecration in Sacrifice.

Up to the present we have envisaged only the part that belongs to man in the constitution of a sacrifice; we must now consider the part played by God. If we keep to the etymology of the word, *sacrificium*, namely, *sacrum facere*, sacrifice consists in rendering sacred the object offered.[3] Now, it is clear that in such a consecra- tion, God's rôle is the primary and principal one, while man's is secondary and instrumental. God alone can consecrate a being.[4] The result of consecration is that the object belongs exclusively to God, so that it cannot be employed for other than divine purposes. This consecration, it is true, admits of different degrees and can assume many different forms. But it is obvious in any case that God alone can thus appropriate an object and set up a real relationship between Himself and it. In this matter all that man can do is to express a desire, or give utterance to a prayer; or, if he be officially deputed by God for this purpose, he can only be the minister or instrument of divine action. "In these matters," writes St. Thomas, "man acts merely as God's instrument."[5]

We know that, in sacrifice, man attempts to transfer part of his own possessions to God in order to give open expression to the recognition of his dependence on God. Sacrifice, therefore, can- not be perfect except God responds to man's desire, accepts the proffered victim, sanctifies it and really consecrates it. In an order of things undisturbed by sin it would seem that God should normally do so, for sacrifice is an act of religion required by the natural law. The act of immolation by which man offers the victim and endeavours to transfer it to God's dominion, becomes

---

[1] *Les religions sémitiques*, p. 261. Cf. also pp. 272-273.
[2] *De Civitate Dei*, Lib. 10, cap. 6.
[3] IIa IIae, Q. 85, a. 3. ad. 3. "Sacrificium dicitur ex hoc quod homo facit aliquid sacrum."
[4] Cf. article by A. Barrois, *Le Sacrifice du Christ au Calvaire*, in *Revue des Sciences philosophiques et théologiques*, April, 1925, pp. 147 and foll.
[5] IIa IIae, Q. 39, a. 3.

then the sign, as it were, of the divine consecration, and therefore of the response and acceptance of God. Nothing prevents us from considering this act of immolation, if performed by a priest, as the instrumental cause of this consecration. Is not the priest himself consecrated and deputed by God for sacrificial worship?

Sacrifice, therefore, appears to us as the joint action of man and God. Man does all in his power to dispossess himself of his own goods in favour of God. God uses man's action to produce by it the consecration of the victim and to accept the sacrifice.

Still, we must never forget that the exterior sacrifice is but the sign of the invisible one, by which man signifies his complete submission to God. By means of the visible sacrifice, man expresses his desire to belong more fully to God and to become more intimate with Him. If he did not succeed in this, his exterior worship would be incomplete and its aim unattained. So God must accept not only the gift of the victim presented to Him, but also the more intimate gift of the soul, of which the victim is but the sign. The divine acceptance consists, of course in a new infusion of grace which strengthens the union of the soul with God. In reply to man's appeal and to his act of worship, God sanctifies him and draws him into closer intimacy with Himself, so that to Him, the Divine Master, glory may be given not only in figure, but in spirit and in truth.

Thus is set up that mysterious cycle of worship, which proceeds from man's soul to God through sacrifice, and which God completes by pouring out benefits on His creature, and by attaching him indefectibly to Himself.

What Sacrifice is Required by the Present State of Humanity?

Taking into consideration the present state of humanity, we must now determine in the concrete what act of worship will best realize all that exterior sacrifice demands. The complexity of the problem is due precisely to man's condition of sinner. If it were merely question of a worship of adoration, praise, thanksgiving, and prayer, to be offered to God by His innocent rational creature, the solution would have been easy. The oblation of any sense-perceptible object, however small, would suffice to express the interior adoration of such a creature and would constitute a sacrifice agreeable to God.

But man is a sinner. Sin has placed him in a state of enmity with God. He is crushed beneath the weight not only of personal faults that are alas! very real, but also by the weight of original sin, which separates him from God from the first moment of his existence. We find it impossible to imagine any individual or any social group, limited by time and space, as being able to cleanse the entire race of the stain of sin. This universal stain, extending to all the generations of the past and the future, renders man's very nature culpable, and receives from that nature an unlimited power of diffusion.

Moreover, if we examine sin in itself, whether personal or social, we shall see that it is always an offence against the infinite majesty of God, and on that account demands equivalent reparation. When I insult one of my equals, my offence is measured by the dignity of the injured person. When I try to repair the injury, the value of my reparation is calculated according to my personal dignity. Hence, if I am to obtain pardon, I shall often need an intercessor more powerful and more worthy of being heard than I am. What reparation could sinful man make in atonement for the infinite offence offered to God? In vain will he seek the most precious victims, those dearest to his heart; in vain will he sacrifice them in uninterrupted hecatombs, all is but a finite symbol of a human feeling still more limited and cannot counterbalance the infinite gravity of the offence.

God, of course, can mitigate the rigours of His justice. He can content Himself with the little we are able to offer, and pardon us because of our goodwill. But He is free to do so or not. To appease His justice He may exact strict reparation of the fault. As a matter of fact, faith teaches us that He has chosen this latter course, and that no satisfaction offered by ordinary men will suffice. But faith reveals at the same time that God, to satisfy both His mercy and His desire to pardon, has Himself presented to humanity a chosen victim, of inestimable price and of incomparable value. The sacrifice of Christ is alone capable of appeasing Divine Justice and of washing away our sins.

The Sacrifice of Christ.

One day, John, who was baptizing at Bethany, beyond the Jordan, saw Jesus coming towards him and said to those around him: "Behold the Lamb of God." By this symbolic title, reminiscent of the ineffectual sacrifices of the Old Law, the Precursor, possibly without being aware of it, defined the essential mission of Christ on earth. The man who was silently approaching, shrouded in mystery, was indeed the Lamb of God, the Holy Victim, far and away superior to the Jewish Paschal Lamb or to the lamb which was offered in sacrifice for Israel every day. John did not speak of Jesus as Elias or as the Prophet or as the Christ. For the Precursor, He was the Lamb, whose immolation was to blot out the sins of the world; He was that Victim which the human race down the centuries had sought for far and wide, the Victim that was to restore it to God's favour.

The primary and essential task of the Divine Victim was, therefore, to reconcile man to God. But, at the same time, it was His duty to institute that sovereign act of homage and adoration by which regenerated humanity could fittingly honour God.

Jesus entered upon His rôle of Victim from the very beginning. Christ said on entering the world: "Holocausts for sin did not please thee: then said I: Behold I come."[1] "He was a victim from

---

[1] *Hebrews*, X, 5-10.

His virginal birth," writes Tertullian.[1] To understand this, we must bear in mind that Christ's personal union with the Divinity gave Him the right to perfect glory, from the first moment of His existence. Jesus enjoyed the vision of the Divine Essence in His highest human faculties, and this happiness of the elect should have overflowed on His whole being, even on His body, and so should have rendered Him immune from suffering and death. Such a state of things would have been most fitting and was called for by the Hypostatic Union. Yet when theologians, in conformity with the Church's teaching, say that the soul of Jesus was in possession of the Beatific Vision, they are also compelled to acknowledge that the glory of the spiritual soul had no repercussion on His lower faculties or on His body. The sensitive part of Our Lord's Sacred Humanity was destined by God to endure suffering and death. He was a Victim from the very beginning of His life, and from the Manger to the Cross the whole development of His life was to be the successive unfolding of His rôle as Victim. This rôle gave unity to the existence which began in the womb of His Blessed Mother and ended on Calvary.

On the other hand, a victim requires to be offered by a priest, and this offering must be made according to rites that are capable of making it a real sacrifice. Who then will offer the Sacred Victim, and how will the sacrifice be accomplished?

When a Jew under the Old Law wished to offer sacrifice to God, he bought a lamb or a dove from the dealers in the Temple and left the accomplishment of the sacred rites to the priest. Because the victim was an irrational creature, it was necessary that another, a rational being, should perform the principal sacrificial acts, namely, immolation and offering. In the case of Our Lord Jesus Christ, we are in presence of a human Victim, fully conscious of His responsible rôle. Because of His infinite dignity, no creature is worthy to offer this Victim to God. God must have a holy priest as well as a stainless victim; and every man, apart from Him who is this Victim, is a sinner. Thus it remains for the Victim to offer Himself in the way laid down from all eternity by Divine Decree. Christ is the Priest of His own sacrifice. But how will He offer Himself to God for the redemption of the human race?

At the beginning of this chapter we stated that sacrifice, as an act of religious worship, had its origin and takes its profound signification from the intimate and mysterious oblation by which a man offers himself to God by an act of free surrender of his being, his will and his faculties. This act implies man's humble acceptance of his condition of absolute and dependent creaturehood. It also implies the recognition of his sinful state and of his debt to the infinite Justice of God, and it directs his activity in accordance with these basic facts. Now Christ also in His human

---

[1] Quoted by Grimal, *La Messe de la terre et la messe du Ciel*, p. 136.

nature is a creature dependent on God. He sees this in the bright light that streams into His intelligence because of His union with the Word. In consequence, what marvellous sentiments of adoration, prayer, obedience, and humility flow from His soul as a pure incense with an agreeable odour ascending to God from the altar of His Humanity! This invisible interior sacrifice manifests itself exteriorly by His complete submission in all things to God's rights over Him, and by His scrupulous fulfilment of the Divine Law.

But in addition, by the will of His Father, Christ is laden with the sins of men, and is destined to work out their salvation. Christ realizes that also, and knows that because of it His Body is subject to the harsh laws of suffering and death. He accepts His lot, and His interior submission to the general laws of the Creator is further perfected by His willing acceptance of God's special designs on Him, and in particular of the life that is marked out for Him till death brings it to a close.

The whole existence of Jesus is summed up in constant submission to His Father's will. On every page of the Gospel we find the affirmation: "I am come to do the will of Him that sent me." And when the thought of His painful death comes before His mind He cries out: "Now is my soul troubled. And what shall I say? Father, save me from this hour. But for this cause I came unto this hour. Father glorify Thy name."[1] In this previous acceptance of death, in this daily submission to a life of labour, of humiliations, of physical hardship and moral suffering, there is really one long sacrifice lasting without interruption from Bethlehem to Calvary. We see this life of sacrifice being lived in the workshop of Nazareth, in the period of fasting in the desert, and in the labours of His public life.

It is in the light of these great realities that the most illustrious representatives of the French Theological School of the seventeenth century—de Bérulle, Condren, Olier—loved to look on the whole life of Christ, from His conception in the womb of the Blessed Virgin Mary to His death on Calvary as a sacrifice. Cardinal de Bérulle writes: "From the first moment of His existence in His mother's womb the Son of God gives Himself up to the life, the cross and the death that are to be His. And this oblation and first act of will on the part of Jesus is not a passing act like ours: it is permanent and endowed, so to speak, with the nature and state of eternity. It is a permanent attitude of mind and will which has never ceased day or night, which has never been interrupted by any other action and which has always been actually present in His heart. As in the heart there is always a continual movement in which life consists, so in the heart and mind of Jesus this interior spiritual movement is ever present."[1] In the article in the *Revue des Sciences philosophiques et théologiques* (April, 1925), already referred to, we also read: "Golgotha is . . . but the culminating point of a sacrifice whose initial act is the Incarnation of the Word."[2]

There is no denying the beauty of such a doctrine. Nevertheless, despite the accuracy of the statements on which it is based, it does not appear to take sufficient account of the altogether special place which the Passion holds in the life of Christ. A glance through the Gospels suffices to show the importance which Jesus Himself attaches to this capital moment of His existence. He has come in view of this hour and He is straitened till it arrives— even though His mortal nature shudders. On different occasions He warns His disciples of the fact that it is incumbent on Him to undergo the sufferings of His Passion. "The Son of Man must be delivered up and scourged. . . ." It is His Father's command. His Body must be delivered up, His Blood must be shed for the sins of men, and in face of this necessity, in presence of this precept of His Father, Christ freely accepts and offers Himself: "Father, Thy will be done."

Nay more, this act of Calvary and it alone, is henceforth to, become the centre of Christian worship by being perpetuated in Holy Mass. Holy Mass is the commemoration and the renewal of the sacrifice of the Cross, and not of any other act of Christ's life. From the Cross flow all the sacraments, the channels by which we share in the merits and satisfactions of Christ. Accordingly, we must draw the conclusion that the Passion and Death of Jesus constitute a sacrifice in a very special sense, and thereby differ from the other events of His earthly life. These latter are not on the same level and have not the same sacrificial value; and it is only on the Cross that Jesus inaugurated the sublime worship of the Christian religion. This is the opinion of St. Thomas, who expresses himself as follows: "By His Passion, Christ inaugurated the rite of the Christian religion, by offering Himself to God as an oblation and a propitiatory victim."[3]

We know, of course, that the Hypostatic Union consecrates the Humanity of Christ absolutely, from the first instant of His conception. This consecration makes Him at once Priest and Victim: Priest, because He is the Mediator par excellence between God and man: Victim, because on the one hand the Humanity of Christ is passible, and therefore capable of dying; and on the other hand because the Hypostatic Union makes the Victim perfectly pleasing to God. Besides, the oblation which Christ makes of Himself on His entry into the world establishes Him actually in the rôle of Priest and Victim for humanity.

---

[1] P. de Bérulle, *Vie de Jésus,* Ch. XXVI.
[2] *Le Sacrifice du Christ au Calvaire,* by A. Barrois.
[3] IIIa P., Q. 62, a.5.

In analysing the foundations on which Christ's Priesthood reposes, we came to the conclusion that it was constituted *radically* by the grace of Union, and *formally* by the Grace of Headship, but we noted also that in order to appreciate it fully, we must take account of the Divine Intention, because it was this alone that determined concretely the mode of exercise of Christ's Priesthood and its scope. The Priesthood of Christ acquires actual efficacy only in accordance with the Divine Intention, which guided it in fulfilling the fixed plan of Redemption. This point of view must never be left out of account, when we are speaking of the sacrifice and the priestly activity of Christ.

God has officially appointed Christ to offer the one perfect sacrifice in the name of sinful humanity. For that purpose He came into the world. In accepting this sacrifice, God also accepts the human race in the spotless Victim offered and reconciles it to Himself. It is certain that the least act of charity and obedience ascending from the soul of Jesus to His Father as a homage to His sovereign majesty, constitutes of itself and in itself a perfect sacrifice, which does not even require an exterior manifestation. The point at issue, however, is not the perfection of such a sacrifice in itself, but whether such a sacrifice is the one willed and determined by God as a condition of renewing His alliance with the human race. Now faith, illumined by the declarations of Scripture, Tradition and the Church, teaches that the sacrifice demanded by God from His Son for the redemption of humanity, was that of Calvary. It is there alone, then, that humanity, in the Person of Christ, was enabled to offer to God the sacrifice of homage and reparation that was to restore it to favour and to give it back the Divine Life of Grace.

The Father's will required that the sacrifice of Christ should not only be interior, but that it should assume a certain external form, namely, that of real and actual immolation, through suffering and death. God willed this, no doubt, in order that the sacrifice of Christ should manifest exteriorly all the loving submission of His soul, but also, and principally, because it was in God's eternal designs to make the act of Calvary the starting point and the centre of the whole Christian worship by perpetuating it down the ages in the Eucharistic Sacrifice.

From this we can understand why Christ, though Priest and Victim from the outset, exercises His Priesthood fully, and is a complete and perfect Victim only on Calvary. It is there, and there alone, that God accepts forever the oblation of His Son and establishes Him as the unique and perpetual Victim of the human race. The other oblations made by Christ during His life can be considered as perfect sacrifices in themselves, but, from the point of view of the Divine Intention, they remain in fact inadequate and incomplete. To have this full efficacy they must be linked up with the perfect oblation of Calvary. From the first moment of His life, Christ moves forward to His Death: all His actions lead

CHRIST'S PRIESTLY ACTIVITY

thereto: and the Gospels warn us on many a page that His gaze is ever fixed on the culminating tragedy of His earthly existence. Accordingly, when offering Himself to His Father in Bethlehem, in Nazareth, on the highroads of Judaea and Galilee, He can never abstract from the term which is the whole *raison d' être* of His earthly pilgrimage. At the first awakening of His intelligence,— coincident with the first moment of His conception—it is towards Calvary that He turns, and in accepting the life of victim marked out for Him, He begins from that very moment the oblation of Calvary. The same applies to all His other oblations. And that is why God accords Him the privilege of dispensing even beforehand the benefits of His anticipated immolation, of exercising over men the prerogatives of His Priesthood, just as God, before the coming of Christ, distributed His graces to humanity in view of the merits and the sacrifice of His Son.

All the sufferings, all the humiliations, all the virtuous acts of Christ, during the rest of His life, exclusive of His Passion, are of value in the eyes of God, but their value as far as the Redemption of the human race is concerned is relative to the Passion, in which they are destined to be completed and consummated. Their sacrificial value, as well as their meritorious and satisfactory value, must be judged from this relative point of view. We must not regard the Passion as superadded to these acts as one quantity is added to another, like a drop of water which causes a vessel to overflow. Raised to a higher level, the Passion is the term towards which the whole life of Jesus is ordained and it is by virtue of this ordered tendency that His life obtains its full value and it complete efficacy. If this astonishes us, we have but to recall the great love of God, which urges Him to spare no pains in the work of our salvation and makes Him send us a Saviour who satisfies for us in a human manner by offering a sacrifice that does away with the ancient rites and observances, and inaugurates a new religion. "And therefore he is the mediator of the new testament: that by means of his death, for the redemption of those transgressions, which were under the former testament, they that are called may receive the promise of eternal inheritance. . . . And every priest indeed standeth daily ministering, and often offering the same sacrifices, which can never take away sins. But this man, offering one sacrifice for sins, for ever sitteth in the right hand of God, from henceforth expecting until his enemies be made his footstool. For by one oblation he had perfected forever them that are sanctified."[1]

---

[1] *Hebrews*, IX, 15, and X, 11-14. In *The Westminster version*, *Hebrews*, X, verses 11-14 are translated as follows: "And every priest standeth forth daily to minister, offering often the same sacrifices which can never take away sin. But He, having offered one sacrifice for sin 'hath taken His seat for ever at the right hand of God,' waiting for the rest, 'until His enemies have been made the footstool of His feet.' For by a single offering He hath for ever perfected those who are made holy."

The Sacrifice of The Cross.

How do the Passion and Death of Christ realize the general idea of sacrifice that we have thus outlined? We know that we are dealing here with a very special sacrifice, one that is incontestably superior to ancient sacrifices, and therefore we must expect to find characteristics in it that are found nowhere else. One such characteristic is the fact that Christ is at the same time Priest and Victim. In ordinary sacrifices, where the priest and the victim are different, there is also a perfect distinction between what we have called the visible and the invisible sacrifice. On the Cross, the distinction is far from being so complete. Of course Christ offers His Humanity to God, or to be more exact offers His Body and Blood, with all the sensitive part of His being destined to suffering and death. But this sensitive Victim is substantially one with the spiritual soul, that invisibly offers itself. Accordingly, strictly speaking, there are not two sacrifices, one visible, the other invisible. There is only one sacrifice, but it presents a twofold aspect; an interior aspect—the oblation Christ made of Himself to God in love and charity; an exterior aspect—the same offering, made manifest by His Passion, His Sufferings and His Death. Such appears to be the mind of St. Thomas, who refuses to apply purely and simply to the sacrifice of the Cross the distinction of visible and invisible sacrifice, which holds good for the sacrifices of the Old Law.[1]

Another special characteristic of Christ's sacrifice is that it takes place on the occasion of a horrible crime, of an odious judicial murder. We cannot then reckon amongst the elements of the sacrifice of Calvary the acts of the executioners who tortured and crucified, for sacrifice is a holy and sacred action. Accordingly, we must ask in what exactly the sacrifice of Calvary consisted. It belongs to the priest to immolate the victim: Christ is the Priest of His own sacrifice. He must therefore immolate Himself. The executioners put Him to death; that is clear, but they do not make of Him an immolated Victim. The state of victimhood or of passive immolation is produced, in ordinary sacrifices, by the action of the priest who lays hold of the victim (generally killed beforehand) and actively immolates it by spilling its blood on the altar. In the same way on Calvary Christ is reduced to a condition of passive immolation when, broken and crucified by His executioners, He accepts His Father's will by an act of love, and willingly pours out His Blood on the Cross. It is the voluntary submission with which Christ accepts these outrages that constitutes His sacerdotal action, His active immolation. The teaching of St. Thomas leaves no room for doubt on this matter. He repeatedly stresses the capital rôle of Christ's will in His obedient acceptance of the sufferings of the Passion. Thus he writes: "Christ offered Himself voluntarily for His Passion, and

[1] IIIa P., Q. 48, a. 3, ad. 2.

for this reason He is a Victim."[1] And again: "It was fitting that the sacrifice of Christ's Passion and Death should proceed from obedience."[2] "The very act by which Christ voluntarily underwent His Passion was sovereignly pleasing to God, because it was animated by charity. Thus it is obvious that the Passion of Christ was a real sacrifice."[3] "On the part of the executioners the Passion of Christ was a heinous crime: on the part of Christ who suffered through love, it was a sacrifice."[4]

This doctrine grows still more luminous if we recall that on Calvary, as in all the acts of His mortal life, Christ enjoyed perfect freedom. Some theologians find it difficult to reconcile the liberty of Jesus with the fact that His Father gave Him a precept to suffer and die. Was not Christ impeccable and thus incapable of rejecting the Divine Command? This problem causes no embarrassment to the disciple of St. Thomas. Efficacious grace though powerful enough to move a soul to what is good, does not deprive it of liberty. And we have already seen that in Christ the Beatific Vision could not prevent Him from meriting freely.

Moreover, it must not be forgotten that, if Christ had wished to work a miracle, He need not have undergone His Passion. He Who had often called the dead from their tombs during His life, could have saved Himself also and could have appealed to His Divine Power at any moment. He affirms this solemnly in the Garden of Olives: "Thinkest thou that I cannot ask my Father, and He will give Me presently more than twelve legions of angels?"[5] And if He allows Himself to be arrested, it is only after having manifested His complete independence. "As soon therefore as He had said to them: I am He: they went backward and fell to the ground."[6] Thus Christ is infinitely superior to the martyrs who have not the power of God at their disposal; and from this fact His immolation receives its full value as a sacrifice freely willed.

These manifestations of His complete independence and voluntary immolation were not without utility. Every sacrifice offered to God must find visible expression and assume a sense-perceptible form. It was necessary, then, that Christ should immolate Himself visibly on the Cross, and that He should offer Himself to His Father as a Victim in a manner that would be absolutely unequivocal. It was not sufficient that His Sufferings and Death should take place before our eyes; it was essential also that we should be able to perceive His submission to His Father's will in the love with which He became a Victim. Now in the words of Jesus, spoken during His Passion, it is easy to discover

---

[1] IIIa P., Q. 22, a. 2.
[2] IIIa P., Q. 47, a, 2.
[3] IIIa P., Q. 48, a. 3.
[4] IIIa P., Q. 48, a. 3, ad. 3.
[5] *St. Matthew*, XXVI, 53.
[6] *St. John*, XVIII, 6.

both free acceptance of the Death which constitutes His active immolation, and complete submission to His Father's will in which consists His loving oblation of Himself. We have already quoted some of His expressions in the Garden of Olives, in which He proclaims that He obeys the will of God, not the will of men. The prayer which, in the Garden, begins the Passion and the one which concludes it on Calvary, suffice to make a perfect oblation: "Father not my will but Thine be done. . . . Into Thy hands I commend my spirit."

On the Cross and during the whole Passion of Christ, we are, therefore, in presence of a real sacrifice, exterior and visible, capable of being the fountainhead, the centre of all true worship and of all true religion. We find in it the broad outlines essential to every sacrifice, together with the transcendent mode of realization peculiar to that of Christ. Its Priest and its Victim are one and the same Person. The Priest immolates the Victim, which is Himself, by freely accepting death: at the same time He offers It to God by subjecting It to His will; as for the Victim, Its passive immolation is to be found in the Blood shed from the Agony to Calvary.

We must also envisage the sacrifice of Christ from God's point of view and ask ourselves what is God's response to the oblation of His Son. Without a shadow of doubt the sacrifice is acceptable to God; but does the Victim on this account receive a new consecration?

In the ordinary sacrifices where there was room for the distinction between the visible and the invisible sacrifice, one could consider from one point of view the consecration bestowed by God on the victim immolated, and from another the sanctification of the soul offering itself to God through the visible sacrifice. These concepts, however, cannot be applied with quite the same signification to the sacrifice of Christ. First of all, we have not here two distinct sacrifices; there is but one Victim whose interior immolation and offering are sensibly manifested to us. Furthermore, Christ possesses the fulness of sanctity from the first moment of His existence so that we cannot see how a new consecration or sanctification can be added to Him. In His human nature He is consecrated in the most perfect way by the Hypostatic Union; and He is sanctified by a grace incapable of increase. For these reasons the adherents of de Bérulle maintain that all the acts of the life of Jesus that are declarative of His interior oblation are not really new sacrifices; they are merely ordinary manifestations of the one interior sacrifice which is perpetuated without interruption from the first instant of His conception in His mother's virginal womb. If we are to avoid this way of looking at things, we must discover in the sacrifice of the Cross a certain consecration of the Victim. This consecration in point of fact does exist and it affects Christ, not in Himself, but in His relation to the whole human race.

On Calvary Christ does not offer Himself alone, but along with Himself and in Himself He offers the whole human race, of which He is the Head and King. His personal consecration and sanctification give Him the right to appear before God in the name of sinful humanity, to offer a homage of reparation and expiation for the crimes committed by humanity and to beg for its complete forgiveness and return to grace. The Humanity of Jesus, immolated on the Cross, cannot but be a sacrifice of agreeable odour; but in it and through it the whole human race is rendered pleasing to God, is reunited to Him and consecrated to Him. It is the inauguration of the new alliance in Christ between God and man. In other words Christ on Calvary is acknowledged and accepted by God as the living and lifegiving Head of the whole Mystical Body; and already, in a certain way, the Mystical Body lives in its Head. This acceptance in Christ of the whole Mystical Body is a real consecration of the Saviour's Humanity. His Grace of Headship is thus crowned and consummated, not of course in its intrinsic perfection—for in this respect it is not capable of increase—but in its order and actual relation to all the members of the Mystical Body. For all that the Divine Will demanded in order to have this grace reach its full efficacy is accomplished: "all is consummated." Heretofore, by His substantial consecration and sanctity Christ was proximately equipped to become the Head of regenerated humanity. On Calvary, however, He becomes the actual Head, and in Him regeneration is carried out; the fulness of His Priesthood has been attained. Sinful man has but to unite himself to the sacrifice of Christ in order to receive the salvation it contains. In a word, the new consecration of Christ on the Cross constitutes Him for ever the spotless Victim in whom the human race is definitely made pleasing to God. "The Priesthood and the Kingship of Christ," says St. Thomas, "find their consummation in His Passion."[1]

The obvious proof of this is the glorification of the Humanity of Jesus which follows His sacrifice immediately and is brought about by the Resurrection and the Ascension. With Christ, humanity penetrates to heaven and recovers the happiness lost by the Fall. If Christ had only had to merit the glorification of His Sacred Humanity that would have been granted to Him from the very beginning, because it was unquestionably due to Him. But Christ is our Head, and "it became Him for Whom are all things and by Whom are all things, who had brought many children into glory, to perfect the author of their salvation by His Passion. For both He that sanctifieth and they that are sanctified are all of one."[2] That is why "God, who is rich in mercy, for His exceeding

---

[1] IIIa. P., Q. 35, a. 7, ad. 1.
[2] *Hebrews*, II, 10-11. "For it behoved Him on account of Whom all things are, when He was bringing many sons to glory, to make perfect through suffering, the author of their salvation" (*Westminster Version*).

I

charity wherewith he loved us, even when we were dead in sins, hath quickened us together in Christ. And hath raised us up together and hath made us sit together in the heavenly places, through Jesus Christ."[1] Hence, St. Paul could write to the Corinthians: "If Christ be not risen again, then is our preaching vain: and your faith is also vain."[2]

The visible sacrifice of Christ on the Cross finds its completion in the visible acceptance by the Father in the Resurrection and Ascension, which are for us the pledges of our restoration to the grace and place of God.

---

[1] *Ephesians*, II, 4-6.
[2] *I Corinthians*, XV, 14.

PART II

CHAPTERS VII—XI

CHRIST IN US

"Know not your own selves that
Christ Jesus is in you."
(*II Corinthians*, XIII, 5).

Chapter VII

OUR PARTICIPATION IN THE HOLINESS OF CHRIST

Man's Response to Christ.

"We have an high priest who is set on the right hand of the throne of majesty in the heavens, a minister of the holies and of the true tabernacle. . . . But now he hath obtained a better ministry, by how much also he is a mediator of a better testament which is established on better promises."[1] "For Jesus is not entered into the Holies made with hands, the patterns of the true: but into Heaven itself, that he may appear now in the presence of God for us."[2] "Having therefore, brethren, a confidence in the entering into the holies by the blood of Christ; a new and living way which he hath dedicated for us through the veil, that is to say, his flesh."[3]

These words from the *Epistle to the Hebrews* are an excellent summary of the conclusions we had reached at the end of the first part of this work. Christ consummated His sacrifice on the Cross, and thenceforth in heaven, as the glorified and accepted Victim, He is the pledge of our regeneration and salvation. "Christ was offered once to exhaust the sins of many."[4] But if He has now to offer Himself no more, He has nevertheless to distribute to us the fruits of His sacrifice. And we, being sinners, have to unite ourselves entirely to our High-Priest, and share in His redemption. It would be indeed strange if our salvation were to be accomplished without our co-operation. As free persons we would protest against such an indignity. We must respond to Christ who has opened to us the way to eternal happiness, by following Him willingly. In the enterprise of our salvation, the initiative belongs to Christ; it is He who calls us and—if we place no obstacle—it is He who restores to us the Divine Life of Grace, by pouring into our souls the graces and benefits bought for us by His Blood. In this way His holy and sanctifying Priesthood is perpetuated

---

[1] *Hebrews*, VIII, 1-2, 6. "Such a High Priest we have, Who 'hath taken his seat at the right hand' of the throne of Majesty in heaven as priestly servant of the sanctuary, and of the 'true' tabernacle, which the Lord, and not man, 'hath set up'. . . . But now He hath attained to a ministry so much the more excellent, as the testament is better whereof He is mediator, which hath been erected on the basis of more important promises" (*Westminster Version*).

[2] *Hebrews*, IX, 24. "For Christ hath not entered into a sanctuary made by hands, a mere type of the true, but into heaven itself, to appear now before the face of God on our behalf" (*Westminster Version*).

[3] *Hebrews*, X. 19, 20. "Since therefore, brethren, we have full freedom to enter the sanctuary in virtue of the blood of Jesus, a new and living way which He hath inaugurated for us through the veil, that is to say, His flesh" (*Westminster Version.*)

[4] *Hebrews*, IX, 28. "Christ 'offered once to bear the sins of many' " (*Westminster Version*).

throughout the centuries; thus is realized "the increase of the body unto the edifying of itself in charity."[1] It is to the building up of this Mystical Body under the divine influence of Christ that we must now turn our attention.

Christ in Heaven is the Cause of Our Salvation.

"By His passion, Christ has delivered us from sin *causaliter*," says St. Thomas.[2] This means that by suffering and dying for us He has instituted a cause by which all sins, past, present, and future, can be blotted out; just as a doctor prescribes a remedy which a patient can procure at will. And again it is St. Thomas who writes: "Though the Passion and Death of Christ are not to be renewed, the power of the Victim remains for all eternity."[3]

It is by the Humanity of Christ, which is actually in heaven, but which always keeps its status as a Victim immolated for the salvation of the world, that the fruits of the Passion and, therefore, our justification are transmitted to us. This Sacred Humanity, still bearing the glorious marks of the sufferings endured, is like a living prayer to the Father, and by it we obtain the graces necessary for our salvation. "For that He continueth for ever, He hath an everlasting priesthood: whereby He is able also to save for ever them that come to God by Him; always living to make intercession for us."[4] And we know too that, according to the Thomists, it is not merely by his moral intercession that Christ saves us, but also by the effective action His Sacred Humanity exercises on us as the instrument of God and the organ of the Divinity. "The Passion," writes Billuart, "lives on in the stigmata which came from it and in the glorious qualities that Christ acquired by it. The Passion may be said to effect our salvation physically, because the Humanity of Christ, being determined, changed and modified by it, physically works out our salvation."[5] Cardinal de Bérulle had already expressed the same thought in the following terms: "We must take into consideration the perpetuity of these mysteries; they belong to the past and took place in certain given circumstances, but looked at from another point of view, they live on and are perpetually present. They are past as regards their accomplishment, but present as regards their efficacy, which is as undying as the love that prompted them. The spirit, the efficacy and the merit of the mystery are ever present. We know that Jesus has found a way of preserving a part of His Passion in His glorified state, by retaining His Wounds; but if He was able to

---

[1] *Ephesians*, IV, 16. "From Him the body deriveth its increase, unto the building up of itself in charity" (*Westminster Version*).

[2] IIIa P., Q. 49, art. 1, ad. 3.

[3] IIIa P., Q. 22, art. 5, ad. 2.

[4] *Hebrews*, VII, 24-25. But Christ "because He remaineth for ever, hath an unchangeable priesthood. Wherefore He can at all times save those who approach God through Him, since He liveth always to make intercession for them" (*Westminster Version*).

[5] *De Incarnatione*, Dissert. 13, a. 2.

keep part of His Passion in His glorified Body, why should He not be able to retain something in His Soul in His consummated state of glory? But what He retains of His Passion both in body and soul is life and glory, and He suffers in neither, and it is what remains in Him of His mysteries that becomes for souls a source of grace that draws to it the souls destined to receive it."[1]

In speaking thus, Cardinal de Bérulle simply gave his own turn to the expressions of St. Thomas. The Angelic Doctor writes: "The resurrection of Christ is the efficient cause of our resurrection; Christ's Humanity, when risen, is in a certain way the instrument of Divinity and operates by the power of that Divinity. And as everything Christ did or suffered in His Humanity is rendered salutary for us by the power of His Divinity, so His resurrection is the efficient cause of our resurrection because of this same Divine Power."[2]

The fact that the Sacred Humanity is far away from us in heaven does not hamper It in Its instrumental efficacy. We have already seen that when God condescends to make use of an instrument He is not bound by the conditions to which we are subject in a like case. His infinite power transcends space and can link together distant objects. There is, therefore, no need for material contact between Christ's Humanity and us. "The Passion of Christ, though corporeal, possesses a spiritual power because of its union with the Divinity."[3] It is this power, this energy, this invisible causality that exercises a mysterious influence on us.

How are we to dispose ourselves to receive Christ's action? The text of the Summa we have just quoted gives the answer: "It is by spiritual contact that the Passion of Christ acquires its efficacy, that is, by faith and the sacraments of faith." Whenever St. Thomas refers to Christ's influence on our souls, he indicates these same two ways of establishing contact between Christ and us—faith and the sacraments of faith.

Our Union with Christ by Faith.

Let us treat of faith first. What is faith but the opening of our minds to all the divine and supernatural realities which Christ represents for us? It would be of little avail for us to have known Jesus during His mortal life and to have seen Him with our bodily eyes. Many had this privilege and yet saw in Him only a man. Faith alone makes us discover Him and understand Him as He is, in His Divinity and in His Humanity, in His redeeming and saving Priesthood. When we look at Him through the eyes of faith, we get in touch with what is most intimate and most real in Him; and nothing is better calculated to establish vital contact between two persons than a genuine mutual understanding.

---

[1] Card. de Bérulle, *Oeuvres de Piété*.
[2] IIIa P., Q. 56, a. 1, ad. 3.
[3] IIIa P., Q. 48, a. 6, ad. 2.

Christ knows us; for, in the vision of God, He sees us as we are. He knows our eternal destiny in Him as He is charged with bringing it about. He takes the initiative in illuminating our minds with His light, and it is at His invitation that we cleave to Him in faith. But our relations with Him do not end there. If knowledge is the indispensable condition for the union of two persons, love is its consummation. There must be fresh outpouring of grace on the part of Christ and additional acquiescence on our part in order that faith may issue in charity. Our justification is actually realized only in perfect adherence to Christ and in the participation in His Divine Life of light and love. Linked with Christ in faith and charity, we are one with Him, we are members of His Mystical Body, acceptable to God for the same reason as our Head is, bearing about with us promises and pledges of eternal life. In this state every good act, every prayer, every suffering, welcomed for love of Jesus, unites us directly to Him, and causes to circulate from Him to us and from us to Him, that Divine Life to which He has raised us, and which He does not cease to foster in our souls.

To express the intimacy of this vital union, we sometimes say that Christ dwells in our hearts. "That Christ may dwell by faith in your hearts . . . rooted and founded in charity."[1] This spiritual indwelling, of which the apostle speaks, serves as an apt expression of our abiding contact with Christ by faith. According to His own words to the Apostles, we live in Him and He in us by this communication of thought and affection, sanctified as we are by our participation in His own sanctity. St. Thomas, commenting on that passage of St. John, explains that we live in Jesus "by our faith, our obedience and our perseverance," and that Jesus lives in us "by the lights, the help and the gift of perseverance He bestows on us."[2]

Our Union with Christ through the Sacraments.

We must not forget that there remains for us yet another way of establishing vital contact with Christ. It consists in having recourse to what we have called with St. Thomas "the sacraments of faith." Its importance is such that it must engage our attention for some time. Not that those two modes of union are strangers one to the other. At first sight it would seem that union with Christ by faith is independent of the union effected by the sacraments; or that at least its practical extension is much more universal. Is not the first call of grace directing the adult towards justification entirely interior? And is not this the case also with that initial submission in faith by which he disposes himself to live by charity? Does not the Christian during the course of a holy life receive invisibly from Christ multiple graces aiding him

---

[1] *Ephesians*, III, 17.
[2] *Commentary on St. John*, XV, 1.

in his progress towards perfection? Again, it may be remarked that the sacraments come into our lives only at more or less distant intervals, whereas the Divine Life flows uninterruptedly from Christ to us, and by the life of our souls we are united to Him at every moment. Moreover, many souls, either through circumstances or because of invincible ignorance, are unable to have recourse to the sacraments; yet their sincere goodwill and their uncompromising fidelity open their souls to the influence of grace and make them members of Christ's Mystical Body.

We may, therefore, be tempted to regard the sacraments as simple external aids, destined to facilitate our relations with Christ, but which could disappear without detriment to the Divine Life within us. That would be a grave illusion. Far from being superfluous in the Christian life, the rôle of the sacraments is, on the contrary, all-important. We know that they are rites instituted by Christ to bestow grace. He brought them into being for reasons we shall soon set forth. Before doing so, however, we must insist on the fact that they form the very framework of our Christian life, and that without them, that life would collapse.

The Rôle of the Sacraments in the Christian Life.

No one can be born again in Christ except by the waters of baptism; that is a universal law which does not admit of any exception. A soul may happen to be justified prior to the reception of this sacrament. But this is because the soul has the intention of being baptized, through the faith which draws it to Christ and the love which urges it to assume the yoke of His law, and thus it receives the sanctification it needs. Moreover, in the growth of charity the sacraments are indispensable. All the other graces and helps which come to us directly from Christ are but consequences of that first orientation to God, imprinted sacramentally on our souls. It is because the sacraments, in their mysterious action on our souls, have assimilated us to Christ and rooted us in Him by faith and love, that our union with Jesus develops along the lines mapped out by them in advance.

It sometimes happens that unbelievers and heretics profess astonishment at this and reproach our religion with its ritualism. They want a worship wholly spiritual and interior, and cannot bring themselves to believe that miserable material things, like water or oil, and simple ready-made formulae can have such efficacy in the production and development of a life so lofty as the Supernatural Life of grace. They even try to prove that there is a connection between the sacramental rites and the magical rites of ancient religions. In addition, they affirm that such a materialistic conception of religion is altogether foreign to the mind of Him who said to the Samaritan woman: "The hour cometh and now is when the true adorers shall adore the Father in spirit and in truth. For the Father also seeketh such to adore Him."[1]

---

[1] *St. John*, IV, 23.

Before formulating such an objection, however, our adversaries should recall to mind that Christ Himself, while on earth, did not hesitate to use the symbolic rites of purification and sanctification. At the beginning of His public life, He submitted to the baptism of John in order "to fulfil all justice."[1] Later on, when sending His disciples to conquer the world, He commanded them to baptize in the name of the Father and of the Son and of the Holy Ghost. On the eve of His death, He took bread and wine, and after having pronounced over them the words which changed them into His Body and Blood, He ordered His Apostles to repeat this ceremony in memory of Him, when He had gone. These different episodes manifested clearly the Saviour's intention to employ rites and symbols and to make them play a part in the religion of the spirit which He came to inaugurate here below.

There is nothing extraordinary in the fact that we need these humble realities to raise us to the Divine Life of grace. Even at the risk of saying what is trite and commonplace we must insist that man is composed of both spirit and matter, and that his action is truly human only on condition of its being the harmonious expression of these two constitutive principles of his nature. Thought needs words and images for its expression. These are still more necessary in the case of a sentiment taking its rise in the soul and unable to be kept pent up within the heart. There does exist a worship in spirit and in truth, but it is not a worship in which the body is deliberately left out of account. It is worship wherein the soul, thanks to the body, can exteriorize its sentiments in suitable words and gestures. Thus, the Divine Master, in instituting sacramental symbols, simply adapted Himself to our nature, at once intellectual and material.

It must be added also that when we enter into contact with God in order to receive from Him the favour of the Divine Life, we need the assurance that this communication is real and effective. Grace is an invisible reality: it does not come within the domain of consciousness. We could never know with certainty that it was being conferred on us, if sense-perceptible signs did not announce it and act as its authentic and infallible herald. Besides, we are sinners, and we generally allow ourselves to be drawn into sin by seeking pleasure and enjoyment in external realities. God, the Divine Educator of our souls, takes account of our weakness. Utilizing the sense-perceptible and material creatures amongst which our lot is cast, with which we cannot dispense, and which are often the objects of our disordered affections, He cleanses and elevates them and converts them into instruments of purification and salvation. What can be more in conformity with Divine Wisdom and transcendent Goodness than thus to transform what is an occasion of stumbling and falling into a source of life and holiness? Are the sacraments then, magic

---

[1] St. Matthew, III, 15.

rites? No: the difference between a sacramental rite and a magic rite is fundamental. The latter is purely utilitarian; it aims at harnessing some preternatural power in view of an earthly advantage, and takes no account of the moral dispositions of him who uses it. The sacramental rite is entirely different; it is ordained essentially to the sanctification of souls; it is efficacious only where it is received with faith, respect, repentance, and love of God. By the very fact of being employed it produces grace. But the soul must prepare to receive this grace, by longing for the Divine Life and desiring supernatural transformation.

A Sacrament is a Sign.

It is certain that the sacraments of the New Law constitute a special order of realities which have absolutely nothing in common with the rites of other religions. The Council of Trent sets forth their true nature when it teaches that the sacraments contain the grace they signify.[1] They are first and foremost signs. The rites that compose them—the use of certain determined material elements, and the employment of certain sacred formulae—serve to direct the minds of the faithful towards something other than themselves—towards a supernatural reality destined to sanctify us. St. Thomas, long before the Council of Trent, had already brought into relief this essential character of the sacrament, and that with a wealth of doctrine too often forgotten in our days. "The sacraments," he writes, "are meant to signify our sanctification. Now, in this sanctification, there are three things to be considered: its cause, which is the Passion of Christ; its form, which consists in grace and the virtues; its ultimate end, which is eternal life. From these three points of view, the sacraments are signs; they recall to our minds the Passion of Christ; they indicate the effect produced in us by this Passion, namely, sanctifying grace; they foretell our future glory."[2] Every sacrament, therefore, is, by its very nature, at once a remembrance of the past, a proof of the present and a pledge of the future. Thus the sacraments introduce us into the supernatural and divine order of our redemption, an order which comes from Christ to us and which enables us to return through Christ to God. For we must always bear in mind that the sacraments come to us from Christ and His Passion, that they are destined to unite us sensibly to Him as to the Source and Author of our salvation, and that they are the instruments of His Priesthood, in applying to us the merits of His sacrifice. We know with what insistence St. Paul teaches the faithful that Baptism, by plunging us into the waters of regeneration, buries us with Christ and makes us die to sin, that we may rise again with Him to a new life. "(You are) buried with Him in baptism, in whom

[1] Session VII, Canon 6.
[2] IIIa P., Q. 60, a. 3.

also you are risen again by the faith of the operation of God, who hath raised Him up from the dead."[1]

All the sacramental rites, then, have but a single purpose—to represent to us by appropriate ceremonies the interior transformation—the fruit of our Saviour's Passion—which is produced in us. On that account St. Thomas calls them sacraments of the faith. They attest in a visible manner the invisible link that faith sets up between Christ and us. "They are signs of the protestation of the faith that justifies," says the Angelic Doctor.[2] They are essentially relative realities, that is, relative to the Passion of Jesus, which they exteriorize, as it were, in order that we may be able to draw from it the salutary fruits it contains.

The Sacrament Effects What It Signifies.

The sacrament is not only a sign. It has another characteristic, no less essential than the former, and by this characteristic it is distinguished from the rites of the Old Law. It is a sign which effects what it signifies. There can be no doubt of its positive efficacity, for it is of faith that the sacraments have not been instituted solely for the purpose of nourishing our faith.[3] It is also defined that they confer grace on those who place no obstacle in the way of their action;[4] that they confer it always and on everyone "ex opere operato," that is, by the very fact of being utilized.[5] The conditions required by the recipient are, faith and attrition for faults in the case of Baptism and Penance; in the case of the other sacraments the state of grace. While these latter augment the Life of Grace in us, the former have as their special rôle to justify sinful man.

Even if the doctrine of instrumental causality as applied to the sacraments has not been the object of a definition by the Teaching Authority of the Church, it is nevertheless quite clear that it throws considerable light on the teaching of the Council of Trent. It is as it were the necessary prolongation of that teaching, so much so that in its absence it would be difficult to maintain in their integrity the strong terms of the Council. The doctrine of instrumental causality is admirably summed up in St. Thomas's expressive formula: "The sacraments effect what they signify."[6]

They effect: that is to say, they are,—like the Humanity of Christ—real instruments of our sanctification in the hands of God. They are, however, in ordered subordination to Christ. Christ, in His Humanity, personally united to the Word, is God's

---

[1] *Colossians*, II, 12. "Along with Him ye were buried in baptism: along with Him also ye had your resurrection through your faith in the power of God, Who raised Him up from the dead" (*Westminster Version*).
[2] IIIa P., Q. 65, a. 4.
[3] Council of Trent, Sess. 7, Canon 5.
[4] Ibid. Canon 6.
[5] Ibid. Canon 7 and 8.
[6] IIIa P., Q. 62, a. 1, ad. 1.

first and immediate instrument, the "conjoined instrument," organic, we may say, after the fashion in which the hand is the instrument of the human intelligence. The sacraments are only secondary or separated instruments, like the chisel in the hands of the sculptor. In addition, Christ is an instrument possessing a real autonomy in the exercise of His instrumental causality. He is the conscious and voluntary agent of God's operations. The sacraments depend on Him and are under His control. It is He who has instituted them, and it is also He who transmits the current of the Divine Life to souls through them. Therefore, just as the sacraments link us to Christ by their signification, so they also unite us with Him by their causality. They are the bond of union between Christ and us. By transmitting the invisible waves of grace, they make us participate efficaciously and surely in the divine influence radiating from Christ. To employ an image beloved of the ancients, they are like the divine fountain gushing forth from the open side of Jesus on the Cross, by which the Church is redeemed.[1]

The sacraments effect what they signify and the divine virtue remains in them as long as they retain their existence as sacraments. To understand this we must consider that the sacraments are not static but dynamic. They consist in the use of a certain matter and the employment of a certain formula, but the efficient cause of the use of that matter and of the employment of that formula is the minister of the sacrament. It is not water, as static, that purifies the baptised soul, but the ablution carried out by the minister by means of the water, and accompanied by words which give to the ablution its complete signification.

All this is perfectly in harmony with what we said of the nature of instrumental causality. An instrument is the cause of the operation of a higher agent only through the exercise of the activity proper to itself. It is this activity that the agent elevates in order to make it produce a higher effect. Now, the sacraments are really actions or ritual gestures, which of themselves, are ordained to the accomplishment of a certain work. The Divine Power passes into these actions, which are entirely directed towards the subjects that are to benefit by them. And thus what was, for example, simply an ablution of the body becomes a purification of the soul.

When, therefore, we profess with the Council of Trent that the sacraments contain grace, we do not mean to affirm that they are inert, motionless receptacles of a supernatural reality locked up in them, so to say. What we mean to convey is rather that they work in virtue of the Divine Power, and that in their very activity they carry that power with them to the soul, thus engendering in it the life of grace.

One sacrament—the Blessed Eucharist—is an exception to this law, because the Body and Blood of Christ are permanently

----

[1] IIIa P., Q. 62, a. 5.

present under the species of bread and wine. The divine virtue therefore, remains in this sacrament as long as Christ Himself is present. "And thus," writes St. Thomas, "while the other sacraments are realized only in the application of their matter to the sanctification of man, the sacrament of the Eucharist is permanently constituted by the very consecration of its matter."[1] This means, of course, a notable superiority on the part of the Eucharist over the other sacraments. To this point we shall return later.

It is now clear that the sacraments, invested with Divine Power, are sacred and sanctifying realities. They are, as it were, the prolongation and extension to us of Christ's action, and in their own way they participate in the very sanctity of their Author.

Finally, if we add that the sacraments effect what they signify, we shall have an adequate idea of their real grandeur. God can use any instrument He wishes to produce grace in us. His action is not limited, like ours, by the creature He condescends to use. But, if He institutes certain sacraments and destines them for our sanctification, He does so in accordance with a special design of His Wisdom. He wills these sacraments to represent visibly the invisible and interior transformation they bring about in us. So His Divine Power, while passing through them, adapts itself after a certain fashion to their mode of being and arrives at a result that is proportionate to them. Thus we find here, deliberately willed by God, one of the conditions of that instrumental causality, to which our defective activity is necessarily subject, and in accordance with which the instrument imprints its own special mark on the ensuing effect. The sacraments, being essentially signs, stamp their own likeness on the soul in producing what they signify. In that respect, it must be remarked, they differ from every other form of divine activity. "It is the same word of God," writes the Angelic Doctor in His treatise on the Blessed Eucharist, "that operates in creation and in the consecration, though it acts differently in the two cases. For here it works sacramentally, that is, according to the power of sanctification of the rite employed."[2]

The special character of the sacraments cannot be over-emphasized, because it makes of them an order of realities apart. Visible links between heaven and earth, their efficacy lies in their power to signify: it is their signification, and that alone, that is raised by God to carry out the supernatural effects it expresses. Since, however, a sacrament is primarily a sign of the Passion of Christ it must first of all reproduce in us something of this Passion. This is perfectly correct. The grace that comes to us through the symbolism of the sacraments is a grace permeated through

---

[1] IIIa P., Q. 73, a. 1, ad. 3.
[2] IIIa P., Q. 78, a. 2, ad. 2.

and through with the sacrifice of Calvary. On the eve of His Death, Jesus said to His Father: "And for them do I sanctify myself: that they also may be sanctified in truth."[1] This sanctification by which Christ gave Himself up to His Father in a humble submission of love, in a total acquiescence to His Divine Will, is transmitted to us by the sacraments. It enables us to enter into the sentiments of Christ, sentiments of detachment from all that is not the will of God, of complete self-oblation to the Father, that He may realize in us His eternal designs. The way by which we must return to God is none other than that by which Christ travelled. It is the way of sacrifice and self-immolation, in which suffering and death itself play their part. It is, therefore, in the highest degree important that we should be assimilated to Christ in His Passion.

This is the work of sacramental grace. If, in its essential nature, sacramental grace is identical with Sanctifying Grace, it yet adds, over and above that Grace, a special resemblance to the holiness of Christ. It is a grace truly and properly Christian.

This resemblance produced by sacramental grace is adapted to the needs of our souls and is different in the seven sacraments, in order to enable us to meet as we ought the vicissitudes of the present life. The man who comes into relation with Christ for the first time and receives from Him a share in the Divine Life, does not require the same aids as he who, living already with the life of Christ, must strengthen that life in himself and defend it against external enemies. The situation of a father of a family is very different from that of a priest who is called upon to continue actively on earth the priestly office of Christ. To the disciple who falls into sin after Baptism there must still be the possibility of having recourse to the expiation of Calvary. And, when the sands of life are running out, when the Christian, like his Master, must make the offering of his life to God, he requires a force and a courage that will not fail.

Thus the different sacraments assimilate us, each in its own special way, to our Divine Head, by communicating to us the graces by which we are enabled to live as His Members. They signify the graces visibly in their ritual gestures and produce them invisibly in the soul .They transform us into other Christs, acting like Him, living like Him, sacrificing ourselves like Him. Baptism inaugurates our life in Christ, by making us children of God in the image of His only-Begotten Son, constituting us His Members, and His brothers and sisters. It applies to us in their fulness the merits and satisfactions of the Saviour, and restores to us in Him the Life of which sin had deprived us. By it we are assured of pardon and favour with God. Confirmation augments this Life of Christ in us and empowers us to defend it valiantly against the assaults of an evil world. Penance raises us up again after our

---

[1] *St. John*, XVII, 19.

falls, and teaches us to mingle our tears of repentance with the Blood of Christ. Matrimony unites man and woman in sacred bonds, bonds that are an image of the mysterious union, which Christ contracted with the Church on Calvary. The sacrament of Holy Orders enables us to fulfil worthily on earth the functions of Christ's Priesthood. Lastly, Extreme Unction disposes us for the passage from death to life by which our eternal union with the Blessed Trinity, through Christ, is consummated.

In their wonderful diversity the sacraments tend towards one end—to establish or tighten the bonds which bind us to Christ who was immolated in order that we might live holy lives and attain eternal felicity. The triple symbolism which, with St. Thomas, we discovered in the sacraments connecting them with the Passion, with grace and with our final end, produces a triple effect on our souls. It assimilates us to Christ suffering, communicates His Sanctity to us, and ordains us to felicity in union with Him as His Members. It is abundantly evident, then, that the sacraments effect what they signify.

The Place of the Blessed Eucharist in the Sacramental System.

When speaking just now of the different sacraments and their various functions, we made no mention of the Blessed Eucharist. The reason was that this sacrament has a pre-eminent place, as it is at once the unifying principle and the end of the whole sacramental system. We must now touch briefly on these matters. We shall envisage the Blessed Eucharist both from the point of view of the interior transformation it operates in our souls, and of the participation it gives us in the holiness of Christ.

The Council of Trent (Can. 3, Sess. 7) condemns those who claim that "all the sacraments are of equal value and that no sacrament is in any way superior to another." In this text there is an obvious allusion to the Blessed Eucharist. Any Christian, who accepts the Real Presence of Our Lord in this sacrament, will have no difficulty in admitting this superiority. Still it would be a mistake to imagine that the dignity of the Blessed Eucharist is such that it has nothing in common with the other sacraments. It also is part of that sacramental symbolism which inaugurates and develops our union with Christ and our holiness. It is a sacrament, that is, a sense-perceptible sign of the wonders it operates in our souls. But it is the sacrament *par excellence*. "What is common to the other sacraments," writes St. Thomas, "must be attributed to it in a special manner, because of its pre-eminent dignity."[1] The Holy Doctor establishes this truth by recalling the three great realities to which every sacrament is ordained, namely. the Passion of Christ, our sanctification, and our future life. "The sacrament of the Eucharist has a three-fold signification: one that refers to the past, because it commemorates the Passion of Christ,

---

[1] IIIa P., Q. 73, a. 4, ad. 2.

which was a real sacrifice; and this is why it is given the name of
sacrifice; another that has reference to the present, that is to the
unity of the Church, because by this sacrament men are gathered
together in unity, and this is why it is called Holy Communion . . .; a third signification looks to the future, in as much as this
sacrament prefigures the joy we shall have in the vision of God in
heaven, our real native land. Hence, its name of Viaticum, since
it opens for us the way that leads to heaven. Finally it is called
Eucharist, that is, excellent or surpassing grace, either because, as
the Apostle says, the grace of God is eternal life: or because it
contains Christ who is full of grace."[1]

The excellence of the Blessed Eucharist, then, consists in this
that it gives us Christ Himself, and not merely His all-powerful
virtue. Nevertheless it is always Christ in His Passion who is
sacramentally communicated to us, and the end towards which
the Blessed Sacrament tends is the union of Christ with all the
members of His Mystical Body, that they may be one in Him and
through this union attain to eternal life. But, while the other
sacraments aim at more particular ends, imposed by the needs of
the present life and the special state in which we happen to be
placed, the Eucharist goes straight to the essential end. It effects
direct and immediate union with Christ Crucified. It gives us in
their substantial reality the Body and Blood sacrificed for us on the
Cross.

This is the proper place to recall that all holiness is directly
dependent on the virtue of religion. If man is sanctified interiorly
by grace and the infused virtues, it is in order that he may direct
all his activity towards God, as revealed to us in the Inner Life of
the Blessed Trinity, that he may freely work out his return to
Him, and make of his whole life a voluntary act of homage to the
Father of Mercies. Holiness is meant to be completed and
perfected by the interior oblation of the soul to God. As a special
virtue, religion commands all the other virtues and all human
action, in view of laying them at the feet of the Divine Majesty
and offering them to Him by a worship in spirit and in truth. All
the sacraments, by giving us the graces and virtues that equip us
for the service of God, prepare for, and in a sense, realize this
interior oblation; but it belongs sovereignly to the Blessed
Eucharist to give the oblation its perfect fulfilment. The Blessed
Eucharist unites us to Christ in the offering He made of Himself
to His Father in obedience and love. It is this very oblation,
commemorated and represented anew by the sacramental rite,
that the Eucharist enables us to make our own and so to offer
ourselves along with Jesus to our Heavenly Father.

For the moment we are not concerned with the exterior cult
realized by the Eucharist under the form of a visible sacramental
sacrifice, and which is the centre of the Christian worship. Our

---

[1] IIIa P., Q. 73, a. 4.

K

point of view is far deeper. We are considering the Eucharist as the sacrament *par excellence* of our union with Christ, and we are looking at it from the point of view of those spiritual realities that the presence of Christ produces in the depths of our souls. Those realities are synthesized, so to say, in the perfect union of all the members of the Mystical Body with their Sovereign Priest, a union which, by sanctifying them, strengthens their oneness with Christ in the interior oblation which He makes of Himself and His members to His Father. On the Cross Jesus offered Himself and along with Himself the whole race which He represented before God. By our participation in the sacrament of the Eucharist, we offer ourselves together with Christ, with the same oblation that was His, and which becomes really and truly ours. Thus the Eucharist concurs effectively in constituting what St. Augustine called "the whole Christ." It augments the real and actual unity of the Mystical Body and makes of it a homage of adoration and praise perpetuated down the centuries.

The Eucharist, The End of the Sacraments.

Such is the dignity and excellence of this mystery of our faith. After what we have said, we need not be astonished that all the other sacraments are ordained to it as to their end. In instituting the sacraments Christ had but one purpose in view, namely, to unite men closely to Himself in order to lead them to God. "That they all may be one, as Thou, Father, in me, and I in Thee . . . that they may be one, as We also are one: I in them and Thou in me."[1]

This is our Lord's great object, His essential mission, the *raison d'être* of His coming down from heaven. When establishing different means for attaining this union, Christ could not lose sight of the principal means, that one which in its perfection contained all the others. And since the imperfect is always ordained to the perfect, He was bound to organize the whole sacramental edifice around the Eucharist. The other sacraments can only be conceived as leading up to the Eucharist, as preparing the more perfect union which it alone realizes. In the mind of their Author their power of sanctification is dependent on the final sanctification which the Eucharist bestows. They are like an anticipated participation of the Eucharist, for it is their centre and they, so to say, gravitate around it.

One may ask why other sacraments were instituted at all since the Eucharist in its perfection contains them all. We must first of of all bear in mind that these sacraments are not strangers to the Eucharist, nor isolated from it. They are, as it were, a foretaste of it, drawing us on to perfect our union with Christ and complete it, by that life of interior holiness and worship in spirit and in truth, which the Blessed Eucharist aims at cultivating in its fulness. Besides, it was fitting that the sacrament *par excellence*

---

[1] *St. John*, XVII, 21, 22, 23.

should express its influence exteriorly in less perfect symbols, just as it is fitting for a universal end to be applied in practice in more particular ends. When several instruments are adapted to the production of one and the same effect, if one of them is thus ordained essentially and of itself, the others only by participation, then these latter are ordained to the former as to their end.

Thus we see, for example, that the spoken tongue is the universal instrument of communication between men. Yet other means of expression—such as writing or the deaf-and-dumb alphabet—have been devised for man's service and help him to exteriorize his thoughts. These latter modes are however dependent on the first-named which is the primary mode of human intercourse; and they are intelligible only to the extent that they approximate to the spoken tongue and share in its perfection. A similar relation exists between the Blessed Eucharist and the other sacraments. By its very nature and by the very fact that it brings us into direct contact with the Sacred Humanity of Christ and with the Blessed Trinity, the Eucharist is first and foremost the sacrament of our mystical life, of our intimate relations with the Divinity. It is the sacrament of love, so that, according to St. Thomas its special effect is to increase the fervour of charity in us. Now, side by side with this life of love which we must live with our Heavenly Father, there are the manifold difficulties of everyday life to be overcome and there are battles to be waged against the world and Satan. Before we can enjoy God's friendship in its fulness, we must traverse the stage of nascent friendship by which we are engendered to a new life; before being received into the divine intimacy, we must be reconciled to the Friend whom we have offended. All these reasons must have weighed with Our Lord in disseminating, so to say, through the other sacraments the riches contained in the Blessed Eucharist.

Far from being useless and superfluous, therefore, the sacraments really initiate our Eucharistic life, and in them Christ—the Sacrament of our salvation—inaugurates the unity of His Mystical Body. And anyone who feels like questioning the authenticity of this doctrine has only to read the words of the Catechism of the Council of Trent: "The Eucharist may be compared to a fountain whose rivulets are the other sacraments. For truly and necessarily it must be regarded as the fount of all grace, because it contains Christ the Source of heavenly charismata and gifts, and the Author of all the sacraments. From Him, as from a fountain, flows all that is good and perfect in the other sacraments. . . . The first grace is granted to none, save on condition of receiving in desire and *in voto* this same sacrament of the Eucharist, for it is the end of all the others."

The Blessed Eucharist is Necessary for Salvation.

The last words we have quoted allude to the doctrine of the necessity of the Eucharist for salvation. This doctrine is well worth a brief treatment before the close of this chapter, for it confirms admirably all we have said on the connection between the Blessed Eucharist and the other sacraments. We are familiar with the words of Our Lord announcing the mystery of the Blessed Eucharist to the Jews: "Amen, Amen, I say unto you. Except you eat the flesh of the son of man and drink his blood, you shall not have life in you."[1] How are these words to be understood? Is the Blessed Eucharist so necessary that without its actual reception salvation is impossible? The Church has always looked on Baptism as the entrance gate of salvation, as being capable of itself of opening the way to life eternal for the Christian. Nevertheless, the words of Jesus are very precise and seem to indicate the absolute and unconditional necessity of the Eucharist. Of course, a sacrament can produce its effects in a soul in two ways: either by actual reception, or in default of this, by the desire of receiving it. Thus the adult who finds it impossible to receive Baptism, can be saved by the very fact of desiring to receive the sacrament. But if we were to interpret this rigorously with regard to the Blessed Eucharist, and thus conclude to its absolute necessity, the consequence would be very grave. It would follow that a baptized child, who has not attained the use of reason and is therefore incapable of consciously and voluntarily desiring the Blessed Eucharist, cannot be saved.

This problem receives a fully satisfactory solution from the consideration of what has already been said concerning the relations between the Eucharist and the other sacraments. Since these are ordained to the Eucharist, the person who receives any sacrament, expresses a desire for or draws nigh to the Blessed Eucharist in some way. One cannot make use of a means without being thereby directed towards the end and without possessing it at least in intention. Every end exercises its causality in the very act that draws us towards it. If, as we have seen, the sacraments are an anticipated participation in the Blessed Eucharist, then the very fact of receiving them unites us to Christ, in a union that is destined to be consummated by the reception of the Body and Blood of the Saviour. It is not necessary that a psychological desire should arise in us. The sacraments of themselves effect this orientation of our souls towards the Blessed Eucharist. The baptized child, precisely because it is baptized, is drawn to it; and that is enough to ensure its salvation.

In other words, in baptism as in the other sacraments, two kinds of causality come into play and concur in our sanctification: efficient causality, by which the sacrament is the instrumental cause of grace; and final causality, which is exercised by the Blessed Eucharist. It is in virtue of its being ordained to the Blessed Eucharist as to its end that every sacrament is the efficient cause of grace in our souls. This does not mean that two

---

[1] St. John, VI, 53.

kinds of grace are produced, one by baptism and the other by the Blessed Eucharist; there is but one—baptismal grace. But in the production of this grace, the Blessed Eucharist acts as final cause; its action is absolutely necessary, so that without it neither baptism nor any other sacrament would be efficacious.

We must be incorporated into Christ, for there is no salvation except through Him. The Blessed Eucharist is the sacrament of this incorporation; it is therefore necessary for salvation. But the other sacraments, being dependent on it, share in its virtue; by them we partake spiritually of the Body and Blood of Christ, and we have Life through Him. Hence, in the measure in which a sacrament is required for our sanctification, in the same measure the Blessed Eucharist is necessary for us. Baptism is absolutely necessary for everyone, Penance is necessary for every baptized sinner. The order to the Blessed Eucharist that they suppose imposes itself on us with the same necessity. The necessity of the other sacraments being less rigorous, less rigorous also is their corresponding intentional relation to the Eucharist. "Without a shadow of doubt," we read in the Decree of Gratian, "each of the faithful becomes a partaker of the Body and Blood of the Lord, when by Baptism he is made a member of the Body of Christ. He is not therefore deprived of the communion of this bread and this chalice, even if, before eating this bread and drinking this chalice, he departs from this world, after having been incorporated into the Body of Christ."[1]

At the close of this study of our participation in the holiness of Christ, we see that the sacraments form an organism with a unity and diversity that is wonderfully adapted to the needs of our souls. Christ lives in and acts through them, and by them makes us participators in His own perfection of Victim immolated for our salvation and accepted by the Father from all eternity. Receiving these effective symbols of our faith and our love, we live and act like Christ and in Him. We form with Him one Mystical Body: "we grow up in Him who is the head unto our edification in charity."

---

[1] IIIa P., Q. 73, a. 3, ad. 1. This text is attributed by St. Thomas to St. Augustine. In point of fact, it belongs to the *Commentary on the First Epistle to the Corinthians* of the Pseudo-Bede, chapter X, v. 77. It has been incorporated into the Decree of Gratian, *De Consecratione*, Dist. 4, canon 131.

CHAPTER VIII

OUR PARTICIPATION
IN THE CONSECRATION OF CHRIST

The Sacraments Form Part of Christian Worship.

The sacrifice of Calvary makes us sharers, through the sacraments, in the graces of regeneration and sanctification which enable us to return to God. In addition, it is a visible homage offered by Christ to the Sovereign Majesty of God, in the name of the whole human race. It is, as St. Thomas remarks, the inaugural rite of the whole Christian religion. We must, therefore, be closely linked with Christ, not only in view of receiving from Him the Divine Life of Grace, but also in order to continue along with Him His adoration of the Father and so to share in the visible worship instituted by Him on Calvary. As we shall see later, the Blessed Eucharist is the real and sacramental commemoration of the sacrifice of the Cross: it is this same sacrifice made present once more in our midst and perpetuated throughout the ages, in order that we may take part in the visible homage of Christ and make it our own.

Under this aspect as well as in the matter of our sanctification, the sacraments are bound up with the Blessed Eucharist. If they produce grace in us, it is not only to empower us to offer to God that interior worship in spirit and in truth whose principle is holiness, but also in order to make us worthy to take part in the Eucharistic cult and to continue here below the religion of Christ. It is true that in offering the Divine Victim, and in partaking of His Body and Blood, we put the finishing touch to our sanctification and our interior oblation. But by this very fact there will mount up to heaven that perfect worship, at once visible and invisible, of which Christ is the Author and in which we are meant to share.

St. Thomas sets forth this teaching as follows: "The sacraments have a twofold purpose: they are meant, first of all, to be a remedy for sin, and then, secondly, to perfect our souls in what concerns the worship of God according to the Christian rite."[1] And the Holy Doctor immediately adds: "Whosoever is deputed to a special office is generally invested with insignia that proclaim to all beholders that this function has been assigned to Him. Thus, in ancient times, soldiers called to military service were marked with corporeal signs or characters, indicative of the fact that they were deputed to a corporeal service. And since, by the sacraments, men are deputed to a spiritual office, connected with the worship of God, it follows that by these same sacraments the

---

[1] IIIa P., Q. 63, a. 1.

faithful will be stamped with a spiritual character, authorising them to take part in the worship of God." In other words, the sacraments are nothing else than the Priesthood of Christ, made visible and permanent under the form of a determined religion and cult. They are ritual actions performed by men in the name of Christ and by virtue of the links that bind them to His Priesthood. Now, no one can attribute to himself the dignity of the priest-hood, even by simple participation, unless he is deputed by God to the office and accepted by Him. We need not be surprised then that in order to take part in the religion of His Divine Master and to perform its rites, a follower of Christ must be stamped by God with a special character giving him the right and the power to do so. This character is the sacramental character, and the study of it that we are about to undertake will complete our idea of the organic whole of the worship of God, which the sacraments constitute.

The Sacramental Character.

The Council of Trent (Sess. VII, Can. 9) imposes as of faith that three sacraments, namely, Baptism, Confirmation, and Holy Orders, imprint on the soul a character, that is, a spiritual and ineffaceable sign, in consequence of which these sacraments cannot be repeated.

The first duty of a theologian, anxious to discover all the doctrinal riches contained in this simple definition of the Church, is to call attention to the fact that the character is not an extra-sacramental reality. On the contrary, it belongs to that harmon-ious group of spiritual realities formed by the sacraments. It draws its origin from them, since it is conferred by three of them—Baptism, Confirmation, Orders. Indeed, by its very nature, it is itself in some way a sacrament, because it is a sacred spiritual sign. What is its exact place then in the sacramental system as a whole?

Theological tradition has always recognized, between the ritual action or sense-perceptible sacramental sign and the supernatural reality of grace to which the sign essentially refers, the existence of an intermediary element which has at one and the same time something of the sign and something of the supernatural reality. In its exterior rite, the sacrament is a sign and nothing more; it is the *sacramentum tantum*—to employ the terminology of the schools. Grace is a supernatural reality and not a sign: it is the *res tantum*. The intermediary element is at the same time a spiritual reality produced by the exterior rite, and a sign of the grace that it calls for and demands: in the technical language of theology, it has been designated *res et sacramentum*.

This distinction is not arbitrary. It is simply an application of the universal law of causality, according to which every created cause, when it produces a form in a subject, begins by disposing the subject for the reception of this form. It enabled the theologians of the Middle Ages, who for the most part admitted the production of grace directly by God, to uphold the instrumental causality of the sacrament, by conceiving it as a causality that prepared the way for grace, as human generation is the cause of the soul, by disposing the matter for the reception of the soul. It is also of distinct utility in explaining conceptually the doctrine of the reviviscence of the sacraments. In the case of several sacraments, it is commonly admitted that if the defective dispositions of the recipient prevent the inflow of grace at the moment of reception the sacraments will nevertheless confer grace as soon as the recipient fulfils the required conditions. Now, the causality of the sacrament endures even when the ritual action is over. This is a conclusion from the general teaching that in any case the sacrament produces in the soul a certain disposition—"a kind of spiritual ornament," St. Thomas calls it—which creates as it were, a demand for grace. This disposition, forming a link so to say, between the sense-perceptible sign and grace, is the *res et sacramentum*.

To the *res et sacramentum* we must have recourse if we are to grasp the nature of the sacramental character. This latter is also a spiritual reality, produced in the soul by the sacrament, a reality that disposes us to receive the grace of Christ. It is, therefore, a sign of this grace, and by that very fact is the certain and authentic mark of our membership of Christ. For, even if it happens that we do not obtain grace, owing to our lack of the proper dispositions, we are still certain of receiving the character with the sacrament. In addition, the sacramental character is remarkable in this that it is ineffaceable. From this it follows that the three sacraments which confer it need never be renewed in order to produce in our souls their full effects of sanctification.

The Sacramental Character is a Sign.

We are now in a position to appreciate the all-important rôle of the character in the organization of Christian worship. The religion of Christ is destined to be perpetuated visibly in the world and to endure unfailingly to the end of time. "Behold I am with you all days even to the consummation of the world," said Our Lord to the Apostles.[1] That presupposes at the very least that the cult inaugurated by Jesus on the Cross shall never cease, as long as there are human beings on this earth. It presupposes also that at every period of the world's history, it will be possible to recognize this visible and exterior religion of Christ, and consequently to distinguish its adherents from those of other religions.

Again, in all organized worship there must be priests and faithful, the former charged with the execution of the religious functions, the latter authorized to take part in them. Moreover, every visible religion is necessarily social, and no society can

---

[1] *St. Matthew*, XXVIII, 20.

exist without order and authority. Besides it is fitting and proper that such a religious society should comprise members specially deputed to safeguard the community against dangers from without. In the face of all these exigencies, the holiness imparted by the sacraments to Christ's members is evidently inadequate and insufficient. Grace is an invisible reality which a simple mortal sin can blot out. No one knows with certainty whether he be worthy of love or hatred in the sight of God; much less has he manifest evidence of how others stand. And though in principle priests should be more perfect than the faithful, actually it may be quite the opposite. Christian worship, therefore, must be founded on some principle other than the sanctity of Christ's members. We shall find this principle in the sacramental character. It is an indelible spiritual mark of our adherence to Christ and His religion. Consequently it distinguishes us from all other men. Because of it we are entitled to take part in Christian worship and have the right to perform the different functions for which it fits us. Christian worship is organized in accordance with these functions. The baptismal character incorporates the faithful into Christ and stamps them with His seal. The character of Confirmation makes them true soldiers of Christ, and gives them the right to defend the interests of Christ's religion. The sacerdotal character is the mark of Christ's priests, who are called to carry on the work of His Priesthood here below.

The question may be asked: how can the character, which is a spiritual and invisible reality, be a true and genuine sign of our incorporation in Christ in view of exterior Christian worship? If a sign is to fulfil its rôle must it not be such as can be perceived by all? We must bear in mind, however, that the character is necessarily and infallibly linked up with the sacrament, and that the latter is a sensible sign. Whoever validly receives Baptism is marked forever with the seal of Christ: the moral dispositions of the recipient, most often uncertain, in no way interfere with this validity. All that is required is that the subject, who presents himself for Baptism, express the wish to conform to the intentions of Christ and His Church in the reception of the sacrament. Hence, we are certain of the existence of the character, whenever we are sure of the existence of the sacrament. And that suffices to make the character a real and true sign of our membership of Christ. The necessary connection between the character and the sense-perceptible sacramental sign is for us the origin of the distinction we make between Christians and non-Christians, as well as between the ordinary faithful and the soldiers and the priests of Christ.

One must not conclude that in thus associating Christian worship with the sacramental character we are leaving out of account the accepted teaching that the *res et sacramentum* of every sacrament is a disposition for and a sign of the grace produced. Christian worship is but the outward expression of the adoration in spirit and in truth which humanity must render to God. Destined by its very nature to sanctify us in Christ, it serves on our side to exteriorize the sentiments of grateful and submissive adoration that we entertain towards God. The character gives us the right to take part in the visible religion of Jesus Christ. It stamps our acts of worship as authentic, as endowed with real Christian value, and by that very fact it creates in us a real need of grace and holiness. It cries out for and demands sanctity; nay, more, in concert with the ritual act with which it is linked, the sacramental character causes holiness, provided we do not place some obstacle in the way. The character is, therefore, the sign and the prelude of sacramental grace. In fact, one may ask if the *res et sacramentum* of every sacrament, even when not raised to the dignity of indelible character, does not consecrate us in some way for Christian worship. According to St. Thomas, each and every sacramental grace not only delivers us from sin, but "perfects our souls for those things that concern the rite of the Christian Life."[1] Now to each of these graces, corresponds, in the mind of the Angelic Doctor, a special *res et sacramentum*. Is it not possible that this *res et sacramentum* modifies in passing the rights and prerogatives conferred by the character, giving them a particular orientation to meet the needs of a particular situation? May it not be in view of this new orientation that sacramental grace is given us, in order, namely, to perfect our souls and make them worthy of the special acts of worship we are called upon to perform?

On the other hand, St. Thomas also remarks that the sacraments which do not confer a character have only an indirect connection with divine worship, of which the principal act is the Eucharistic Sacrifice. This is because none of them confers a new power of worship distinct from the three powers bestowed by those conferring a character. Nevertheless, the baptized person who receives Extreme Unction, for instance, is assimilated by this sacrament to his Divine Master in His Sufferings and Death, and is consequently raised to the dignity of a suffering member of Christ. His participation in the worship of God has undergone a modification. Though always based on the rights conferred by baptismal character, his participation is now invested with this additional formality, namely, that it is the worship of a suffering member of Christ and recognised as such by the whole Christian Body. In the same way Christian spouses, by their sacramental union, symbolize before the world the mystical union of Christ and His Church. There is no reason, it would seem, to abstract from this aspect and this Christian social quality, in their active participation in the religion of Christ. Thus, too, the adoration and worship of the repentant sinner, who has been restored to grace by sacramental absolution, is characterized by a sincere

---

[1] IIIa P., Q. 63, a. 1.

sorrow for the past and a desire to make fitting atonement for his sins.

Accordingly, the sacraments not only sanctify us, but give us a share either directly or indirectly in the divine worship instituted by Christ, and enable us to take part in it in varying degrees. Yet the sacramental character alone constitutes the solid framework of this worship. It alone organizes and guides socially our exterior religious acts by imprinting on our souls the indelible mark of our membership of Christ.

The Sacramental Character is a Consecration.

We have seen that the sacramental character is a sign. It is however more than that. It is also a spiritual reality. The notion of sign, in fact, expresses simply a relation to the thing signified. Now, rather than admit, in opposition to the common opinion of theologians, that the character is a simple relation of reason, a purely nominal deputation to acts of Christian worship, we must hold that the right and the dignity it confers have a real foundation in the soul of the recipient. "The character is impressed upon the soul," says the Council of Trent. Such teaching is difficult to explain if the character is not something real, What then is the nature of this spiritual reality, which, entering into our souls, ordains us to the worship of God?

When studying Christ's sacerdotal power, we remarked that the Hypostatic Union, by the substantial consecration it conferred on our Saviour's Humanity, was the ultimate foundation of His Priesthood. It is properly speaking this consecration that gives Christ His priestly character, and makes Him the Mediator *par excellence* between God and man. Moreover, it imparts to His actions their absolute value as the sovereign homage of a creature to its Creator. The worship thus established by Christ is one which draws its unique and transcendent value from the substantial consecration of the Humanity of Jesus. It belongs in some degree not only to the supernatural order of grace, but to the order of the Hypostatic Union. It is the cult and the religion of the God-man.

On the other hand, the whole of humanity is called to participate in this cult. Christ is ours: so also is His religion. Consequently, in order that a man may make the worship of Jesus his own, it is not enough that he should be sanctified by grace, indispensable though that be for worthily approaching God. He must also be sanctified, or more exactly, consecrated, in the way Christ Himself is consecrated by the Hypostatic Union. This, of course, does not imply that man must become God. What is required, however, is that the Christian's acts of worship as such have a value analogous to that of Christ's own. They must belong to the order of the Hypostatic Union, because God wills that there be but one cult and one religion in the world. Man's acts of worship must be not only supernatural, but fully and truly Christian, so that they may form a homage acceptable to God.

That is, they must be principles of interior sanctification like the Passion of Christ, of which they take the place. If it is true that the organic whole formed by the sacraments is simply Christ's worship placed within our reach, then man must have the power of realizing this worship is such wise as to give it its proper value of homage and sanctification, analogous to the homage and the sanctification of the Sovereign High-Priest who is True God and True Man. The sacramental character satisfies perfectly these lofty demands of Christian worship. By dedicating us irrevocably to Christian worship, it links us in a very special manner with Christ and with God. It effects a real consecration of our whole being. St. Thomas repeats this several times: "By these sacraments which imprint a character, a man receives a special consecration which deputes him to the worship of God."[1] Of course, there can be no question here of a substantial consecration, identical with the Hypostatic Union; but, just as the Hypostatic Union consecrated Christ and deputed Him to the most perfect form of worship possible, so does the character consecrate a man and enable him to take part in this same perfect worship of Jesus. The character is as it were a derivation from the substantial consecration of the Hypostatic Union. Man's acts of worship are of value only in so far as they reproduce those of Christ. It is in view of giving them this value that the character confers a consecration on man that is derived from and linked up with Our Saviour's substantial consecration.

In other words, it is because Christ belongs to God in a way altogether transcendent that He can offer the perfect homage due to the Divine Majesty. To associate us with this homage and enable us to make it our own, the character links us too with God in a derived and accidental manner, it is true, but yet in a way which enables us to offer a worship wherein God sees the worship of His only-Begotten Son, Jesus Christ, and which He finds acceptable for that reason. What the Hypostatic Union is to the Priesthood of Jesus, the character is to our priesthood; and, because the latter is only a continuation of Christ's Priesthood, the character too takes its origin from the Hypostatic Consecration in some way. Hence, St. Thomas is not satisfied with stating that the sacramental character is a consecration, but affirms at the same time that it is a participation in Christ's Priesthood.

Christ evidently plays a part in the production of the character in our souls, through the sacrament. But it belongs primarily to God, as principal cause, to produce it. The Sacred Humanity of Jesus is the instrumental cause. It is also true to say that by imprinting the character on our souls God stamps us, so to speak, with Christ's effigy. We then bear on our souls the mark that is special to Christians, a mark that is indelible, because it partakes of the perennial nature of Christ's consecration and is a reflexion

[1] IIIa P., Q. 63, a. 6, ad. 2.

of it. This mark distinguishes us from all other men, even from those who may be sanctified by the Divine Life of Grace but who, not being baptized and therefore not stamped with the character of Christ, do not belong to His visible religion and cannot take part in His worship.

The Sacramental Character is a Power.

Besides being a consecration dedicating man to the worship of God, offered by a humanity united substantially to God in the Person of its Head, the character is also a power. It enables us to posit acts of worship that are truly Christian. It is a power of participation in Christian worship. What exactly does that mean?

We are already acquainted with the organization of this worship. It is immediately linked up with the sacrifice of Calvary by the Blessed Eucharist which perpetuates the sacrifice of the Cross, and by the sacraments which communicate to us its sanctifying virtue and enable us to take part in the Eucharistic worship. Christian worship, therefore, consists essentially in the Blessed Eucharist and the Sacraments; but it comprises in addition all the ceremonies and public prayers instituted by the Church. These add to its splendour as the sublime official protestation of our faith in Christ the Saviour and in the thrice-Holy God, eternally glorified in Jesus.

There is this difference between the sacraments and the ceremonies which accompany them. The sacraments have been instituted by Christ and are, as it were, the action of Christ reproduced amongst us, with the same value of homage and the same power of sanctification. The ceremonies on the other hand are of ecclesiastical origin and are acts of worship of Christ's members, precisely in as much as they are His Members and are personally and socially associated with the worship of their Head. Sacramental actions are the very actions of Christ, and he who performs them does so, as St. Thomas points out, "in the name and in the person of Christ." The purely liturgical actions are the actions of Christ's Mystical Body, which, united with the Head expresses visibly the part it takes in His worship.

Accordingly, a hierarchical order can be set up between these actions as follows: the sacramental actions have an excellence beyond comparison and are holy with the holiness of Our Lord Himself; the liturgical actions are holy with the holiness which belongs to the Mystical Body because of its actual connection and close union with its Head. They are sacred actions also, but they have not the same value as those of Christ; His actions are sacred because His Humanity is immediately united to God, while the actions of His members are sacred in virtue of the bond which links them with Christ, and through Christ with God.

Now, since the sacramental character has consecrated us in the same manner as Christ Himself, it enables us to reproduce the very actions of Christ, the sacramental actions, or at least to receive them and derive benefit from their all-powerful influence. In virtue of this same character we are, moreover, empowered to accomplish the liturgical actions of the Mystical Body and make of them the authentic prayer of the Church. It is quite evident that there can be no difficulty in admitting the existence of the latter power, if we admit the reality of the former—"*qui potest plus, potest minus*," in the same order. We are here in the order of Christian worship in which Christ as Head, and all His Members with Him, render to God the homage He has the right to expect from the human race. It is therefore on the first power that we must especially insist, if we are to get an accurate idea of the nature of the sacramental character.

The sacramental action can be viewed from two points of view, from that of the minister of the sacrament and from that of the recipient. In both cases it is essential that the action be really that of Christ; hence the necessity of a power relating to the production of this act and of another referring to its reception. It is not surprising, therefore, to find ourselves in presence of three different characters, of which one, the sacerdotal character, enables the person endowed with it to reproduce the sacramental actions of Christ; while the other two, namely those of baptism and confirmation, permit us to receive such actions and to derive spiritual benefits from them.

We thus see that the character is not only a power, but an active or passive power according to the circumstances: "Divine worship," writes St. Thomas, "consists in receiving divine things or in transmitting them to others. In both cases a certain power is required: because to deliver a thing to another, a certain active ability is indispensable: and to receive a thing, a passive one. Hence the character implies a certain spiritual power ordained to the worship of God."[1]

The Character is an Active Power.

We are obliged to pursue our study further, and to declare with St. Thomas that the character is an instrumental power. There is no difficulty in admitting this when it is question of the character as an active power. In this case, its rôle is to enable us to perform an action of sacramental value, that is, an action which is, as it were, the prolongation of the very action of Christ, and is therefore sanctified and consecrated like His. There is question, then, of an act ennobled by a special sanctification. Is the character or rather the person possessing it to be taken as principal or instrumental cause of this special sanctification? We answer that he can be only the instrumental cause. To understand this, it will suffice to compare the production of this sacramental act with the production of one that is supernaturalized by the Divine Life of Grace or by an infused virtue.

---

[1] IIIa P., Q. 63, a. 2.

When the will, informed by the virtue of charity, elicits an act of love of God, it acts as principal cause. The supernatural habitus or virtue of charity elevates the will in the order of action so that what was a simple power to love God as known by the light of reason, becomes by charity a faculty capable of loving God in Three Divine Persons with supernatural love. In both cases, it is by its own activity that it attains its object: it is the principal cause of its action. In like manner when the intelligence of the Blessed in heaven is raised by the light of glory to the point of knowing the Divine Essence directly and in Itself, it is as principal cause that it produces the act of the Beatific Vision; for it is the intelligence which by its own activity, apprehends and beholds God in Three Divine Persons. The elevation of the faculty is intrinsic to the faculty; it is its own activity, as such, which is transformed and directed towards a superior object.

In the case of the sacramental character, things are quite different. The character does not transform the activity of a faculty so as to enable it to attain an object beyond its range. It is question rather of a well-defined rite to be carried out in accordance with the intentions of Christ and His Church. This is an act of the practical intelligence of which every man is capable, once he has attained the use of reason. Whether the intelligence is stamped with the character or not, it can perform such a ritual act by accomplishing it in accordance with Christ's intentions. For that reason we can understand why a sacrament like baptism, which is absolutely indispensable for everyone, can be validly administered by one without the faith.

Accordingly, the sanctification, conferred on the intelligence by the character, does not affect that faculty in its activity: it does not transform its activity. Like every consecration, it affects the being of the subject, not its operations. We have already remarked that the Hypostatic Union, by its substantial consecration of Christ's Humanity, did not confer on Him the power to act supernaturally. Here, too, we must confess that because of His sacramental character the minister belongs in a special way to God; he acts under God's impulse and domination. Nevertheless, the activity of his intelligence is not intrinsically changed on that account. Every being whose activity is exercised in the full radiance of the noonday sun, for example, elicits visible acts; nevertheless he cannot correctly be said to be the cause of the visibility of his acts.

A man with the sacramental character is consecrated to God. His acts of worship for which this character ordains him, reflect this consecration; they also are sanctified. But we cannot say that the intelligence, which is the cause of these acts, is also the principle of their sanctification; it is only the instrumental cause. For, just as the instrument communicates the perfection of the principal agent to the effect, so the intelligence, sanctified by God through the sacramental character, transmits this same sanctification to its acts of worship. We must add, however, that the minister, whose intelligence is thus consecrated by the character, is a free and conscious instrument. He can posit at will ritual acts, which are both sanctified and sacred. He is thus the ministerial cause of his acts of worship as such.

As is clear, the concept of instrument is here employed analogically to indicate the nature of that mysterious reality, the sacramental character, and to express the fact that an intellectual faculty produces an effect beyond its innate capacity. The difficulty in this case is to conceive an instrument which, while remaining such, participates in permanent fashion in the virtue of the principal cause. Is it not a matter of common knowledge that an instrument shares in the power of the principal agent only while being used by the principal agent? The virtue or force received by the instrument is essentially transient.

To find the solution of this difficulty we have only to recall what is meant by consecration. Consecration is the surrender of a thing into the ownership of God, either total as in Christ's case, or partial as in the case of the minister of the sacraments. In consequence, every act posited in virtue of this consecration belongs to God and is consecrated to Him. All the acts of Jesus are holy with an absolute holiness, because they are the acts of the Man-God. All the acts that man accomplishes as the minister of Christ and of God are holy with this same sanctity, which has been conferred on him by consecration. When God takes possession of a creature, His domination extends to all its acts. We have only to examine the question whether the domination is total, or whether it extends to certain faculties only.

This way of envisaging the production of the sacramental act applies also to the production of the other liturgical acts. They are holy, though with a lesser sanctity, as they are the acts of the Church of Christ. The character enables a person to elicit them and to bestow on them their special consecration. Its potency, in their regard, is active and instrumental.

To sum up: the sacramental character, as an active power, enables a person to accomplish valid acts of worship in the religion of Christ, acts that are holy and sanctifying; it is the cause of their validity.

The Character is a Passive Power.

The problem becomes much more difficult when we come to examine the instrumentality of the character considered as a passive power. Does not the very notion of instrument demand efficient and active causality? And in what way can the recipient of a sacrament be the instrumental cause of this act of worship? How can he contribute to make of it a rite that is at once sacred and valid?

First of all, we must remark, with the best commentators of the Angelic Doctor, Cajetan and John of St. Thomas, that it is always a question of a living instrument, and therefore, of one that is not completely inert and passive, but which is capable of freely placing itself under the influence of sacramental action. Again, it is not with regard to the action, considered as a merely natural entity, that the subject is an instrument, but rather with regard to its sanctifying power and sacramental efficacy. This is equivalent to saying that because of the character, the sacrament, from the point of view of its value as a sacrament, depends on the recipient as on its material cause. In point of fact, every transitive action depends, for its very existence, not only on the agent that performs it, but also on the subject that receives it. The agent is not actually an agent in reality, if no subject is really modified as a result of its action. So that if a sacrament is to exist with the perfection that is proper to it, there must be not only a power capable of actively administering it, but also matter that is apt to receive it. It is by the character that the matter is rendered apt for modification by sacramental action.

We are here in presence of the state of things that we have already met, when we were studying the character as an active power. The faculty or power which receives the sacrament is not raised higher in its natural capacity to the point of becoming a proper material cause, as happens, for example, in the case of the human eye when its visual receptivity is increased by optical instruments. More precisely, the intelligence of a person receiving a sacrament is not enriched by the character from the purely intellectual point of view; it is simply sanctified in its being, so that by fitting a subject for the reception of a sacrament, it enables him to receive it validly, that is to say, as a sacred and sanctifying action. Or, to push the matter further, just as the intelligence through the action of the active intellect or *intellectus agens*[1] is prepared to receive the *species impressa*, so the Christian, by an act of the practical intelligence, submits to the ceremonies involved in the reception of the sacraments. But whilst in the act of speculative knowledge, the intelligence offers its own natural passivity to the object which is to inform it, in the reception of a sacrament, the Christian offers to the minister a borrowed passivity, one that comes from outside and remains extrinsic, so to

---

[1] "We employ the word *intellect* to describe the power of forming concepts. . . . This power is distinguished in a twofold manner because of the dual rôle that it must perform in the conceptual procedure. Thus *active intellect* prepares the materials of sense knowledge for their elaboration into ideas. Those materials are still palpable or concrete data, and are only potentially understandable. . . . To *active intellect* St. Thomas assigns the task of stripping the contents of sense of their material aspects by revealing the naked nature that lies underneath. . . . Immediately on the appearance of the phantasm *active intellect* penetrates to its inner core and discloses the essence that lies hidden beneath its surface characteristics. To the product of this abstractive process St. Thomas has given the name *species impressa*. The whole purpose and function of such a product is to stimulate passive intellect which, in giving conscious expression to it, produces a *species expressa* or concept" (*General Psychology*, by R. E. Brennan, O.P., pp. 327-329).

speak, since the receptive capacity of his intelligence is not thereby elevated. This borrowed passivity is nothing else than the character.

Accordingly, at the starting point of sacramental action we place the character as an active power; and, at its term, the character as a passive power. On the one hand, the intelligence of the minister of the sacrament, stamped with the character, directs and commands the inferior faculties in the carrying out of the ceremonies; on the other hand, the intelligence of the recipient, adorned also with the character, submits to these rites with full knowledge and understanding. The sacramental action is the intermediary between the principle and the term. It is the sense-perceptible link between them and it receives from both its special value of sacred and sanctifying action. It is true that God could do without these active and passive instrumental powers which we know as the characters of Order, Baptism and Confirmation. If he uses them, it is precisely because the whole social hierarchy of Christian worship, the priests and the faithful, is established by the character. Only those who are marked with the baptismal character have the right to share in the worship of His visible society. Only those who possess the priestly character can direct that worship, or officially accomplish its rites. Thus the whole organization and the harmonious arrangement of Christian worship is based on the character.

It is well also to draw attention to the fact, that if the character, as a passive power, makes us capable of receiving the sacraments validly, it also enables us to open our souls to the action of all the other liturgical rites and to benefit by their supernaturalizing influence. The baptized Christian can profit by every public prayer and liturgical ceremony of the Church. He may even take a more or less active part in them.

The Sacramental Character is a Participation in Christ's Priesthood.

We are now in a position to appreciate the full force of St. Thomas's statement: "The sacramental character is a participation in the Priesthood of Christ." Just as the substantial consecration bestowed on Christ by the Hypostatic Union constitutes Him the One True Priest of humanity, thus giving him full power to institute the worship of God, and to inaugurate it personally on the Cross, so the character consecrates man and gives him the power of sharing in the worship established by Christ, of continuing it on earth, and of propagating it until the end of time. This cult must necessarily be visible, social and hierarchical. The character organizes the cult, creates priests and members of the Mystical Body and thereby constitutes a visible and objective organism. Perpetuity is, moreover, assured to this organism by the fact that the character is indelible. In this worship everything comes from Christ and everything passes through Christ to God. The character sets up union with Christ in the order of worship, because it makes of all our ritual acts sacred operations, analogous to those of Christ Himself, in as much as they are performed in His name and person. There are not two cults: that of Christ and that of the Church. There is but one, namely, that of Christ and of the Church united to Him by the sacramental character. As St. Thomas puts it: "The whole rite of the Christian religion is derived from the Priesthood of Christ. Accordingly, it is clear that the sacramental character is in a special way the character of Christ to whose Priesthood the faithful are configured by the sacramental characters, which are nothing else than participations in the Priesthood of Christ, derived from Christ Himself."[1]

The Baptismal Character.

To complete this study we must now examine the nature of the three sacramental charaters, setting forth in particular the powers peculiar to each. This we shall do as briefly as possible.

From what has preceded, the conclusion can readily be drawn that the baptismal character is the first consecration which gives us the right of entry into Christian worship and enables us to take part therein. It constitutes us official and visible members of the Church. Consequently, it is primarily and principally a passive power enabling us to receive the other sacraments validly and especially to unite ourselves in Holy Communion with the Divine Victim immolated on the altar. It is furthermore a passive power with respect to all the spiritual benefits to be obtained from the prayers and liturgical ceremonies which the Church offers to God in union with Christ, her Head. Finally, our baptismal character gives us the right to be offered by the Priest in the Holy Sacrifice of the Mass with the rest of the faithful; for, in Holy Mass it is not Christ alone who is offered by the priest; it is the "whole Christ," to use St. Augustine's phrase, that is, Christ and the Church.

From certain points of view, the baptismal character is also an active power. This, however, presents no difficulty. Thanks to the character with which it is adorned the same faculty can concur passively or actively in the consecration or validation of determined ritual acts, because its activity or passivity belongs to the instrumental order in the sense we have already explained. The same faculty cannot of course be active and passive in regard to the same act at the same time. In the sacrament of Matrimony, the baptismal character is an active power even in the sacramental order, for the baptized spouses are themselves the ministers of the sacrament. The same holds good in regard to the liturgy, because those who are baptized have the right to take an active part in the prayers and ceremonies of the Church, and to unite themselves with the oblation of the Divine Victim and of all

---

[1] IIIa P., Q. 63, a. 3.

united to Him as His Members, which the priest makes in the name of the Church.

It must be remarked, however, that in all the activity they exercise in the name of the baptismal character, Christians are always subject to the Church's hierarchy. It is only under their control that the baptized are ministers of the sacrament of Matrimony; and it is by ranging themselves in order under them and by their intervention that they send up prayers and oblations to God. The baptismal character never gives the ordinary faithful the rôle of leaders in the organization and the carrying out of Christian worship.

The Sacerdotal Character.

In opposition to the baptismal character, the sacerdotal character is by its very nature an active power. The priest upon whose soul it is impressed can accomplish in the name and in the person of Christ, all the sacramental rites destined for the sanctification of the faithful. He can offer the Eucharistic sacrifice, which is the centre of Christian worship, and thus daily renew the sacrifice of Calvary on the altar. In regard to liturgical functions, the priest is the leader of the Christian community. He has the mission of praying and acting in its name, of offering the Holy Sacrifice for the whole Church and of presenting to God the oblations of the baptized. It is under his direction that the community takes part in public worship. He unites the Members of Christ, to link them with their Head and thus lead them to God. In the exercise of the priestly office here below, he takes the place of Christ Himself.

Accordingly, when a priest posits a sacerdotal act, when, for example, he administers a sacrament, or prays in the name of the whole people, or blesses the assembled community, his act is holy and sacred, and the consecration which makes of it, as it were, an act of Christ, also gives it a real and authentic value of homage, in the eyes of God. This act, thus consecrated, calls down grace and benefits of all kinds from the infinite Mercy of God, and if it is a question of a sacramental act, it becomes by the very fact the channel and infallible instrument of the sanctification of souls. The participation in the Priesthood of Christ conferred by the sacramental character differs, however, according as the person in question is a priest or merely a baptized Christian. We may express the matter succinctly as follows: Christ alone has the plenitude of the priesthood; He bestows a first participation in that plenitude on the priest, who becomes in a certain sense another Christ. Then by the medium of the priest the faithful share in Christ's Priesthood and are thus made one with Him in that perfect religion of which He is the principle and the foundation.

It must be remarked, however, that between the priest and the faithful, there exists in the Church of Christ a whole hierarchy of powers of offering worship. These are inferior to the sacerdotal power, though ordained to it as to their end. Actually, the sacrament of Order is divided into seven different orders, amongst which the priesthood holds the highest rank, the others being more or less restricted participations of it. These latter are the orders of porter, lector, exorcist, acolyte, subdeacon and deacon. All are connected, directly or indirectly, with the Eucharistic sacrifice, and each confers a special character which enables its possessor to assist the priest and aid him actively in sacred and liturgical functions.

The Character of Confirmation.

If it is easy to ascertain the nature of the baptismal and sacerdotal characters, it is quite the opposite with regard to that of Confirmation. In certain respects, more especially in all that pertains to the reception of the other sacraments, this character seems to be rather a passive power. When, however, it is a question of defending the One True Faith, it stands out quite clearly as an active power. It will be worth our while to examine this problem at some length, and in the light of Thomistic teaching, to set forth in broad outline its main features.

The character of Confirmation, like that of Baptism and Holy Orders, has necessarily for object certain sacred actions connected with divine worship. By Baptism we are reborn as Christians. It incorporates us into the Mystical Body of Christ and enables us to profit by all its spiritual treasures, in particular, to receive the other sacraments validly and fruitfully. But because Baptism makes us newborn children in the Christian life, and because it is fitting that everything in a family be placed at the service of the newly-born infant, it is especially for his own spiritual profit that the baptized Christian concurs passively through the baptismal character in holy and sacred actions. In the words of St. Thomas *"quasi singulariter sibi ipsi vivit."*[1] Confirmation, as the word implies, comes to strengthen, to reinforce, to complete and to perfect the spiritual life inaugurated at baptism. It represents the adult stage of the spiritual life, when a Christian begins to live and to act not only for his personal profit, but for the general good of the community. "One who has arrived at man's estate begins to give others a share in the results of his labours.[2]

Therefore, while Baptism ordains us to live and act as befits Christians in view of the development of the Divine Life within us, Confirmation directs our activity for the common good. "In Baptism," writes St. Thomas in another article, "man, living for himself, receives the power to do what is required for his personal salvation; but in Confirmation he is commissioned to take his place in the spiritual combat being waged against the enemies of

---

[1] IIIa P., Q. 72, a. 2. "He, as it were, lives for Himself alone."
[2] IIIa P., Q. 72, a. 2.

the faith."[1] The confirmed Christian is empowered to make public confession of the faith that is in him for the defence of Christ's visible religion. By the character of Confirmation the baptized boy or girl is deputed and consecrated to proclaim publicly and *quasi ex officio*[2] the vitality of the worship of Christ's Mystical Body. While the characters of Baptism and Orders tend to constitute the acts indispensable for worship, namely, the sacraments, so that without them the sacraments simply would not exist, the character of Confirmation has a different end in view. It has the rôle of defending, preserving, conserving and strengthening the worship already instituted. It constitutes its recipient a firm and official defender of Christian worship.

The act of defence posited by a confirmed Christian is, in its way, an act of worship, even if it be only because of its immediate reference to the worship it protects. Because it proclaims the truth and sanctity of the Christian religion, it is a homage rendered to God; and it is also an action holy and sacred, having of itself an objective value for the preservation of Christian worship.

In what precisely does this action consist? According to the teaching of St. Thomas, set forth in the *Commentary on the Sentences* and the *Summa Theologica*, it is primarily an oral protestation of one's faith, of which the perfect model is to be found in the confessions of Christians before their judges in times of persecution. "The confirmed person receives the power to profess his faith in Christ publicly and orally, and that *quasi ex officio*."[3] "Accordingly, in times of persecutions, members of the flock were chosen to remain in the area of persecution that they might publicly confess the name of Christ, while the rest of the faithful went into hiding."[4] "All are not called upon to take part in this combat, but only those who are confirmed."[5]

It belongs to the confirmed person, then, and to him alone, to profess his faith officially in the presence of the enemies of Christianity; and his profession has a sacred and objective value which the protestation of one who is only baptized could not have. In case of necessity the latter would evidently be obliged to proclaim himself a follower of Christ, but he would then be acting as a private person, so to say, not as one officially designated to defend the Christian Community.

It is easy to understand why the Church of Christ must have official defenders. The religion of Christ, the Catholic Church, is a visible and external society which has received from its Divine Founder the mandate to vindicate openly its claims and extend its influence throughout the world. Accordingly, it must

---

[1] IIIa P., Q. 72, a. 5.
[2] IIIa P., Q. 72, a. 5 and 2.
[3] IIIa P., Q. 72, a. 5 and 2.
[4] *Commentary on the Sentences*, Book 4, dist. 7, Q. 2, a. 1, sol. 1.
[5] Ibid.

boldly proclaim its message and reveal itself to all. This duty is especially incumbent in times of crisis when the Church's very existence is threatened. The time of persecution is an extreme instance, but it is not the only occasion when the confirmed Catholic is called upon to act in virtue of the character he bears. Every time that he finds himself in presence of enemies of the Catholic Faith and that the interests of the community are involved, he can rely upon the union with Christ which results from the seal imprinted on his soul by Confirmation to elicit those acts which duty imposes. On such occasions his acts are of them-selves holy and sacred.

Besides verbal protestations of faith there are others also. Every act of worship, by its very nature, constitutes a certain exterior profession of faith, and St. Thomas points out that all the sacraments are such. But these protestations are common to the baptized and the confirmed alike, and do not, properly speaking, form part of the official function of the latter. One must envisage things from another point of view, if one wishes to understand the rôle of the character of Confirmation in the reception of the sacraments.

It is evident at a glance that this character gives the recipient a right to a grace of special fortitude, which raises him to the dignity of a perfect adult Christian by bestowing on him the fulness of spiritual vigour. By this it renders the soul more apt to receive the other sacraments instituted by Our Divine Lord. Several of these sacraments presuppose that the baptized Christian has come of age spiritually, and for that reason the Church requires that, prior to their reception, the person con-cerned should have already received Confirmation. "The character of Baptism," says Cajetan, "makes the baptized, absolutely speaking, a subject for the other sacraments ; the character of Confirmation makes him a free and perfect subject." In this respect the character of Confirmation appears to be a passive power whose function it is to perfect that of Baptism; it works in the same way and under similar conditions. That is why St. Thomas writes: "By Baptism, man acquires the power to receive the other sacraments. . . . In a certain sense Confirmation is ordained to the same end."[1]

Nevertheless it is clear that for the Angelic Doctor, the character of Confirmation is primarily an active power, a power of social defence and preservation, whereby the Mystical Body of Christ asserts its vitality in presence of its enemies. And it is under this special aspect, which marks it off clearly from the other sacramental characters, that it is interesting to study it.

In order that a gesture of protestation or defence be really worthy of the name and attain its object, it must be characterized by firmness in its accomplishment. It should of its very nature

---

[1] IIIa P., Q. 63, a. 6.

command the respect of those to whom it is directed. In what consists this special firmness, which all theologians demand in the act posited by the confirmed Christian in virtue of his character? The difficulty with regard to this point lies in distinguishing between the strength of soul possessed by the confirmed Christian by reason of the character of Confirmation and that which he enjoys because of sacramental grace. It is quite certain that Confirmation gives a person who is well-disposed a very special grace of fortitude, enabling him to proclaim his faith courageously in all circumstances, and thus rendering him capable of discharging the functions assigned him by the character he bears. Yet we must not forget that Christian worship in its organic constitution and for its continuance does not depend on the subjective holiness of its adherents. We know that the baptismal and sacerdotal characters produce their proper effects independently of the moral dispositions of those who have them. For the character is an instrumental power and the minister of the sacrament acts as the instrument of Christ and of God. If he intends to accomplish what Christ wills and if he carries out the prescribed rites, that suffices. His act is sacred and valid; it is an act of worship which perpetuates the Priesthood of Christ in our midst.

The same should hold good for the character of Confirmation. Officially charged with the protection of Christian worship against external destructive elements, the confirmed person must be capable of fulfilling his duties independently of the grace of fortitude conferred by the sacrament when received in the proper dispositions. In defending the worship of the Mystical Body of Christ, the confirmed person is not a principal cause. He is acting only as the instrument of Our Lord. How then are we to explain the special firmness and courage that accompany his act when he proclaims his faith?

One might conceive the soldier of Christ as possessing, in virtue of the character stamped on his soul, the right to certain actual graces which would give him the psychological strength necessary for the defence of his faith. In truth, however, this supposition merely reiterates the confusion between the character and sacramental grace. All are agreed that sacramental grace confers the right to receive from God the special actual helps corresponding to the sacrament in question. According to the above explanation, therefore, the character would be no longer a mere instrumental power. The soldier of Christ's Mystical Body protecting Christian worship, would thus be the proper cause of the efficacy of his action. This is opposed to the Thomistic teaching on the sacramental character.

We must hold, then, as a general principle, applicable to every case, that the character has for object a sacred action of which the value is completely objective and independent of the moral dispositions of the subject who performs it. In Baptism and Holy

Orders this value is one of sanctification or homage to God; in Confirmation, it is one of defence of Christian worship, so that this defence is endowed with a special confidence and firmness. Consequently, if we are not to play havoc with the very notion of character, we must admit that these qualities of firmness and assurance, this underlying strength that is to be found in the assertions of the confirmed Christian do not come from him as from their proper and principal source; neither do they spring from sacramental grace. But just as the priest is not the proper principle of the sanctification he transmits through a sacrament, so neither is the confirmed Christian the source of that firmness in his profession of the Faith, which overawes the enemies of Christ. It is Christ Himself as chief Minister, and ultimately as God and First Cause, who makes use of the confirmed Catholic as an instrument or secondary minister and communicates to his external act a fitting strength and vigour.

On different occasions in the course of His public life, and principally during His Passion, Christ affirmed in the face of His enemies, the truth of His mission and of the Kingdom of God He had come to inaugurate on earth. The Hypostatic Union not only communicated an altogether exceptional sanctity and efficacy to His acts, but also gave His Words an entirely divine power and authority. If the holiness and efficacy of His acts pass into those of His minister, when the latter acts in His name, why should not the power and authority of His words resound in the words of the soldier of the Mystical Body, when he vindicates the rights of Christian worship in the name of Christ? The character, as we have seen is an accidental participation in the Hypostatic Union. It permits man to reproduce in the order of worship effects analogous to those realized by Christ in virtue of His substantial consecration. When the priest administers a sacrament there is no need to ascertain whether or not he is in the state of grace; the holiness permeating his act is a consecration which does not change its physical nature, but which makes the act belong in a special way to Christ and to God. Because of this consecration a divine power passes through it and produces the Divine Life of Grace in the soul if the latter is rightly disposed.

Something similar occurs when a confirmed Catholic is called upon to make profession of his faith. Christ has willed that His disciples bear witness to Him: this is essential to the maintenance of Christian worship. The confirmed Christian must give this testimony not in his own name, but in that of Our Lord Jesus Christ. His testimony is therefore sacred, like the act of conferring a sacrament. Thus consecrated, it demands by its very nature the divine virtue which, passing through it, brings home to the external enemies of the Mystical Body, its strength and power. Absolutely speaking, it is not necessary for the confirmed person to be in the state of grace; it is not even required that his testimony should be upheld by the virtues of faith and religion. Whatever his personal unworthiness, if he is conscious of the rôle assigned to him by the Church, of his dignity as a soldier of Christ, and consents to fill this rôle, then his words share in the strength and vigour of those of Christ. He is but the channel or instrument which transmits this power of affirmation, precisely as the priest is the channel of the sanctifying virtue that animates the sacramental action and produces Divine Grace in the soul of the recipient.

If the confirmed Catholic is to be capable of bearing witness to his faith in this manner, especially at the risk of his life, he must have sufficiently developed intellectual powers. Considered in itself independently of the increase of power that comes from Our Divine Lord and does not affect the faculties as such, to bear witness to the faith demands a real effort of intellect and will. Yet any confirmed Christian may be capable of such an effort in virtue of his merely natural qualities, and absolutely speaking, they are sufficient to enable such a person to speak in the name of Christ. Sacramental grace is there to supplement and reinforce these natural qualities when they are defective. Besides, the case is not peculiar to the character of Confirmation. The administration of a sacrament by a priest also demands certain natural qualities of practical intelligence and *savoir faire,* and sacerdotal grace helps the priest to carry on his ministry becomingly.

In every case, then, the exercise of the character supposes the mental equipment of the minister, though this is only a prerequisite condition of the action through which will pass the Divine Power.

This is the doctrine exposed by John of St. Thomas. "When a person professes the faith, as principal cause, with greater firmness of will and intensity of conviction, that comes physically from the *habitus* of faith. When, on the contrary, one professes the faith firmly, with a sacramental firmness, that is to say, as a minister deputed for that and merely fulfilling one's duty as a minister, the firmness does not come from the *habitus,* but rather from that sacramental faculty called the character. . . . The character of Confirmation is bestowed in order to enable a person to confess the faith with sacramental, not with habitual or intensive, firmness. Sacramental or ministerial fortitude does not spring from the *habitus,* but from the special function assigned by Our Lord Jesus Christ to the confirmed Catholic through the bestowal of the character. In virtue of his function, the confirmed person may fulfil his duty and profess the faith unworthily, either through vainglory or because he happens to be in the state of mortal sin. In such a case his action, being sinful, cannot proceed from the supernatural *habitus* of faith."[1]

We must always keep in mind that this profession of faith is not demanded for the confirmed Catholic's personal advantage, but

---

[1] *Cursus Theologicus, De Sacramentis,* Disp. 25.

for the general good of the Christian community. It is required for social reasons. We have seen that St. Thomas exemplified this by the fact that, during the persecution of the first centuries, to certain Christians was assigned the duty of proclaiming their faith publicly, while the others went into hiding. It belongs to the Church to select officially certain members for the public proclamation of their faith, when she sees that the common good demands it. In this way the character of Confirmation takes its place in the hierarchy of worship and is subordinated, in practice, to the leaders of this hierarchy. It is not a character equipping for leadership, like the priestly character. It is rather a character that empowers a member of the Mystical Body to be and to act as a soldier of Christ. Of course, cases of urgent necessity may arise wherein it may be incumbent upon a Catholic to defend his religion for the sake of the common good. Usually it pertains to the Rulers of the Mystical Body to select confirmed members for this duty, when the community is in danger. On all other occasions of more restricted interest, it is by sacramental grace that confirmed Catholics find the help and strength necessary to prevent their being ashamed of Christ, and to enable them courageously to proclaim their faith in Him in the face of His enemies.

Lastly, it is noteworthy that this idea of the Holy Ghost conferring a very special Divine Power on the words of Catholics is not merely a theological conclusion. We find it affirmed in Holy Scripture, particularly in the Acts of the Apostles and in the Epistles, in reference to the preaching of the first disciples of Jesus. In those pages of the Inspired Books we often find mention of a certain firmness or confidence—"*fiducia*," and of a kind of power—"*virtus*," which characterized the words of the Apostles bearing witness to the truth of the Gospel and of the religion of Christ. This firmness and power were superhuman, and came directly from God. As an example let us take the prayer of the Christian community on the eve of the day when Saints Peter and John were to appear before the Sanhedrin: "For of a truth there assembled together in this city against thy holy child Jesus, whom thou hast anointed, Herod, and Pontius Pilate, with the Gentiles and the people of Israel. . . . And now, Lord, behold their threatenings, and grant unto thy servants, that with all confidence they may speak thy word." And the sacred text adds immediately: "When they had prayed, the place was moved wherein they were assembled; and they were all filled with the Holy Ghost, and they spoke the word of God with confidence."[1] "And I, brethren," St. Paul writes later to the Corinthians, "when I came to you, came not in loftiness of speech or of wisdom; declaring unto you the testimony of Christ. . . . I was with you in weakness, and in fear, and in much trembling. And

---

[1] *Acts*, IV, 27-31.

my speech and my preaching was not in the persuasive words of human wisdom, but in showing of the spirit and power; That your faith might not stand on the wisdom of men, but on the power of God."[1] And to the Thessalonians he writes: "Our gospel hath not been unto you in word only, but in power also, and in the Holy Ghost, and in much fulness."[2]

The religion of Christ crucified has not ceased to be "unto the Jews a stumbling block, unto the Gentiles foolishness."[3] To make headway in the world it requires a force not to be found in human reasoning or human wisdom; it needs the strength of the Holy Spirit, and it is not in vain that Confirmation has always been regarded by the Church as the sacrament which gives the Holy Ghost in full measure, and bestows with Him the power to engage and vanquish the enemies of Our Lord Jesus Christ.

Thus by our participation in the consecration of Christ through the three characters of Baptism, Confirmation and Holy Orders, we perpetuate Christ's worship here below; we affirm its all-powerful vitality and its indefectibility in the world. When sending the Apostles to evangelize the nations in the name of the Father, Son and Holy Ghost, Jesus said to them: "Behold, I am with you all days, even to the consummation of the world."[4] The character is the essential element of stability which assures this permanence of Christ in our midst, and which guarantees the continuity of His action on our souls, to bring them to the feet of God in unending homage and adoration.

---

[1] *I Corinthians*, II, 1-5.
[2] *I Thessalonians*, I, 5.
[3] *I Corinthians*, I, 23.
[4] *St. Matthew*, XXVIII, 20.

CHAPTER IX

OUR PARTICIPATION IN THE KINGSHIP OF CHRIST

The Kingship of Christ in the Church.

The study of Our Lord's Headship of His Mystical Body led us to attribute to Him a twofold rôle of Priest and King. As Priest, He offers to God the sacrifice of His Body and Blood for the redemption of mankind and the sanctification of souls; as King, He governs souls, guides them to God by His teaching and His precepts, and controls the distribution of the gifts of grace among them. "The head," writes St. Thomas, "exercises a twofold influence on the members: an *interior* influence, because the head transmits to the other members the power of moving and feeling; and an *exterior* influence of government, because by the sense of sight and the other senses that reside in the head, a man is guided in his external activity."[1]

Now, it is essential that the Priesthood of Christ be perpetuated through the medium of Christian worship and by means of the sacramental character, which consecrates the members of Christ and dedicates them to His worship. A similar necessity arises in regard to Christ's Kingship. This Kingship would not be effective in the world without a visible and permanent inter-mediary, capable of assuring to the human beings of all ages and of all countries the directions they need in their journey to the vision of the Blessed Trinity in heaven. "It is evident that all the sacraments of the Church are conferred by Christ. It is Christ who baptizes, who remits sins, who, as the real Priest, offered Himself on the altar of the Cross, and by whose power the con-secration of His Body is daily effected on our altars; but, because He was not to remain corporally present amongst us He selected ministers to dispense the sacraments to the faithful. For the same reason, and because He was to deprive the Church of His bodily presence, He had to select someone who would assume, in His stead, the office of governing the universal Church."[2]

It is to the Rulers of His Church that Christ confided this mission, charging them to govern the whole Mystical Body in His name. The Pope and the Bishops are the mandatories of Christ, the lieutenants of His spiritual Kingdom. Their duty is to hold up before the eyes of men, from age to age, the common ideal to be sought after, to explain the laws and precepts that make its attain-ment possible, to regulate the distribution of spiritual benefits, to impose the requisite sanctions, and finally, to carry on the struggle, after the example of Christ, against the forces of evil.

---

[1] IIIa P., Q. 8, a. 6.
[2] *Summa contra Gentiles,* Book IV, Ch. LXXVI.

Priesthood and Kingship of Christ in the Chruch.

St. Thomas rightly remarks that the Church's participation in the royalty of Christ is very different from the part she plays in the sanctification of souls. "The inpouring of Divine Grace must be the exclusive work of Christ whose sacred Humanity, owing to its union with the Divinity, has the power of justification. But the influence which Christ exerts in His external government can be communicated to others. These are the heads of the Church. . . . They are heads in the sense that they hold the place of Christ (dicuntur capita in quantum vicem gerunt Christi)."[1]

On the one hand, then, when the Church governs in the name of Christ, she does so as proper, though subordinate, cause. Spouse of Christ and true regent of souls here on earth, she is entitled to have her authority recognized and respected. On the other hand, when the Church, through the Priesthood and the Sacraments, transmits the Supernatural Life of Grace to us, she is simply an instrument utilized by Christ to vivify souls. There is a manifest parallelism between this double dependence of the Church in relation to Christ, and the dependence we have already remarked in Christ in regard to God. The difference between them lies in this that because the Sacred Humanity is immediately united to the Word, His Kingship and His Priesthood receive therefrom an amplitude, an universality and a perfection which the Church can share only in a limited degree. The men of all times, all places and all states, as St. Thomas remarks, are subject to Our Lord. The heads of the Church govern only in particular places, as is the case with Bishops; or over the whole Church though only during a certain limited period, as is the case with the Pope; and in all cases their power of ruling extends only to those living on earth. Moreover, it is by His own power and authority that Christ rules. All are subject to Him with the exception of Him "who put all things under Him."[2] But the heads of the Church have no authority other than that bestowed on them by Christ.

It must be also remarked that, in His Priesthood, Our Lord's Sacred Humanity is the specially appropriated instrument of the Word, or as St. Thomas expresses it, the instrument united to the Word. The Church, in its ministers, is only the secondary, exterior, visible instrument, needed without doubt for uniting us normally and with certitude to Christ, but which He is not obliged to use in order to pour His gifts of grace into our souls. Again, Christ is the sole Mediator whose merits and infinite satisfactions save the world; He is the sovereign Priest of the only sacrifice acceptable to God. The mediation exercised by the Church is relative and dependent on that of Christ. Her priests have power to offer that sacrifice only because they act in the

---

[1] IIIa P., Q. 8, a. 6.
[2] *I Cor.*, XV, 27.

person of Christ, and because Christ really acts in them and by them.

Finally, the influence that Christ exercises upon the world by His Priesthood and His Kingship, surpasses in extent, even here below, the influence of the visible Church. St. Thomas teaches that all men, even pagans and heretics, belong to Christ. He can act invisibly on them, giving them the graces they require for conversion, and even raising them to the Supernatural Life of Grace, if invincible ignorance keeps them outside the One True Church. It must be admitted, however, that this mode of salvation exemplified in the case of those souls is imperfect and abnormal. The Church is the centre from which Christ's Divine fecundity is diffused in its plenitude; by right, the Church is universal and her influence on earth properly tends to be coextensive with that of Her Divine Founder. It is possible to be subject to the Priesthood and the Kingship of Christ outside the Church, but in order to reap the full benefit of such subjection for the spiritual life, one must be a child of that Church to which Christ confided the infinite riches of His redemption.

The Constitution of the Church.

How exactly does the Church exercise her kingship in the realm of souls? On the other hand, what are the relations between her priesthood and her powers of government? These are the two problems which must now be investigated. The answers to them will complete our teaching on the organization and the hierarchical constitution of the Church of Christ.

It was not without a precise and well-defined purpose that Our Divine Lord, at the beginning of His public ministry, chose from among His disciples, twelve who were to be His Apostles. "And he made that twelve should be with him, and that he might send them to preach. And he gave them power to heal sicknesses, and to cast out devils."[1] In this choice of the Divine Master, there is clearly manifested the will to establish His Church, appoint her leaders and thereby provide the faithful with a guilding power other than their own interior spirit and the fervour of the early days. Thus the primitive Church understood matters. In the Cenacle, where the disciples gathered together after the Ascension, the Apostles occupied a preponderant place; they acted as the unquestioned directors and responsible leaders of the spiritual society grouped about them. In order to accord with the intentions of the Master, who had chosen them twelve in number, their first concern was to replace Judas the traitor. The goods of the community were laid at their feet. Soon afterwards, they organized the preaching of the gospel throughout the world; and when a practical difficulty arose with regard to this Apostolate, it was to them that St. Paul, "the least of the Apostles," turned for a definitive decision.

---

[1] *St. Mark*, III, 13, 14.

It is clear that such an organization, established by the will of Christ, was meant to continue after the Apostles. Our Divine Lord had promised His disciples that He would be with them until the end of time, and, since the Apostles were destined to die before the end of the world, it was evidently indispensable that they should have successors. That is a natural law for any society intended to endure. The Apostles themselves took care to appoint rulers over the Churches they founded. St. Paul, addressing the bishops and priests of the Church of Ephesus, said: "Take heed to yourselves and to the whole flock, wherein the Holy Ghost hath placed you bishops, to rule the Church of God."[1] And St. Peter wrote in the same strain to the presbyters of the Churches of Asia Minor: "Feed the flock of God which is among you."[2] The two *Epistles of St. Paul to Timothy* and the *Epistle to Titus* will repay study with regard to this point. They set forth the organization of the Churches by the Apostles. They indicate the transmission, by the imposition of hands, of hierarchical powers, to the rulers charged with safeguarding the doctrine of the Church, her discipline and the organization of her worship.

After the Apostolic Age, it belonged to the Church to perpetuate the government established by Our Divine Lord, and with His unfailing assistance to complete her organization by erecting dioceses and appointing bishops to rule them as the true successors of the Apostles.

But Our Divine Lord did not content Himself with setting apostles over the spiritual society He had come to found here below: He willed also that the Apostles should have a head in the person of St. Peter. "Thou art Peter; and upon this rock I will build my church, and the gates of hell shall not prevail against it. And I will give to thee the keys of the kingdom of heaven. And whatsoever thou shalt bind upon earth, it shall be bound also in heaven; and whatsoever thou shalt loose on earth, it shall be loosed also in heaven."[3] Unquestionably, the other Apostles also had this power to bind and to loose: they were also made pillars of the Church by Christ. But the fact that Jesus addressed Himself in a very special way to Peter to confer these prerogatives upon him indicates that this Apostle possessed them with primacy over the others. Moreover, to him was confided the duty of confirming his brethren in the faith,[4] of feeding not only the lambs of Christ but the sheep.[5] After Jesus, and in His stead, Peter was definitely appointed pastor of the whole flock.

This is why, in the Apostolic College, Peter always occupies the first place. He presides over the election of Matthias[6], he

---

[1] *Acts of the Apostles*, XX, 28.
[2] *I St. Peter*, V, 2. "Be shepherds to the flock God has given you." (*The New Testament*, Mgr. R. A. Knox).
[3] *St. Matthew*, XVI, 18-19.
[4] Cf. *St. Luke*, XXII, 32.
[5] Cf. *St. John*, XXI, 15-17.
[6] Cf. *Acts of the Apostles*, I, 15-26.

inaugurates the preaching of the Apostles.[1] All through the Acts
of the Apostles, we find him exercising the primacy with which
Christ had invested him, and the Apostles were the first to
acknowledge this. Thus, for example, St. Paul goes up to
Jerusalem to see Peter and to tarry with him fifteen days.[2]

This primacy, willed by Christ, and instituted by Him, Peter
was to transmit to his successors, because the establishment of the
Apostolic College under a single head was evidently the keystone
of the whole hierarchical structure of the Church. The Pope,
successor of St. Peter, the bishops, successors of the Apostles and
subject to the Pope as the Apostles were to Peter, such is the
Church of Christ, a graded and organized society, by which the
faithful are governed spiritually and conducted in perfect security
to eternal life. "Wherever there are several authorities directed to
one purpose, there must needs be one universal authority over
the particular authorities, because in all virtues and acts the order
is according to the order of their ends (*Ethics*, Book I, chaps. 1 and
2). Now the common good is more divine than the particular
good. Wherefore above the governing power which aims at a
particular good there must be a universal governing power in
respect of the common good, otherwise there would be no
coherent tendency towards the one object. Hence, since the whole
Church is one body, it behoves, if its entity is to be preserved, that
there be a governing power in respect of the whole Church, above
the episcopal whereby each particular Church is governed, and
this is the power of the Pope. Consequently, those who deny this
power are called schismatics, because they rend or divide the
unity of the Church."[3]

The Church's Power of Teaching.

To understand the rôle of the Pope and the bishops in the
government of the Church, we must remember that it would have
been impossible for Christ to lead men to share in one worship
and one sacrifice, without first instructing them with regard to the
eternal designs of God on the world. It was necessary that they
should know who Christ was, the mystery of the Incarnation and
Redemption, and the mystery of the eternal life of God, which we
are destined to share. It was necessary, moreover, that the voice of
Christ should resound to the very ends of the earth and be re-
echoed amongst the generations as yet unborn. Therefore, when
Christ sent His Apostles to baptize all peoples, He warned them
first to teach them. The rôle of the Church on earth, then, is
primarily a teaching rôle. It is the duty of the Pope and the
bishops, who have received the deposit of Revelation from Christ

---

[1] Ibid, II, 14-41.
[2] Cf. *Epistle to the Galatians*, I, 18.
[3] III P., Supplement, Q. 40, a. 6. The Translation of the English Dominican
Fathers has been utilized.

M

and the Apostles, to preserve that deposit intact, safeguard it from error, and transmit it unsullied to the world.

"I shall be with you all days even to the consummation of the world," said the Saviour. It is not only the perpetuity of divine worship which is guaranteed by these words, but also the unshakeable solidarity of its foundation, namely, the preaching of the Church. What would a religion be like that would rest on the unstable foundation of a doctrine subject to variations? The Pope and the bishops have received from Christ the power to teach, and that with an infallible authority. Perpetual assistance has been promised them by Him to Whom has been given "all power on heaven and on earth," and Whose "words shall not pass away." "If anyone preach to you a gospel besides that which you have received, let him be anathema."[1] Thus speaks St. Paul with full consciousness of his doctrinal authority. The Church does but use this same authority, when she excludes from her bosom all the germs of divisions, all the seeds of error.

That this teaching may preserve its unity, it must be committed to the care of one undisputed authority. The primacy of St. Peter in the government of the Church is first of all a doctrinal primacy. "I have prayed for thee that thy faith fail not: and thou being once converted, confirm they brethren."[2] This is the origin of the privilege of infallibility which faith obliges us recognize as belonging to the Pope on the one hand, and to the bishops united with the Pope on the other. The Pope is immune from error whenever as Supreme Pastor and Teacher of the faithful he makes a solemn doctrinal decision. The bishops in their turn, whenever they propose, in union with the Pope, a common doctrine to the flock of Christ, are likewise assisted by the Holy Spirit, and so are free from error. Thus the divine light brought by Christ to this world is effectively transmitted to us by the teaching of the Church. Like her Divine Founder with whom she is one, the Church is the way and the truth that lead to God. And those who follow her can go forward with the certainty of never making a false step on the way to eternal life.

The Church's Power of Jurisdiction.

The Kingship of the Church comprises not only the right to teach, but also, the power of jurisdiction. After having commanded the Apostles to go teach all nations, baptizing them in the name of the Father and of the Son and of the Holy Ghost, Our Lord Jesus Christ added immediately: "Teach them to observe all things whatsoever I have commanded you." The Church, then, in the person of its rulers, is charged with transmitting the precepts of Christ to the faithful; and by that very fact, with interpreting and expounding them, and applying them in

---

[1] *Epistle to the Galatians*, I, 9.
[2] *St Luke*, XXII, 32.

more precise regulations, according to the diversity of times, places and circumstances. Christ's command would be vain if it did not bestow on the Church the power to legislate in every matter that concerns the spiritual welfare of the faithful. And the Apostles, from the earliest days of their mission, never hesitated to make use of this power. At the Council of Jerusalem, they promulgated an edict concerning the use of meats sacrificed in the idolatrous worship of the Gentiles.[1] St. Paul gave orders and precepts to His Churches: he regulated the Eucharistic liturgy: he laid down rules for the charismata.[2] And why did he do all this? Because there was question of guiding the faithful in the way of salvation, of training them in the observance of Christ's commandments, and of inculcating in them the spirit that should animate their daily participation in Christian worship. Only a competent authority could decide these matters and impose a strict obligation in the name of Christ. By this authority, the Church participates in the Kingship of Christ. Thus the Pope is empowered to make laws for the Universal Church and the bishops for their several dioceses. Likewise the Pope and the bishops assembled in council rule the whole Church and enact laws for its well-being.

The power to make laws carries with it the right to insist on their observance. It supposes, therefore, the power to pass judgment on delinquents and to mete out condign punishment. We have already seen with St. Thomas that judicial power is an essential attribute of royal authority. Here again Christ has given full authority to His Church: "Amen, I say to you, whatsoever you shall bind upon earth, shall be bound also in heaven; and whatsoever you shall loose upon earth, shall be loosed also in heaven."[3] The Apostles from the first made use of this power to sanction laws and punish the guilty. This is illustrated by the episode of Ananias and Saphira in the *Acts of the Apostles*,[4] and by St. Paul's excommunication of the incestuous man at Corinth.[5] When the Church brings her judgments and her sanctions to bear on those who contravene her orders, she is simply fulfilling the wishes of Christ and exercising a power which she possesses equally with that of legislating for or instructing the faithful. And if the Church has the power to condemn, she also has the power to absolve and to remove the penalties inflicted. Whether she binds or looses, her decision is sovereign and is ratified in heaven.

Participation in the Kingship of Christ, then, supposes in the Church an established and hierarchical government, capable of instructing the faithful without error, of commanding with

---

[1] Cf. *Acts of the Apostles*, XV, 24-29.
[2] *I Epistle to Corinthians*, X, 16-21; XI, 18-34; XII, 1-31; XIII, 1-40.
[3] *St. Matthew*, XVIII, 18.
[4] Chapter V, 1-11.
[5] *I Corinthians*, V, 1-7.

authority, and of punishing disobedience. The Pope, the successor of St. Peter, and the bishops, the successors of the Apostles, form this government. The Pope as head of the Church and the bishops in union with him are endowed with the very authority of Christ. They hold His place here below, and they rule the Church in His name. "He who hears you hears Me, and he who despises you, despises Me."[1] Such is the great divine reality at the foundation of Ecclesiastical authority; such is the basis of the participation of the Church's rulers in the Kingship of Christ.

The Indirect Power of the Church.

There still remains the question of the Church's right to intervene in temporal affairs, a right she possesses by the fact that she is charged with continuing the work of Christ on earth. In this case also, we are in presence of a participated power, limited in its nature and in its scope to safeguarding the spiritual interests of the visible society of the faithful. Yet, if it be admitted that the heads of the Church are truly the representatives of Christ, that they take His place, that they have received authority and jurisdiction from Him, then the conclusion formulated by Pope Leo XIII, in his Encyclical Letter, *Immortale Dei*, necessarily follows: "Whatever in human affairs is of a sacred character, whatever belongs either of its own nature or by reason of the end to which it is referred, to the salvation of souls, or to the worship of God, is subject to the power and authority of the Church."

The Spiritual Kingship of the Church is Ordained to Her Priesthood.

We would have a very incomplete notion of the Church's government, if we were to regard it in itself without considering the end it pursues and the object for which it has been instituted. We must never be deluded into believing that the mission of Christ here below is other than sacerdotal. Jesus came on earth to save men, to sanctify them, to unite them to God by grace, that they might with Him return to their Creator and offer Him the homage of their adoration and their worship. His spiritual Royalty itself, in as much as it is an effective Kingship, tends to render possible this sanctification and this worship: it is entirely directed to His Priesthood. Doubtless the final end towards which the Incarnation and the Redemption are ordained, is the glory of Christ and ultimately the glory of God. This glorification is as it were the apotheosis of Christ's Kingship and of the supreme honour it confers upon Him. Looked at from this point of view, the royal dignity of Christ, which makes Him Sovereign Master of all creatures, is superior to His priestly function which only establishes Him as Mediator between God and man. But kingship, by its very notion, implies exercise of government. The king is he who guides his subjects towards their common end. From

---

[1] *St. Luke*, X, 16.

this point of view the king is at the service of the end. It is only afterwards, when the end has been attained that the magnificent success of his efforts will redound to the glory of his royal dignity. It is to this that St. Paul alludes when he writes: "Thou hast made him a little lower than the angels: thou hast crowned him with glory and honour. Thou hast subjected all things under his feet.... For it became Him, for Whom are all things, and by Whom are all things, Who had brought many children into glory, to perfect the author of their salvation, by his Passion."[1]

When we say, then, that the Kingship of Christ is ordained to His Priesthood, we are referring to the actual exercise of government by which Christ directs His followers to their end—union with God. This union can only be realized in and by His Priesthood, because Christ is the official Mediator of Supernatural Life between God and man. It is in view of communicating the Divine Life of union and consummating His Priesthood that Christ rules the faithful.

So it is, too, with the rulers of the Church to whom Christ confided the task of perpetuating His spiritual Kingship on earth. These rulers teach the faithful exclusively in order that they may show them the way to God; they draft laws and sanction precepts only that they may facilitate the progress of their subjects towards the Life of the Beatific Vision. But the road to heaven is found and progress is achieved only through the means of sanctification placed at the disposal of the faithful by the whole order of worship and the sacraments. The sole aim of the Church's government is to assure the faithful a participation in the Priesthood of Christ in the worship established by Him.

Now, Christian worship, inaugurated by Christ, has as its centre, the Blessed Eucharist, which perpetuates the sacrifice of the Cross amongst us. From that centre, it is radiated in the sacraments, which are, as it were, derivations of the Blessed Eucharist, and in some way communicate its sanctifying virtue to us. The framework of this visible worship is constituted by the three characters of Baptism, Confirmation and Holy Orders. Baptism recruits members, Confirmation designates its defenders, and the sacrament of Order consecrates its priests. A visible, organized society, such is the religion of Christ.

The Relations Between Church Government and Catholic Worship.

What are the relations that exist between the governing hierarchy and the organized worship of the Mystical Body of

[1] *Epistle to the Hebrews*, II, 7, 8, 9, 10. "Thou hast made Him but a little lower than the angels, with glory and honour Thou hast crowned Him: and Thou has set Him over the works of Thy hands: thou hast put all things beneath His feet.... But Him who was made a little lower than the angels, even Jesus, we see crowned with glory and honour because of the sufferings of death.... For it behoved Him on account of Whom all things are, and through Whom all things are, when He was bringing many sons to glory, to make perfect through suffering, the author of their salvation" (*Westminster Version*).

Christ? Have the rulers of the Church no other rôle than that of guiding the faithful, as it were externally, towards this worship, and do they then remain strangers to it? Evidently not? The religion of Christ is one: it cannot be composed of two separate and independent organisms. If the Church's power of ruling is ordained to her priesthood, then this same priesthood is in some way subject to those invested with hierarchical power. That same authority which teaches the faithful and gives them laws to guide their moral conduct, must also regulate Christian worship. Besides, was it not to the Apostles that Our Lord Jesus Christ gave the injunction to baptize as well as to teach and to legislate? Was it not to them He spoke the night before His death, confiding to them the charge of perpetuating the Eucharistic worship in the sacrifice of the Mass: "Do this in commemoration of Me?"

It is true that in regard to certain points Christian worship cannot always be controlled by the ecclesiastical hierarchy. Since the character is a permanent participation in the Priesthood of Christ, it follows that once a person's soul is sealed with this character, he can always validly exercise its special acts. A baptized Christian can always validly receive the sacraments to which his baptism ordains him; an act posited by a confirmed person in virtue of his character will always be clothed with a special sanctity: a priest can validly consecrate the Blessed Eucharist whenever he wishes. But it is clear that for their lawful exercise, such acts must be controlled by the rulers of the Church. To act outside their control is to revolt against their legitimate authority: it is to deprive oneself, *ipso facto*, of the fruits of grace and holiness which the sacraments and Catholic worship produce in well-disposed souls. The sacramental action accomplished by a priest or received by a baptized person against the will of the Church is undoubtedly valid, and from the standpoint of worship, is holy and sacred; but because of the absence of submission on the part of its author or recipient it does not achieve its ultimate effect, namely, the sanctification of the soul. It thus constitutes a real abuse of sacred things, and renders its minister and the recipient guilty of sacrilege.

In addition, the validity of the sacrament of Penance does not depend on the character alone, but also on the jurisdiction received from the rulers of the Church. The priest can absolve souls only by passing judgment on them. Now, "judicial power is a consequence of kingship."[1] The priest, therefore, must receive from his ecclesiastical superiors authorisation to pass judgment on souls, so that he may absolve them and communicate grace effectively to them. It is true that the character, of itself, ordains him to sanctify souls, even by the sacrament of Penance. But, at the same time, given the nature of this sacrament, in which the sinner submits his faults to the judgment of the Church, it is

---

[1] IIIa P., Q. 59, a. 4. ad. 1.

impossible for the priest to administer it without having received a real power of jurisdiction over the faithful.

The Power of Order and the Power of Jurisdiction.

One might be inclined to think that in Catholic worship, the priest, by virtue of his character, has a real prerogative of headship, and that he exercises the functions of a ruler. This is perfectly correct, if by that we mean that the priest is empowered to offer to God the Sacred Victim of the altar, not only in his own name, but in the name of all the faithful; or again, if we mean that the faithful after a certain fashion have to pass to God through the priest and that it is for him to gather them together and unite them in one oblation and in one worship; or if, lastly, we mean to say that the priest, after having offered the Eucharistic Sacrifice at the altar, can pour out the treasures of Christ's satisfactions and merits liberally on the people by means of the sacraments. "Sacramental grace," writes St. Thomas, "descends on the Mystical Body from the Head; on that account, every sacramental operation on the Mystical Body, by which grace is communicated, depends on the sacramental operation on the Body of the Lord."[1]

This remark is of very great importance. It throws a vivid light on the nature of the power conferred by the sacerdotal character. By the character the priest receives direct and immediate power over the real Body of Christ; he can transubstantiate bread and wine into the Body and Blood of Our Lord Jesus Christ and offer them in sacrifice to God, thus renewing the sacrifice of Calvary. That is his proper and principal function. From this power over the Body of Christ in the Blessed Eucharist flows his right to sanctify souls by the other sacraments; for, being charged with the Eucharistic worship of God, it is for him to prepare souls for fitting participation in it. The sacraments have been instituted precisely in order to direct members of Christ towards the Eucharist. Accordingly, the priest can administer them in view of uniting souls more closely with Our Lord in the Eucharistic Sacrifice and Communion. Between the priest's power over the Body of Christ in the Blessed Eucharist and his power over Our Lord's Mystical Body, there exists the same order as between the Blessed Eucharist and the other sacraments. The Blessed Eucharist is the end of the sacraments. The priest's power over the Most Holy Sacrament is the end and the *raison d'etre* of his power over the other sacraments. Properly speaking, it is not a participation in Christ's Kingship but rather a power of sanctifying His Mystical Body, a participation in His Priesthood.

---

[1] *Commentary on the Sentences*, Book IV, Dist. 7, Q. 3, a. 1, ad. 3. "A priest has two acts: one is principal, namely, to consecrate the Body of Christ; the other is secondary, namely, to prepare God's people for the reception of this sacrament" (Suppl. Q. 40, art. 4).

Hence, as often as the sacraments, by their nature, postulate for their valid administration, not only the power of sanctification but also authority to rule, something more is required in the minister than the sacerdotal character. This is what we find in the case of Penance; it is also what we see in a much higher way, in the conferring of Orders and Confirmation.

In addition to sanctifying souls, the sacraments, by the three characters they confer, establish an organic society for divine worship, composed of ordinary members, authorized defenders and priests. To organize such a society, and to confer on some of its members a dignity which marks them off from others, the sacerdotal power of sanctification is not sufficient. Direct power over the Mystical Body of Christ, involving the right to rule and govern its members is also required. It is true that, as Baptism is destined for those who are not yet members of the Church and are not subject to her authority, it does not demand for its administration the power of government. A simple priest can give admittance into the Church to anyone who so desires. But once a man enters the Catholic Church, he becomes—thanks to his baptismal character—subject to those who rule and guide it. Consequently, when, in the Mystical Body, the question arises not only of sanctifying souls but of raising them to a dignity which makes them share more intimately in the Priesthood of Christ, the ordinary priest cannot, of himself, effect this elevation. He must be clothed with an authority which gives him direct and immediate power over the members of the Mystical Body. "By Order and Confirmation," writes St. Thomas, "the faithful of Christ are deputed to special functions; to depute in this wise is the exclusive prerogative of a ruling authority. That is why the conferring oı these sacraments belongs to the bishop alone who discharges in the Church the functions of a prince."[1]

Be it noted that it is not here question merely of liceity. In that respect every priest is subject to the control of the Church in the administration of the sacraments. It is the validity of the sacraments that is in question. By reason of their particular nature,—which is to confer a certain dignity in regard to the worship of the Blessed Trinity,—Confirmation and Holy Orders presuppose for their valid administration an authority which the bishop alone possesses.

In the sacrament of Penance the power of jurisdiction is required in order to give to the absolution of the priest the value of a judicial sentence, pronounced in full knowledge of the case and ratified before God's tribunal. According to St. Thomas, the penitents themselves are the matter of this sacrament, and they can be subjected to a judgment, that is, the form of the sacrament can be applied to the matter, only thanks to competent jurisdiction. In this respect, absolution is in strict and necessary

---

[1] IIIa P., Q. 65, a. 3, ad. 2.

dependence on the legimate authority of the Church, which alone can legislate for and sanction the acts of the faithful. Absolution is not a mere declaratory sentence; it is a sacramental act, that confers grace instrumentally, and it sanctifies the soul by the blotting out of its faults. Looked at from this point of view, it depends exclusively on the sacerdotal character; jurisdiction is extrinsic to it and is only an indispensable condition for it. "Every spiritual power is conferred by some form of consecration," writes St. Thomas, "hence the power of the keys is given together with the sacrament of Order. But the exercise of the power requires appropriated or designated matter, and the faithful made subject to the priest's jurisdiction are the matter. Therefore, before he receives jurisdiction, the priest has the power of the keys, but not the right to exercise that power."[1] Accordingly, though every priest, because of his sacerdotal character, has the power of absolving from sin, nevertheless, the efficacious exercise of this power depends on the reception of jurisdiction from legitimate authority. Now, in the question of jurisdiction, as in that of legislation and teaching, the Pope and the bishops in union with the Pope are the legimate authority. Consequently, only the Catholic Church can authorise a priest to administer efficaciously the sacrament of Penance; this sacrament as such is *none the less* the work of the priest, and an immediate effect of his sacramental character.

Quite other conditions obtain in the case of the sacraments of Holy Orders and Confirmation: the sacramental act which constitutes them not only confers grace, but also deputes to the functions and responsibilities of Christian worship. To transmit such a deputation to members of Christ, it is not sufficient to have power over the Eucharistic Body of Christ, nor the power of sanctification which flows from it and is conferred by the sacerdotal character. It does not even suffice to possess more or less extensive jurisdiction, for there is no question of passing judgments or laying down sanctions. It is absolutely necessary to have, in the very order of worship itself, a hierarchical power authorizing the sacramental conferring on members of the Mystical Body of an office or function relating to Catholic worship. This power is the episcopal power.

The Bishop's Power of Order.

Because of what has been said, we may be tempted to ask if the episcopate is not really and truly a sacrament, like the priesthood and the other inferior orders. The sacrament of Order is divided into several orders, unified by their relation to the Blessed Eucharist and by the fact that the inferior orders are participations of the supreme Order.[2] Is the episcopate this supreme

---

[1] *Supplement.*, Q. 17, a. 2, Sol. 2.
[2] *Supplement.*, Q. 37, a. 1, ad. 2.

Order? Many modern theologians, following Peter Soto, are of this opinion. But St. Thomas thinks otherwise. For him the sacrament of order has a direct and immediate relation to the Blessed Eucharist; the powers it confers refer primarily to the real Body of Christ offered on our altars. It is only in a secondary and derived manner that the sacrament of Order ordains us to the Mystical Body, in view of disposing souls for divine worship. Now, with regard to the Blessed Eucharist, the powers of a bishop are not greater than those of a priest. He consecrates and offers the Divine Victim as the priest does, and he can do no more. Accordingly, the episcopate is not—as one might be led to believe—the sacrament of Order in its supreme degree.

On the other hand, the episcopate invests the bishop with a dignity which ordains him directly to the government of the Mystical Body. This dignity is a consecration, quite different, however, from that conferred by the sacramental character. The character dedicates us to God directly and immediately, and unites us to Him after the manner in which the Sacred Humanity of Our Lord is united to the Word, thus enabling us to take part in the acts of His Priesthood. The episcopate consecrates and dedicates the bishop for the government of the Mystical Body, which is also a Divine Reality, since it is linked with God by its Head, Jesus Christ. The bishop's dedication to God, however, is indirect, since it is first and foremost to the Mystical Body that his consecration dedicates him. This consecration obviously confers on him a hierarchical power, a right to rule of the highest order. "By promotion to the episcopate," writes St. Thomas, "the bishop receives a power which remains his for ever. It cannot, however, be called a character, for by episcopal power a man is not directly dedicated to God, but to the Mystical Body of Christ. Yet this power is nonetheless indelible like the character, and it is conferred by consecration."[1]

By episcopal consecration, then, a bishop is made a true ruler of the Mystical Body and of its members. And by that very fact, he has the authority requisite to rule the members of Christ and to appoint them officially to the different functions of Christian worship. He can nominate the defenders of that worship, and he can select its priests and ministers. Of course, it is in virtue of his sacerdotal character that he will consecrate them and sacramentally confer on them the power to discharge their respective functions. But it is essential that his priestly character be elevated beforehand to that of a ruler and a prince of the Church. The episcopal consecration effects this elevation. Thus the Kingship of Christ raises his priesthood to the point of enabling it to exercise its functions with perfect autonomy.

Since episcopal consecration is as indelible as the character it elevates, it follows that the bishop, once consecrated, can

---

[1] *Supplement.*, Q. 38, a. 2, ad. 2.

always confer the sacrament of Order and Confirmation validly, if not licitly. His power over these sacraments, like that of the priest over the Blessed Eucharist, is to some extent, outside the supreme jurisdiction of the Church. Hence in certain churches—called schismatic,—which refuse to acknowledge the spiritual supremacy of the Roman Pontiff, genuine Christian worship still continues, and produces fruits of holiness in souls in good faith, who are invincibly ignorant of the truth.

The Bishop's Power of Order and Power of Jurisdiction.

From what has been said already, it is easy to understand why the bishop's power of ruling is ordinarily divided into the power of order and the power of jurisdiction. The former power comes to him both from his sacerdotal character and his episcopal consecration. It is a hierarchical power which makes him a ruler in the matter of Catholic worship and gives him the right to rule sacramentally the members of the Mystical Body. It even extends to the Blessed Eucharist, in the sense that it enables the bishop to consecrate objects required for the celebration of Mass and the Eucharistic liturgy in general, such as, chalices, altars, churches. "If the episcopal power," writes St. Thomas, "does not surpass the sacerdotal power as regards the consecration of the Body of the Lord, it is nevertheless superior to it in all that concerns the faithful. For the priestly power itself is derived from the episcopal, and all the important acts concerning the faithful are reserved to bishops. Again, it is by their authority that priests fulfil the functions confided to them. Hence, in these functions, priests use objects consecrated by bishops, such as, the chalice, the altar, the palls, employed in the consecration of the Blessed Eucharist."[1]

Accordingly, St. Thomas has no difficulty in admitting that the episcopate is really an order, not in the sacramental sense of the word, but in the sense of grade or hierarchical dignity. And it is doubtless of this kind of dignity he is thinking, when, along with the pseudo-Dionysius, he distinguishes in Christian worship three hierarchical powers, namely, those of deacons, priests and bishops.

It may be of interest to inquire to what extent ordinary priests can participate by delegation, in the hierarchical power of a bishop. It is a well known fact that the Sovereign Pontiff sometimes delegates a simple priest to administer Confirmation or Minor Orders.[2] This point St. Thomas explains as follows: "The Pope, having the plenitude of episcopal power, can confide to one who is not a bishop anything pertaining to the episcopal dignity,

---

[1] *Summa contra Gentiles*, Lib. IV, ch. LXXVI.
[2] Translator's Note: Cf. Can. 782, 2, also the recent decree of the Sacred Congregation of the Sacraments *Spiritus Sancti Munera* (Sept. 14th, 1946), which authorizes and obliges parish priests to administer the sacrament of Confirmation to the faithful who are in proximate danger death from a grave illness.

provided that it does not bear an immediate relation with the true Body of Christ. Hence, by delegation, an ordinary priest can confer Minor Orders and administer Confirmation: one who is not a priest cannot do so. A priest cannot confer those higher orders which have an immediate relation to the Body of Christ, for, with regard to the consecration of the Blessed Eucharist, the Pope's power is not greater than that of a simple priest."[1] The supreme power of jurisdiction possessed by the Sovereign Pontiff extends to all the faithful, even in their functions pertaining to worship, at least when those are not in direct relation to the consecration of the Blessed Eucharist. It is for this reason that he can delegate an ordinary priest to administer Confirmation and to confer Minor Orders. The delegation is analogous to that received for the sacrament of Penance, except that jurisdiction is an essential condition for the latter, while in the case of Confirmation and Minor Orders, it only takes the place of the hierarchical power normally required in the person who confers these sacraments. It can be seen at once that a simple priest, who is not consecrated and who acts only in virtue of the delegation he has received, can never validly exercise the powers thus confided to him, apart from the authority of the Pope.

The bishop's power of jurisdiction, with which must be linked that of teaching, is quite distinct from his power of order. It is true that the latter, owing to the fact that it confers a royal dignity upon him and makes him a prince of the Church, creates in him a radical aptitude to govern and instruct Christ's members. But because government and teaching have real value and efficacy only in so far as bishops are in union with the Sovereign Pontiff, it is to the Pope and to him alone that it belongs to confer jurisdiction on a bishop. Jurisdiction is not essentially dependent upon hierarchical power. A bishop has jurisdiction as soon as he is nominated by the Sovereign Pontiff to rule a diocese, and even before his consecration. He forfeits it, even after his consecration, if he withdraws from submission to the Pope and falls into schism. For it is one thing to teach, to legislate and to judge Christ's members; and quite another to have control over divine worship and the functions that are necessary for it. The former belongs to the power of jurisdiction bestowed by Christ on St. Peter and the Apostles, and transmitted, by authentic succession, to the Pope and the bishops. The latter is a hierarchical power, conferred by consecration and intimately bound up with the sacerdotal character. The Pope and the bishops are not merely teachers, legislators and judges; they are consecrated hierarchically and sacerdotally. While the Pope is superior to the bishops from the point of view of jurisdiction, he is their equal in regard to hierarchical consecration. And while the Pope and the bishops are superior to ordinary priests both by their jurisdiction and

---

[1] *Supplement*, Q. 38, a. 1, ad. 3.

their hierarchical power, they are on the same level with them as regards the proper object of their priestly power, the consecration of the Blessed Eucharist.

Such is the kingship of the Church, a direct participation in the Kingship of Christ. However complex its organization may seem, it is endowed with a very definite unity by its ultimate orientation towards the Blessed Eucharist. We have already seen that all the sacraments and all the powers that are participations in the Priesthood of Christ converge towards the Eucharistic Sacrifice. It is towards that same sacrifice that all the Church's powers of ruling really tend directly or indirectly. The Mass is the centre and the consummation of divine worship here below; it is the cornerstone of the whole visible spiritual society established by Christ to carry on His work in this world.

CHAPTER X

OUR PARTICIPATION
IN OUR DIVINE LORD'S SACRIFICE

The Doctrine of Faith.

"I have received from the Lord that which also I delivered unto you, that the Lord Jesus, the same night in which he was betrayed, took bread, and giving thanks, broke and said: Take ye and eat: this is my body which shall be delivered for you: this do for the commemoration of me. In like manner also the chalice, after he had supped, saying: This chalice is the new testament in my blood: this do ye, as often as you shall drink, for the commemoration of me. For as often as you shall eat this bread, and drink this chalice, you shall show the death of the Lord, until he come."[1]

Such is the Mass in the mind of St. Paul: a memorial of the death of the Lord: a rite by which we seal, in the Blood of Christ, the new alliance between God and humanity. The Passion and Death of Christ constituted the perfect sacrifice by which we have been redeemed and saved. Holy Mass perpetuates amongst us this Passion and Death and gives us an opportunity of taking part in the sacrifice. It is, as it were, a sense-perceptible transposition of this sacrifice.

Christian tradition has always unanimously considered the Mass to be a true sacrifice, identical with that of the Cross. And the Council of Trent solemnly confirms this belief by imposing it as of faith. In the first two chapters of the twenty-second session we read this fine exposition of Catholic doctrine: "Jesus Christ, our God and our Lord, who was on the point of offering Himself once on the altar of the Cross to the Eternal Father through death, with a view of bringing about their eternal redemption, at the Last Supper on the night in which He was being betrayed, offered up to God the Father His Body and His Blood under the appearances of bread and wine. This He did in order not to let His priesthood come to an end through death, and thus He gave to His beloved Bride, the Church, a visible sacrifice in keeping with the exigencies of the nature of man. His object was this, that the bloody sacrifice which was on the point of being accomplished

---

[1] *I Corinthians*, XI, 23-26. "The tradition which I received from the Lord, and handed on to you, is that the Lord Jesus on the night when he was being betrayed, took bread, and gave thanks, and broke it, and said, Take, eat; for this is My body, given up for you. Do this for a commemoration of Me. And so with the cup, when supper was ended. This cup, He said, is the new testament, in My blood. Do this, whenever you drink it, for a commemoration of Me. So it is the Lord's death that you are heralding, whenever you eat this bread and drink this cup, until He comes" (*The New Testament*, Mgr. R. A. Knox).

on the Cross should be represented; that its memory should remain to the end of the world, and that its saving power should be applied (to us) unto remission of those sins which are committed by us daily; and in acting thus He declared Himself to be constituted a priest according to the order of Melchisedech for ever.

"Moreover He gave His Body and Blood under the symbols of the same things to His Apostles for their food making them priests of the same New Testament. Furthermore, He gave them a precept to offer up in sacrifice His Body and Blood, and in their name to their successors in the priesthood. This precept was conveyed in the following words: 'Do this in memory of me.' Such has always been the understanding and the doctrine of the Catholic Church. After celebrating that old Pasch which the multitude of the Children of Israel were wont to immolate in memory of their flight from Egypt, Christ instituted the new Pasch, namely Himself, to be immolated by the Church through her priests, under visible signs, in memory of His own passage from the world to the Father, that passage in which He redeemed us through the pouring out of His Blood. . . . And as in this divine sacrifice which is celebrated at Mass the very same Christ is contained and immolated in a bloodless fashion who had offered Himself up once on the Altar of the Cross in a bloody manner, it is the teaching of this Holy Synod that this sacrifice (of the Mass) is truly the sacrifice of propitiation . . . for it is one and the same victim; the same is offering now through the ministry of the priests who then offered Himself on the Cross, the difference being only in the mode of offering."[1]

Theological Explanations.

St. Thomas insists upon this great truth of the Christian Faith. In his treatise on the Blessed Eucharist, in the *Summa Theologica,* he repeatedly remarks that this sacrament must be regarded as a sacrifice, because it contains the Body and Blood of the Saviour. It is noteworthy that he has not treated apart this question of the Eucharistic sacrifice. The sacrificial and sacramental points of view are closely linked together in his work, and quite obviously, for him, there was no need for an independent treatment of the two questions. This is an important point which will be very useful to us in our study.

Modern theologians have adopted a different method. They generally deal with the Blessed Eucharist as a sacrament in one treatise and as a sacrifice in another. The reason for this mode of procedure can be readily grasped. In face of Protestant denials, the Council of Trent had affirmed the reality of the Eucharistic sacrifice. Accordingly, to maintain the sacrifice in the purely

---

[1] For this text of the Council of Trent, the translation given in *A Key to the Doctrine of the Eucharist* (p. 153), by Dom A. Vonier, O.S.B., has been utilized.

sacramental order was to run the risk of making it a simple sign, an image of the sacrifice of the Cross, and of thus seeming to favour heretical tenets. A simple sign of something is not that thing itself; it commemorates it, no doubt, but does not reproduce it in its reality. Now if the mystery of our faith is really a sacrifice, the essential elements of every sacrifice should be found in it in an absolute, not in a relative, manner. These elements are immolation and oblation. Suarez, Bellarmine and de Lugo tried to discover a real immolation in the Mass. It is outside the scope of this work to expose and discuss these doctrines. We shall, therefore, refer to them only in so far as they help to throw light on the Thomistic teaching.

For Suarez, this real Eucharistic immolation consists in the change undergone by the bread and wine, which, by being transubstantiated into the Body and Blood of Christ, are so to speak, destroyed and annihilated. For Bellarmine, it is to be found in the Communion, because the consumption of the sacred species causes also the disappearance of Christ in His sacramental reality. De Lugo on his side holds that there is a real immolation in Christ's state of annihilation and apparent death under the sacred species.

It has long been objected to these theories that they fail to attain their object, namely to discover a real immolation of Christ in the Blessed Eucharist. If the change effected in the bread by the consecration is a destruction of the bread, it is not an immolation of Christ. Moreover, neither the Communion nor the Consecration annihilate Christ in the proper sense of the word, for He remains whole and impassible under the sacred species as long as these subsist. Lastly, if we were to admit that such acts bring about a true immolation, then we would have a new sacrifice, distinct essentially from that of the Cross.

To obviate these difficulties, other authors have tried to show that there is no need to postulate a real immolation in the Mass. For them, sacrifice is above all an oblation, and it is sufficient to find in the Mass the oblation of Calvary in order to have the same real sacrifice. With regard to immolation, it suffices, according to M. Lepin, if it be represented on the altar by the separate consecration of the bread into the Body and of the wine into the Blood of the Saviour. Père de la Taille holds that as Christ—whose sacrificial act on Calvary was acceptable to God—still retains in His glorified Body the state of immolated victim and is thus offered in the Mass, such an offering constitutes by the very fact a true sacrifice.

These theories have the advantage of not making the Mass an entirely different sacrifice from that of Calvary; but in the sacrifice of the Mass they suppress the active immolation, reducing it to the rôle of a simple oblation.

Other theologians adhere more closely to the sacramental conception of the Mass and find in the sacrament itself the sacrificial immolation of Christ. The words of consecration, by making the Body of Christ present under the appearance of bread, and His Blood under the appearance of wine, separate them in some way. The separation is not real, but virtual or mystical. Sometimes, as in the opinion of Vasquez, this separation is regarded as being simply figurative. Sometimes, an effort is made to show that the consecration has the power to bring about the real separation of the Body and Blood, and the law of concomitance alone prevents this separation from taking place. Such is the teaching of Gonet and Hugon. We shall return to this last point to show that there are no grounds for thinking that the consecration has the power to bring about the death of Christ. Thus there seems to be left only the theory of Vasquez. Must we in despair support this theory of relative sacrifice? The question is all the more poignant because of these words of St. Thomas: "The celebration of this sacrament is a certain image representative of the Passion of Christ, which is a real immolation."[1]

The Mass Belongs to the Sacramental Order.

We may well ask ourselves whether the multitude of hypotheses put forward since the Council of Trent does not arise from the fact that theologians have not kept sufficiently in view the great doctrinal realities of which the Eucharistic Sacrifice is the centre. If Christ instituted the Blessed Eucharist before His death, He did so in order that we might be able to associate ourselves with the sacrifice of Calvary by sense-perceptible rites, capable of effectively communicating its fruits to us and at the same time of constituting a real homage to God such as was rendered by Christ on the Cross. The religion of Christ is visible and external, a sign of that invisible religion by which our return to God is effected. That is why the worship inaugurated by Christ is a sacramental worship, composed of efficacious rites and of signs that produce what they signify.

The Blessed Eucharist, therefore, is also a sacrament destined to nourish the Divine Life of our souls by the Body and Blood of the Saviour. If its excellence is such that it is also a true sacrifice that is no reason for thinking that it thereby ceases to belong to the sacramental order. Far from transporting us into a new and extra-sacramental world, the Blessed Eucharist as a sacrifice, is the end and consummation of Christian worship. Two facts confirm this point of view. On the one hand, according to most theologians the consecration of the Blessed Eucharist realizes at one and the same time the sacrament and the sacrifice On the other hand, Holy Communion, in which we receive the sacrament, is at the same time a participation in the victim of the sacrifice. In the Blessed Eucharist, then, the sacramental and the sacrificial aspects are closely linked together, and the study of the latter is intimately connected with that of the former.

---

[1] *Summa Theol.* III, Q. 83, a. 1.

N

It is important to remember that the notion of sacrifice we form from a study of ancient sacrifices cannot be rigorously applied to the mysteries of Revelation. Already, in dealing with the sacrifice of the Cross, we remarked that it should not be judged by the sacrifices of the Old Law, since the image can never be equated to the reality. We saw, besides, that its unique and absolutely transcendent character demanded very special conditions for its realization. The same must be said of the Blessed Eucharist. The Eucharistic Sacrifice is a replica of that of the Cross, adapted, however, to our needs in the sacramental and sacrificial order. As well as sharing in the transcendency of Calvary, it constitutes, like the whole body of Christian worship, a reality without analogy or parallel. It is a mystery imposed by God on our faith, and we can only hope to catch a glimpse of part of the treasures it contains.

The work of research we are about to undertake is chiefly a study of the Blessed Eucharist as a sacrament. This line of approach is adopted in the hope that it will help us to elucidate the sacrificial character of the Blessed Eucharist. We are convinced that the conclusions at which we shall arrive will amply justify this mode of procedure. In addition we shall be faithfully following St. Thomas, according to whom the sacrament itself should be called a sacrifice. "This sacrament," he writes, "commemorates the Passion of Our Divine Lord, which was a true sacrifice, and under this aspect we give it the name of sacrifice."[1] And again: "This sacrament differs from the others in this, that it is a sacrifice."[2]

The Blessed Eucharist is a Permanent Sacrament.

When we speak of the Blessed Eucharist as a sacrament in contradistinction to the Eucharistic Sacrifice, we are inclined to dwell exclusively on the act by which the grace proper to the sacrament is communicated to us, namely, Holy Communion. Yet it is incorrect to think that Holy Communion of itself constitutes the sacrament. True, every sacrament is a sense-perceptible sign which effects what it signifies; yet, it should be borne in mind that every sacramental rite realizes this general definition, each in its own way. Baptism is conferred by way of ablution; Penance is administered under the form of a judgment, while Matrimony assumes the character of a contract. The Blessed Eucharist, which by reason of its proper perfection transcends all the other sacraments—*potissimum inter alia sacramenta*,—is realized in an altogether special way.

"A sacrament," we read in St. Thomas, "is so called because it contains something sacred. Now, a thing can be sacred in a

---

[1] *Summa Theol.*, III, Q. 73, a. 4.

[2] *Summa Theol.*, IIIa, Q. 79, a. 7, ad. 1. This explanation of the Eucharistic Sacrifice, arrived at by the study of the Sacrament, has been very clearly expounded by Dom Anscar Vonier in his work, *A Key to the Doctrine of the Eucharist.*"

twofold manner, either absolutely or relatively. The difference between the Blessed Eucharist and the other sacraments lies in this, that whereas the Blessed Eucharist contains something which is sacred absolutely, namely, Christ Himself, the water of Baptism (for example) contains something which is sacred relatively, namely, the power of sanctifying. The same is true of holy chrism and the matter of the other sacraments. That is why the sacrament of the Eucharist is perfected in the very consecration of the matter, while the other sacraments are completed only in the application of the matter to the sanctification of a human person."[1] In other words, the other sacraments exist only at the moment the minister makes use of the matter proper to each, pronouncing over it the sacramental formula, which determines its signification and ordains it to the particular spiritual end of each sacrament. Indeed, it is only at that moment that the sacrament is the instrument of the Divine Power, which passes through it without inhering in it. Like every action that is relative to its term, the sacrament is, therefore, sacred only relatively, and the Divine Energy it contains tends wholly towards the effect, the sanctification of the human person.

The Blessed Eucharist, on the contrary, contains Christ Himself, who is the holy and sacred Reality *par excellence*. There can be no question here of a mere relation to the sanctification of a soul. Though the Blessed Eucharist is destined to produce the Supernatural Life of grace in our souls, nevertheless, it is first and foremost the sacrament that really contains the Body and Blood of the Lord, not in a passing manner but permanently, in a way that lasts as long as the species of bread and wine remain in their integrity. Unlike the other sacraments, which consist essentially in a transient action, the Blessed Eucharist is a permanent sacrament, constituted by the consecration of the matter itself.

The Res et Sacramentum of the Blessed Eucharist.

"From this," continues St. Thomas, "there follows another difference. In the sacrament of the Eucharist what we have called the *res et sacramentum* (reality and sacrament) is found in the matter itself: and what we call the *res tantum* (reality only), that is, the grace conferred, is found in the person who receives the sacrament. In Baptism, on the contrary, both elements are found in the recipient, namely, the character, which is the *res et sacramentum,* and the grace of remission of sins, which is the *res tantum.*"[2]

The doctrine set forth in the foregoing passage of the Angelic Doctor is most important and will serve as an excellent starting-point for our study of the Blessed Eucharist as a sacrifice.

In treating of the sacraments, we, in common with the ancient theologians, envisaged in them three distinct elements: the

---

[1] *Summa Theol.*, IIIa, Q. 73, a. 1, ad. 3.
[2] IIIa, Q. 73, a. 1, ad. 3.

sacramentum tantum (sacrament only), which is the sense-perceptible sign, symbolizing the invisible realities it produces; the *res tantum* (reality only), which is sacramental grace; and between the two, the *res et sacramentum*, (reality and sacrament), which has in it something of the sign and something of the supernatural reality. Although invisible and spiritual, it is a sign because it is indissolubly linked with the sense-perceptible sign itself, and is, as it were, its imprint. It is also a spiritual reality, which we conceive as a disposition or preparation of the soul for grace and an ordination to divine worship. The character is the most perfect type of this disposition or preparation for grace.

In the Blessed Eucharist, the sense-perceptible sign is permanently constituted by the consecration; it is the species of bread and wine. It is not surprising, then, that this sign refers immediately to the *res et sacramentum*, which it contains in an equally permanent manner. This *res et sacramentum* is nothing else than the Body and Blood of Christ present under the appearances of bread and wine. "In this sacrament," says St. Thomas, "we can consider three things, namely, that which is sacrament only (*sacramentum tantum*), and this is the bread and wine; that which is both reality and sacrament (*res et sacramentum*), to wit, Christ's true Body; and lastly, that which is reality only (*res tantum*), namely, the effect of this sacrament."[1]

The bread is the sense-perceptible sign of the Body of Christ offered as food for our souls; the wine is the sense-perceptible sign of the Blood, offered as drink. The Body and Blood, in their turn, are supremely holy and spiritual realities, heralding that mysterious union, which is effected between Christ and the members of His Mystical Body in Holy Communion.

The Blessed Eucharist, Symbol of the Passion of Christ.

We must remember also, that for St. Thomas the sacrament has a three-fold signification. It symbolizes the past, that is, the Passion of Christ; the present, which is Divine Grace, the fruit of the Passion; the future, that is, Eternal Life, of which grace is the beginning. This threefold symbolism is found both in the simple, sense-perceptible, sacramental sign and in the *res et sacramentum* (reality and sacrament), because both are truly sacraments. Needless to say, since the Blessed Eucharist is the sacrament *par excellence*, this symbolism is found realized in it most perfectly and comprehensively. St. Thomas has taken care to make his mind clear on the subject. "This sacrament," he writes, "has a threefold significance, one with regard to the past, in as much as it is commemorative of Our Lord's Passion, which was a true sacrifice, and in this respect it is called a Sacrifice. With regard to the present it has another meaning, namely, that of Ecclesiastical Unity, in which men are united together through this sacrament;

---

[1] IIIa., Q. 73, a. 6. Translation of the English Dominican Fathers.

and in this respect it is called Communion or Synaxis. . . . With regard to the future it has a third meaning, inasmuch as this sacrament prefigures the enjoyment of God, which we shall have in our heavenly home; hence its title of *Viaticum*, because it opens the way to Eternal Life."[1]

The Blessed Eucharist contains Christ in His Passion.

It is evidently the first signification that demands our attention at this juncture. This sacramental signification directs us immediately to the notion of sacrifice, and thus clearly brings before us the connection of the Blessed Eucharist as a sacrifice with the Blessed Eucharist as a sacrament. We must strive to acquire as perfect an understanding as possible of this point.

Let us first inquire why the name of sacrifice has not been given to the other sacraments although they, too, signify Christ's Passion. To this St. Thomas replies that "what is common to all the sacraments is attributed antonomastically to the Blessed Eucharist on account of its excellence."[2] This is but another way of stating that what is proper to the Blessed Eucharist, is only shared in by the other sacraments. "The sacrament of the Blessed Eucharist," writes St. Thomas, "is the greatest of all the sacraments . . . because it contains Christ Himself substantially; whereas the other sacraments contain a certain instrumental power which is a share of Christ's power."[3] Now, what we say of Christ, we must also say of His Passion: "The Blessed Eucharist is the perfect sacrament of the Lord's Passion, because it contains Christ Himself in His Passion (*tamquam continens ipsum Christum passum*)."[4]

How is the Passion of Christ contained in the Blessed Eucharist? Evidently not in its material reality. We are here in the sacramental world, a world of signs. The Passion of Christ is, therefore, signified or rather represented by this sacrament. Christ died on the Cross by shedding His Blood for us. Holy Scripture, particularly the Epistle to the Hebrews, insists on the fact of the Blood being shed and thus separated from the Body. It sees therein the sense-perceptible element of the sacrifice and immolation of Calvary. Now, in the Blessed Eucharist, the consecration of the bread into the Body of Christ and of the wine into His Blood, turns our minds at once to the separation of the Body and the Blood of Christ on Calvary. In addition, the words themselves, which accompany the consecration and bring it about, clearly set up this relationship. It is not without purpose, as St. Thomas points out, that we have a twofold consecration in the Blessed Eucharist, "for this serves to represent the Passion of Christ, in which the Blood was separated from the Body: hence,

---

[1] IIIa., Q. 73, a. 4.
[2] IIIa., Q. 73, a. 4.
[3] IIIa., Q. 65, a. 3.
[4] IIIa., Q. 73, a. 5, ad. 2.

N*

in the form of the consecration of the Blood mention is made of its shedding."[1]

Are we to conclude, then, that the Eucharistic Sacrifice is nothing more than a pure sign, more perfect than the other sacraments because more representative, but yet a mere symbol of the Passion of Christ? If we had only the sense-perceptible sign, composed of matter and form, to which we gave the name of sacrament only (*sacramentum tantum*), the reply would not be in doubt. The whole value of the Eucharistic Sacrifice would lie in the fact of its being a more adequate representation of the drama of Calvary. But there is another sign contained in this sacrament, the reality and sacrament (*res et sacramentum*), which is both a spiritual sign and a most perfect reality, for it is the Body and Blood of Christ. These are separated in a certain sense on the altar and therefore, reproduce in a mysterious manner their separation on the Cross. It is in this separation, without a shadow of doubt, that the true Eucharistic Sacrifice is to be found: it is connected with the mode of presence peculiar to the Body and Blood under the appearances of bread and wine, a mode of presence brought about by the consecration. If we would penetrate deeper into the mystery, we must analyse the nature of the Eucharistic consecration and study its effects.

The Mystery of Transubstantiation.

The Council of Trent teaches that the consecration of the Blessed Eucharist is effected by transubstantiation. In virtue of the words pronounced by the priest, the whole substance of the bread is changed into the whole substance of the Body of Christ, and the whole substance of the wine into the whole substance of the Blood of Christ. After the consecration there remain on the altar only the appearances or accidents of the bread and the wine, which contain respectively the Body and the Blood of Christ. The Church has not specified how precisely this substantial change occurs. She confides to her theologians the solution of the difficulty in so far as it is possible for the human mind to elucidate it. The Scotist explanation, therefore, according to which the substance of the bread is annihilated by God, and the substance of the Body of Christ put in its place by local movement, is not condemned. It gives rise, however, to many difficulties which we cannot now dwell upon. It is particularly unsatisfactory in this that it takes from transubstantiation its proper character of real conversion and substitutes a simple succession of different realities in one and the same place.

The doctrine of St. Thomas is completely different. His point of departure is the notion of change or conversion of one reality into another. In the ordinary course of events we encounter changes and conversions of form only. As every corporeal being is

---

[1] IIIa., Q. 76, a. 2, ad. 1.

composed of matter and form, we say that a thing is substantially changed into another when, the matter remaining the same, the substantial form is replaced by another. Every chemical combination which issues in a new body is an example of formal substantial conversion. But in the Blessed Eucharist, the change is not only formal; it is total. The entire substance of the bread, that is to say, its matter and form, is changed into the entire substance (matter and form) of the Body of Christ. In this case no common reality underlies the change.

A change is not, however, a mere succession. It supposes a unique action on the part of the operator; this action, while bringing about the appearance of a new form, causes the old form to disappear. The disappearance of one is formally dependent on the appearance of the other. The cause that actuates the matter, which is in passive potency to divers forms, brings one of these forms to act; and the immediate physical consequence of this actuation is the destruction of the original form. The mystery of the Blessed Eucharist consists precisely in this that, while the destruction of the substance of the bread is dependent on the production of the Body of Christ under the accidents of the bread, we can conceive no passive potency or primary matter remaining common and identical in the process of change.

We must bear in mind that the author of the Eucharistic conversion is God, and that God does not act on things after the manner of a mere creature. Created causes cannot act on primary matter, which of its nature lies outside their range. In fact, they cannot get in touch with reality except from without, and then it is only indirectly, by the aid of successive accidental transformations, that they succeed in bringing about substantial transformations. God, on the contrary, acts on the inmost being of things. He can reach down to the depths of form and primary matter, for he is the Author of both one and the other. He can, therefore, so act that the non-being of bread should be placed in a relation of immediate and intrinsic dependence on the being of Christ's Body. This means that by one and the same act of His omnipotence, God effects such a change in the being of the bread that it is converted into the being of Christ's Body. When this conversion is accomplished, what was hitherto the bread is now the Body of Christ, or inversely, the Body of Christ is what was the bread. The Body of Christ is in such a relation to the non-being of the bread that one can say that it comes from the bread; this is the *Christus ex pane* of the theologians.

There is no question, then, of a local movement, by which the Body of Christ leaves its place in heaven to descend upon our altars. The whole change takes place in the substance of the bread, which the Divine Omnipotence puts in such a relation to Christ's Body that it loses its being as bread and becomes, from the point of view of being, Christ's Body. It is God, Being Itself, who sets up this relation of dependence between the non-being of the bread and the being of Christ's Body. In changes made by creatures, the passive potency concurs with the active power of the creature in setting up a relation between the non-being of one form and the being of a new form. In the Blessed Eucharist, the substance of the bread offers to God only its obedient potentiality, which makes it susceptible of complete conversion into everything that is being, and which, as such, is dependent on the Creator of all things.

Austere though this conceptual elaboration be, it enables us, nevertheless, to stammer something of the mystery, instead of indulging in sterile imaginings. It enables us, in particular, to draw certain conclusions concerning Christ's mode of being in the Blessed Eucharist.

Nature of the Eucharistic Presence.

First of all, we must note that the term of the Eucharistic conversion is the substance of Christ's Body—or of His Blood if there is question of the conversion of the wine—and, therefore, not the quantity or the accidents of the Body and Blood. Christ is present under the appearances of bread and wine, after the manner of a substance. The substance of a body is wholly in the body and wholly in each of its parts; thus, the Body of Christ is whole and indivisible in the Host and in each of its parts. Christ's Body is not in the Host as in a place that circumscribes and measures the parts of quantified and extended matter. The quantity and the other accidents of Christ's Body are in the Blessed Eucharist of course. Nevertheless, because the conversion has for object to render present the substance, which alone is brought into relation with the non-being of the bread, the accidents are there only by way of consequence and in a manner adapted to the mode of being of the substance. Accordingly, they are not extended in the place where they are.

The Law of Concomitance.

It is the same with the other elements that constitute Christ's Being. The species of bread and wine contain the whole Christ; not only His Body and Blood in their integrity, but also His Soul and Divinity. Yet these divers elements are not present on an equal footing. The Blessed Eucharist is a sacrament, and therefore a sensible sign, effecting what it signifies. Now the words of consecration signify exclusively the conversion of the bread into the Body of Christ and of the wine into His Blood. If we keep to these sacramental words, through which the force of Divine Omnipotence passes, it is the Body, and not the Blood, that they render present under the species of the bread; and it is the Blood, and not the Body, that they render present under the species of the wine. If the Body and Blood were separated in the reality, as they were during Christ's sojourn in the tomb, we would have only the Body of Christ under the bread and His Blood under the species of the wine. Accordingly, it is only because all the elements of Christ's Being are inseparably united that we have the whole Christ under the appearances of either bread or wine. Yet, it is none the less true that the power of the words, by which the bread is consecrated, for instance, has for primary and direct object Christ's Body; and His Blood, Soul and Divinity, only by way of consequence and because of their natural connection with the Body. In the same way, the Blood of Christ is the primary and direct object of the consecration of the wine, and thus the Body, Soul and Divinity of Our Lord are present only by way of consequence. Such is the law of Eucharistic concomitance, which the Council of Trent expresses in the following words: "It was always the faith of the Church that immediately after the consecration, the real Body of Our Lord and His real Blood, as well as His Soul and Divinity, exist under the species of the bread and the wine. But the Body is present under the species of the bread, and the Blood under the species of the wine, in virtue of the words. On the contrary, the Body and the Soul are under the species of the wine and the Blood and the Soul under the species of the bread, only in virtue of that natural connection and concomitance, through which the parts of the Lord Jesus Christ, who has already risen from the dead and dieth now no more, are linked together among themselves."[1]

We certainly do not mean to assert that the words of the consecration have the power to effect a real separation of Christ's Body and Blood in His natural being. If this were so, Christ would have brought about His own death in instituting the Blessed Eucharist, since He was not then immortal. The words of consecration have no effect on Christ's natural being; all the Divine Power that passes through them acts upon the bread and the wine; and it is these material substances that undergo a real change in their natural being. They are transubstantiated into the Body and Blood of Christ in such wise that their non-being instantly entails the presence of Christ's Body and Blood under the species. The being of the bread becomes the being of Christ's Body; the being of the wine becomes the being of Christ's Blood. But the same act of conversion brings with it, as a consequence, all the other elements which are naturally connected with the Body and the Blood; for this action cannot prevent concomitance. So true indeed is this, that many Thomists hold that God Himself, even by His absolute Power, could not oppose this law of Eucharistic concomitance.[2]

The Sacramental Separation of the Body and Blood of Christ.

Since the conversive action has for its proper object the changing of the bread into the Body alone, and of the wine into the Blood alone; and since, moreover, such a substantial change

---

[1] Sess. XIII, ch. V.
[2] Cf. Salmanticenses, *Cursus Theologicus; De Eucharist, Disp.* 7, *dub. 4.*

entails for Christ a very special sacramental mode of being (*Christus ex pane, Christus ex vino*), we must admit that the words of consecration effect a true sacramental separation of the Body and Blood, under the species of bread and wine. We say sacramental separation, because it is produced in a way that does not affect the natural being of Christ, but which nevertheless symbolizes His natural death. It is a true separation because, since Christ is present under the species of bread by means of His Body (*Christus ex pane*), and under the species of wine by means of His Blood (*Christus ex vino*), His sacramental being is not the same in the two cases, and from the strictly sacramental standpoint, this being is really divided. We have these two different modes of being having their origin in the nature of the sacrament, and affecting Christ only in His relation to the bread and the wine; we are, therefore, in presence of a true sacramental separation. In all probability it is to this St. Thomas alludes when he writes: "The being which Christ has in Himself is not the same as the being He has in the Sacrament; for, when we say that He is in the Sacrament, we signify a certain relation that Christ has with it."[1]

Our study of the Eucharistic consecration leads us, then, to conceive the Body and Blood of Christ as sacramentally separated under the species of bread and wine. There is a wealth of doctrine expressed in this formula, an ensemble of mysterious realities far surpassing the ideas of image or sign at first evoked by the word sacrament. The Passion of Christ is represented by this sacramental separation; but here the symbol and the reality are closely linked together. It is Christ Himself who by His sacramental mode of being, expresses anew and realizes in an altogether special way that condition of death in which He offered Himself to His Father on the Cross. The sign and the reality—*res et sacramentum*—are so intimately connected that we can truly say with St. Thomas: "The Eucharist is the perfect sacrament of the Lord's Passion, because it contains Christ Himself in His Passion."[2]

The Eucharistic Sacrifice.

Accordingly, whenever we speak of the Eucharistic sacrifice, we must always remain in the domain of sacramental realities, and keep constantly before our minds the definition of a sacrament already given; a sacrament is a sign which effects what signifies. The Blessed Eucharist signifies the separation of Christ's Body and Blood, and effects that separation in its own way by giving this Body and this Blood a sacramental mode of being which is completely bound up with their special relation to the bread and the wine. The Blessed Eucharist also signifies the

---

[1] IIIa., Q. 76, a. 6.
[2] IIIa., Q. 73, a. 5, ad. 2.

Passion of Christ, and this, too, it produces; or rather it reproduces it in its own way by separating the Body and Blood of Christ, which were separated on Calvary. But while on the Cross the separation affected Christ in His natural being and existence, here it is restricted to His sacramental being, which by its very nature as reality and sacrament (*res et sacramentum*) is ordained to signify and to recall to mind the Blood shed on the Cross. With the aid of the principles outlined in the preceding section, we shall find it easy to rediscover in the sacramental order those great realities which, in the natural order, constituted the sacrifice of Christ on Calvary.

We know that the sacrifice of Calvary is conditioned by the fact that the same person, Christ, is both Priest and Victim. If the Eucharistic Sacrifice is the sacrifice of the Cross made present to us in a sacramental fashion, then we must necessarily find this basic condition realized in it. For this reason, some authors maintain that Christ, the Priest of the sacrifice, is Christ present in the sacred species offering Himself invisibly to His Father as He offered Himself on Calvary. This opinion seems to be without foundation, for it makes the Eucharistic Sacrifice invisible, at least in its principal part. Besides, the sacrifice is thus removed from the sacramental order, to which it essentially belongs. In addition, what is expressed by the words of consecration is the presence of Christ's Body and Blood under the sacred species, and not His interior, invisible oblation. But if the Eucharistic Sacrifice is a sacramental sacrifice, we may not, in order to judge of its nature, go beyond the immediate data of the sacrament.

"This sacrament," we read in St. Thomas, "is directly representative of the Lord's Passion, in which Christ as Priest and Victim, offered Himself to God on the altar of the Cross. Now, the Victim which the priest offers is really the same as the one Christ offered, since it really contains Christ. As for the minister who offers, he is not really the same; but he must be the same representatively. That is why the priest, consecrating in the person of Christ, (*prout gerit personam Christi*), pronounces the words of consecration in narrative form, in the name of Christ (*ex persona Christi*), so that no one may think that the Victim is different."[1] The Council of Trent teaches the same doctrine: "It is one and the same Victim, and the same Priest, who offers Himself now by the ministry of priests, after having formerly offered Himself on the Cross, the manner of offering alone being different."[2]

The priest of the Eucharistic Sacrifice, then, is Christ, sacramentally represented by the ministers of our altars. And there is nothing vague or indefinite about this representation. The sacerdotal Character, which invests the priest with the power to

---

[1] *Comment. in Sent.*, Lib. 4, Dist. 8, Q. 2, a. 1, sol. 4.
[2] Sess. 22, ch. 11.

speak and act in the name and person of Christ, is that form of reality, which we have designated by the term, "reality and sacrament" (*res et sacramentum*). It is a sign, but it is also a real consecration and a power; and thus, the priest who possesses it is really, though sacramentally, Christ Himself. His sacerdotal consecration assimilates him to the Sovereign Priest and gives him the power to take the place of the Sovereign Priest in the Eucharistic oblation.

There is no difficulty in recognizing that the Victim in the sacrifice is also Christ. It must be remarked, however, that the Victim is also a *res et sacramentum*, a reality-sign. But there is this difference, that in the Blessed Eucharist the reality is no longer a mere assimilation to Christ, but is His own Body and Blood. Thus, without ever leaving the plane of sacramental realities, we can hope to find in the Blessed Eucharist that true and visible sacrifice which we are seeking.

The Active Immolation in the Eucharistic Sacrifice.

In every sacrifice we have distinguished between the active immolation, the passive immolation and the oblation. How is active immolation to be found in the Eucharistic sacrifice? Some authors, as we have already said, try to discover in the Mass a destruction of Christ analogous to that carried out by the executioners on Calvary. Is not this to forget that the act of the executioners could not be in any way an integral part of Christ's sacrifice? Sacrificial immolation is the work of the priest; it could, therefore, be carried out on Calvary only by Christ Himself. We know that it consisted in the act of will, by which the Saviour, who could have delivered Himself from death by His Omnipotence, accepted to shed His Blood and die. "This voluntary enduring of the Passion was most acceptable to God, as proceeding from supreme charity. Therefore, it is evident that Christ's Passion was a true sacrifice."[1] It is to this will of Christ that we must turn, if we are to find, from the sacramental point of view, its counterpart in the Blessed Eucharist.

At the Last Supper, Christ clearly and effectively expressed His willingness to die by changing bread into His Body, which was about to be delivered up, and wine into His Blood, which was soon to be shed for the salvation of men. By the sacramental separation He accomplished already, by means of sense-perceptible rites, the morrow's immolation. It was not a solemn promise or a vow to deliver Himself up, as some have imagined. Christ from the very beginning was determined to obey His Father. From the outset He had interiorly made the sacrifice of Himself. Entering into the world He said: "Behold I come to do Thy Will O God."[2] And this will, which He made His own, He expressed

---

[1] IIIa., Q. 48, a. 3.
[2] *Hebrews*, X. 9.

sensibly and ritually, by accomplishing in sacramental form, the great act of the morrow. He, who need not have died, separated His Body and Blood sacramentally, in order to manifest His resolve to shed His Blood on the Cross.

Moreover, in saying to His priests: "Do this in commemoration of me," Jesus confided to them the mission of renewing His great act, and, by means of this same sacramental separation carried out in His name and by His power, of expressing again this same Will to shed His Blood for the salvation of mankind. It is, therefore, the act of immolation on Calvary, that the priest reproduces in his turn by doing as Jesus did in the Supper-room, that is, by changing bread into His Body and wine into His Blood. Although the separation carried out on the sacramental being of Christ does not affect Him in His natural being, still it is amply sufficient to express Christ's willingness to accept the death by which He actively immolated Himself on Calvary and consummated His sacrifice.

Oblation and Passive Immolation.

At the same time that it realizes in its own sacramental way the active immolation of Calvary, the Eucharistic consecration is an oblation to God of the Body of Christ delivered to death and of the Blood shed for us. For this will to die, by which Christ immolates Himself, is a free acceptance of God's eternal intentions and designs in His regard. It is an act of complete, loving obedience, and such a submission cannot fail to be supremely acceptable to God. "His willing acceptance of the Passion was most agreeable to God," writes St. Thomas.[1] In sacrifice, the same action of the priest is an active immolation in as much as it has for object the victim, and an oblation in as much as it is referred to God. The priest of the New Law sacramentally renewing the immolation of Christ in the Eucharistic consecration, renews also by the very fact the oblation of Christ to His Father in this same immolation. This Eucharistic oblation remains sacramental like the separation of the Body and Blood, and, accordingly, does not constitute a new oblation in addition to that of the Cross. It is in the sacramental order what that of the Cross was in the physical order.

Finally, oblation and active immolation derive all their meaning from their object which is the passive immolation of the Victim. In the Blessed Eucharist Christ is sacramentally immolated, and this separation of His Body and Blood has no other aim than that of expressing in sense-perceptible fashion the natural separation that took place on Calvary. Here, again, such a separation adds nothing to that of the Cross; it simply reproduces it, makes it present again in a manner that is special, unique and without parallel. But it preserves, nevertheless, the

[1] IIIa., Q. 48, a. 3.

value of a transcendent reality, which gives to the Eucharistic oblation all its worth.

The Eucharistic Sacrifice is, in a word, the same act as the sacrifice of Calvary, but accomplished in another order—the sacramental order. Essentially it refers to the Cross, not by simple signs, but by realities that are signs, and which, as such, reproduce really and truly before our eyes the great drama of Calvary. Thus Holy Mass or the Eucharistic Sacrifice is the ritual act which is perfectly proportioned to the needs of Christian worship.

We now see that it is incorrect to strive to make the Eucharistic consecration in the Supper-room an integral part of the sacrifice of Calvary, as if it were merely the oblation of that sacrifice. By so doing, one unites in a single sacrificial act two realities of different orders. The sacramental order belongs to a world apart, and the physical order is very different from it. The former is essentially ordained to the latter; it signifies, represents and reproduces it, but in a way that is proper to itself and which must never be confounded with the physical order.

The Consummation of the Eucharistic Sacrifice.

A sacrifice is perfect only on the assumption that it is agreeable to God. We have already seen that this Divine Complacency connotes a certain consecration of the Victim. Christ Himself, although consecrated from the first moment of His existence, was specially acceptable to God in consequence of His obedience unto death on Calvary. There He was definitively acknowledged by God and glorified as Head of the whole Mystical Body. The glorification of Our Lord Jesus Christ in heaven means the acceptance of the whole human race in the Person of its Head, and the recognition that, by His Sacrifice, peace has been re-established between the Blessed Trinity and mankind. Still, this acceptance applies only to the race as a whole; it has to be made effective for every individual human being and every generation down to the end of time.

At the beginning of the second part of this book, we stated that the aim of the sacraments is to communicate to us the Supernatural Life of Grace and thereby give us access to the benefits that are ours in virtue of the fact that in Christ, our Head, we have been reconciled to God, our Father. Now, the sacraments are ordained to the Blessed Eucharist; and in the Holy Sacrament of the Altar the sacrificial aspect dominates and appears as the end of the whole order of Christian worship. Hence it follows that it is the function of the Eucharistic Sacrifice to effect that union of our souls with Christ, and thus bring about the acceptance of the whole Mystical Body. Christ and the Mystical Body are one; on Calvary Christ was acceptable to God as Head, that is, as the principle of salvation of the whole Body. At Mass the Mystical Body is accepted in its members, and it is Christ again who is the object of this acceptance, that is, "the whole Christ," to use St. Augustine's beautiful expression.

As a sacramental sacrifice, the Blessed Eucharist effects what it signifies, and because it signifies the oblation of Christ in His death on Calvary, it produces in souls the fruits of this oblation. "If any one says that the sacrifice of the Mass is only a sacrifice of praise and thanksgiving, or a mere commemoration of the sacrifice accomplished on the Cross, and not a propitiatory sacrifice; or that it is useful only to him who communicates and that it should not be offered for the living and the dead, for sins, punishments, satisfactions and other necessities, let him be anathema."[1]

All the effects of Calvary are, therefore, transmitted to us by the Mass, and their one aim is to unite us with Christ and make us sharers in His Redemption. These effects, however, can be produced directly or indirectly: directly, when there is question of atonement and of the remission of the temporal punishment due to sin or of obtaining the spiritual or temporal favours we need; indirectly, through the sacraments, which justify us and infuse sanctifying grace into our souls. For the sacraments are the instruments of the Passion of Christ; and since the Eucharistic Sacrifice contains Christ in His Passion, it is to be expected that they (the sacraments) should be at the service of this same sacrifice. Through them we receive our share of the fruits of sanctification which the immolation of Calvary merited for us, and which become ours actually and immediately through the Eucharistic immolation. Thus sanctified, we are enabled to unite our oblation to that of Christ on the altar and worthily to render to God the perfect homage of praise, adoration and thanksgiving which is His due.

Nevertheless, it is only in Holy Communion that our acceptance by God in the Eucharistic Sacrifice is really completed and consummated. It was not without reason that Christ, at the Last Supper, chose bread and wine in order to change them into His Body and Blood. As well as thus signifying His bloody immolation and giving us the power to reproduce it, He gave Himself to us as food, so that we could unite ourselves in the most real way possible to the holy Victim of the sacrifice. For, even in Holy Communion, one cannot dissociate the sacrifice from the sacrament. It is not any Christ whom we receive, but Christ immolated for us, whose Flesh we eat and whose Blood we drink. "For as often as you shall eat this bread and drink the chalice, you shall show forth the death of the Lord until He come."[2]

We find here again one of the chief rites by which man, in sacrifice, strives to establish a more intimate union with God and

---

[1] Council of Trent, Sess. 22, c. 3.
[2] *I Cor.*, XI, 26. 'For as often as ye eat the bread and drink of the cup, ye proclaim the death of the Lord, until He come" (*Westminster Version*).

endeavours to enter into His society, by eating before Him the remains of the immolated and consecrated victim. But how far above anything man had hoped for is the Eucharistic reality! Through Christ's Body and Blood God comes to us and unites us with Himself in an undreamt of outpouring of the Divine Life of Grace that is the pledge and the principle of union for all eternity. "I in them and Thou in Me": this is the unity of the Mystical Body desired by Christ, inaugurated on Calvary, and realized by the Blessed Eucharist as sacrament-sacrifice. Thus the total oblation of the Head and the members is consummated in loving union with the Triune God.

The Mass and the Heavenly Sacrifice.

The line of approach adopted in the preceding pages reveals the Holy Sacrifice of the Mass as linked up with what has been rather improperly called the heavenly sacrifice. In heaven Christ is the holy Victim, always pleasing to God, who stands before the heavenly Father to bear witness by the glorious marks of His Passion to the reconciliation accomplished in His Blood. He has no longer to offer Himself, having done so once for all on the altar of the Cross. "But this man offering one sacrifice for sins, for ever sitteth on the right hand of God. . . . For by one oblation He hath perfected forever them that are sanctified."[1] Yet it remains for Christ to present to God the infinite value of His merits and atonement, to intercede for us, and to transmit to us those favours which He is entitled to solicit on our behalf. From this point of view the Mass is nothing other than this same intercession of Christ, based on His sufferings and death, which we lay hold of, as it were, and make our own. It is, so to say, a reflection of the heavenly sacrifice, and enables us to draw copiously from the inexhaustible treasury of grace with which the Sacred Humanity of Christ is enriched. The Holy Sacrifice of the Mass is truly the link between heaven and earth, and it is, therefore, fitting that all our efforts to return through Christ to God should centre round it.

The Church's Sacrifice.

It is obvious from what has been said that the members of the Mystical Body are intended to take a very active part in the Holy Sacrifice of the Mass. It is absolutely essential that they should unite themselves to the sacramental oblation of the Divine Victim and offer themselves with it, so that in it and by it, they may be effectively made acceptable to God. The Holy Sacrifice of the Mass is primarily, of course, Christ's sacrifice; but it is also the sacrifice of the Church authentically united to Christ. The priest

---

[1] *Hebrew* X, 12-14. "But He, having offered one sacrifice for sin, 'hath taken His seat forever at the right hand of God.' . . . For by a single offering He hath forever perfected those who are made holy" (*Westminster Version*).

of the New Law acts in the name of Christ, but he acts also in the name of the whole Church Militant. On Calvary, Christ offered Himself with His Mystical Body, whose Head and authorized Representative He was; on the altar it is the Mystical Body which offers itself with Christ, whose oblation it renews, as it has full powers to act in His name and person. Accordingly, it is the whole Church, the whole community of Christ's Members, stamped with His character, that offers its own immolation to God by the ministry of the priest, in union with the immolation of its Head, in order that the Divine forgiveness and the gifts of God's munificence may descend upon it. It is the whole Church which, by the ministry of the priest, communicates in the Body and Blood of the Saviour, and so realizes the perfect unity of the Mystical Body. Finally, it is the whole Church which, by the ministry of the priest, sends up to the throne of God that perfect adoration, which, united with the praises of the Heavenly Jerusalem, associates earth with heaven in one and the same worship, the worship of Christ. It behoves the faithful to unite themselves with their priest, so that he may transmit their offerings to God, and communicate to them the Divine Victim, the pledge of their solidarity and union with their Head; so that together with Him they may lift their hearts to God in fervent acts of adoration, praise and thanksgiving.

We have seen that the Mystical Body is visibly constituted by means of the sacramental character and that this gives it a participation in the Priesthood of Christ. We have seen that it is organized under the government and guidance of pastors charged by the Divine Shepherd with the care of the flock. We have seen that it is sanctified by the sacraments, and so becomes an oblation to God "in an odour of sweetness." The Eucharistic Sacrifice, by raising the Mystical Body up to God in one tremendous movement and strengthening in Holy Communion the bonds that unite it to Christ, consolidates the union of man with God in charity. "You are a chosen generation, a kingly priesthood, a holy nation, a purchased people; that you may declare His virtues, Who hath called you out of darkness into His marvellous light."[1]

---

[1] *I St. Peter* II, 9. "But ye are a chosen race, a royal priesthood, a holy nation, God's own people, that ye may proclaim the perfections of Him Who hath called you out of darkness into His wondrous light" (*Westminster Version*).

CHAPTER XI

THE ETERNAL PRIESTHOOD

"Jesus Christ yesterday, and today, and the same forever."[1]

As Priest of that sacrifice to which His sublime mission destined Him, Christ, having entered heaven and seated Himself at the right hand of the Father, continues to exercise His sovereign Priesthood. He was Priest yesterday; He is Priest today; He will be Priest forever. Not that there is any question of a new immolation. God has accepted once for all the oblation of His Son. The Man-God reigns henceforth in glory, and in Him mankind is elevated to the throne of the Divine Majesty. The way His sacrifice opened to Him, and by which we pass in His wake, has brought Him to the pinnacle of honour and glory. "But we see Jesus, who was made a little lower than the angels, for the suffering of death, crowned with glory and honour. . . . And being consummated, He became, to all that obey Him, the cause of eternal salvation."[2]

The exercise of Christ's Priesthood in heaven consists in communicating to us here below the fruits of His redemption through the medium of Christian worship. Sometimes these fruits are transmitted apart from this worship but not independently of it. The infidels, who turn to God in good faith, not knowing that they are outside the One True Church, gravitate unconsciously around this source of light and love, which is the society founded by Christ; and it is in virtue of their tendency towards His Church that Our Lord bestows the Divine Life of Grace upon them.

The Priesthood of Christ is brought into action also in welcoming us into His Kingdom at the conclusion of our earthly life, and in conferring on us the gift of the Beatific Vision. Thus, even in eternity, Christ does not cease to act as our sovereign High-Priest. Signs and symbols will pass away; the sacramental worship will cease with this world of trials and difficulties. In the world beyond the grave, Christ will bring us to the consummation of eternal life by associating us with His own beatitude. "The saints in heaven," says St. Thomas, "will not need any further expiation through the exercise of Christ's Priesthood, but, having expiated, they will need to have the final reward conferred on them by Christ, on whom their glory depends. Hence we read in the Apocalypse (XXI, 23): 'The glory of God hath enlightened it—

---

[1] *Hebrews*, XIII, 8.

[2] *Hebrews*, II, 9; V, 9. "We can see One Who was made a little lower than the angels, I mean Jesus, crowned now with glory and honour because of the death He underwent. . . . And now, His full achievement reached, He wins eternal salvation for all those who render obedience to Him" (*The New Testament*, Mgr. R. A. Knox).

that is, the city of the saints—and the Lamb is the lamp thereof.' "[1]

The members of the Mystical Body continue to be united to their Head in heaven, and there receive from Him that plenitude of the Divine Life in which the happiness of the Blessed consists. And just as the Priesthood of Christ is eternal, so the reflections of and the participations in that Priesthood are eternal: "The Priesthood of Christ is eternal, according to Psalm CIX, 4: 'Thou art a priest for ever, according to the order of Melchisedech.' Consequently, every consecration, which is wrought by His Priesthood, is perpetual, enduring as long as the consecrated object itself. Since, therefore, the subject of the character is the soul according to its intellective part, where faith resides, as stated above (art. 4 ad. 3.), it is clear that, as the intellect is perpetual and incorruptible, the character remains indelibly stamped on the soul. . . . Although external worship does not continue after this life, nevertheless its end remains. Consequently, after this life the character remains, in the good for their glory, in the wicked for their shame: just as the military character remains in soldiers after victory, adding to the glory of the conquered and the shame of the vanquished."[2]

Our Lord Jesus Christ, Priest and King, has conquered the world, and for that victory He is supremely honoured in heaven. But they also share in the triumph of the Lamb who "bear his name on their foreheads";[3] who, marked with the seal of Christ, have shared in His Priesthood here below, and have offered with Him the sacrifice of His Body and Blood. They, and along with them, all those who are saved, including those whose union with Christian worship was only in desire, send up to the throne of God and His Christ that paean of eternal praise of which the Apocalypse speaks: "I saw a great multitude, which no man could number, of all nations, and tribes, and peoples and tongues, standing before the throne and in sight of the Lamb, clothed with white robes and palms in their hands. And they cried with a loud voice saying: 'Salvation to our God, who sitteth upon the throne, and to the Lamb.' And all the angels stood round about the throne, and the ancients, and the four living creatures; and they fell down before the throne upon their faces, and adored God saying: 'Amen. Benediction, and glory, and wisdom, and thanksgiving, honour, and praise, and strength to our God, for ever and ever. Amen.' "[4].

---

[1] IIIa, Q. 22, a. 5, ad. 1.   [2] IIIa, Q. 63, a. 5, c. and ad. 3.

[3] *Apocalypse*, XXII, 4.

[4] *Apocalypse*, VII, 9-12. "And then I saw a great multitude, past all counting, taken from all nations and tribes and peoples and languages. These stood before the throne in the Lamb's presence, clothed in white robes, with palm-branches in their hands, and cried with a loud voice: To our God, who sits on the throne, and to the Lamb, all saving power belongs. And all the angels that were standing round the throne, round the elders and the living figures, fell prostrate before the throne and paid God worship: Amen, they cried, blessing and glory and wisdom and thanksgiving and honour and power and strength belong to our God through endless ages, Amen" (*The New Testament*, Mgr. R. A. Knox).

BIBLIOGRAPHY

The following works may be found useful for the under-standing of the teaching set forth in this volume. The list does not pretend to be exhaustive and is limited to the more recent treatises on the question of Christ and His Church. For the most part, they are faithful to the doctrine of St. Thomas.

THOMAS PEGUES, O.P.—*Commentaire français littéral de la Somme Théologique de Saint Thomas d'Aquin*, Tome XV, *Le Rédempteur:* Tome XVI, *La Rédemption*. (Toulouse, Privat, 1924, 1926).

Ch. V. HÉRIS, O.P.—*Le Verbe Incarné*, Tomes I et II, French Translation of the Third Part of the *Summa Theologica*, QQ. 1-15. (Editions de la *Revue des Jeunes*. Paris, Desclée, 1927-1928).

L. HUGON, O.P.—*Le Mystère de l'Incarnation*. (Paris, Téqui, 1913). *Le Mystère de la Rédemption*. (Ibid). *La causalité instrumentale en Théologie*. (Ibid). *La sainte Eucharistie*. (Ibid).

L. GRIMAL, S.S.—*Jésus-Christ étudié et médité*. (Paris, 1910).

SCHWALM, O.P.—*Le Christ d'après saint Thomas d'Aquin*. (Paris, Lethielleux, 1910).

DOM MARMION, O.S.B.—*Christ the Life of the Soul. Christ in His Mysteries*.

Mgr. CHOLLET—*La psychologie du Christ*. (Paris, Lethielleux, 1903).

A. TANQUEREY, S.S.—*Les dogmes générateurs de la piété*. (Paris Mignard, 1924).

A.-D. SERTILLANGES, O.P.—*L'Eglise*, 2 vols. (Paris, Lecoffre, 1917).

A. de POULPIQUET, O.P.—*L'Eglise Catholique*. (Paris, Editions de la *Revue des Jeunes*, 1923).

UN PROFESSEUR DE GRAND SÉMINAIRE—*Le corps de Jésus-Christ présent dans l'Eucharistie*. (Avignon, Aubanel, 1926).

A. VONIER, O.S.B.—*A Key to the Doctrine of the Eucharist*. (London, Burns & Oates, 1925).

G. GASQUE—*L' Eucharistie et le Corps Mystique*. (Paris, Editions Spes, 1925).

M. DE LA TAILLE, S.J.—*Esquisse du Mystère de la Foi*. (Paris, Beauchesne, 1924).

M. LEPIN, S.S.—*L'idée du sacrifice de la Messe d'apres les Théologiens depuis l'origine jusqu'à nos jours*. (Paris, Beauchesne, 1926).

SAINT THOMAS AQUINAS

The principal works in which St. Thomas has treated at length the questions concerning Our Lord Jesus Christ and the Sacraments of the Church are:—

(i) *The Commentary on the Sentences*, Books III & IV.
(ii) *The Summa contra Gentiles*, Book IV, chap. 27-78.
(iii) *The Compendium Theologiae*, Chap. 190-242.
(iv) *The Summa Theologica*, IIIa, QQ. 1-90.

The other works of St. Thomas, in which he treats of the subject-matter of this book, are given below in the order of the chapters.

CHAPTER I. De rationibus fidei, cap. 5; Declarat. Q. 36, art. 23; I Tim., cap. 1, lect, 4; Cont. error. Graec., cap. 5; In psalm. 45.

CHAPTER II. Quodlib. 9, art. 2-5; De Unione Verbi Incarnati, art. 1-5; De Symb. Apost; De rat. fidei, cap. 6; De articulis fidei; Cont. error. Graec., cap. 16-24; Ad Philipp., cap. 2, lect. 2; Ad Rom. cap. 1, lect 2; In Joann., cap. 1, lect. 7.

CHAPTER III. Quodl. 3, art. 3; Quodl. 7, art. 7; De Verit. Q. 20, Q. 29, art. 1-3; In Joann., cap. 3, lect. 6; Ad Rom., c. 4, lect. 3.

CHAPTER IV. De Verit., Q. 29, art. 4-8; I Cor., cap. 11, lect. 1; Ad Ephes., cap. 1, lect. 8; Ad Coloss., cap. 1, lect. 5.

CHAPTER V. De Symb. Apost.; Quodl. 10, art. 2; De Veritate, Q. 29, art. 4; In Joann., cap. 5, lect. 4-5; In Matth., cap. 25; Ad Rom., cap. 14, lect. 1; II Cor., cap. 5, lect. 11.

CHAPTER VI. Quodl. 1, art. 3; Quodl. 2, art 1-2; De Symb. Apost; Ad Ephes., cap. 5, lect. 1; Ad Hebr., cap. 7, lect. 1.

CHAPTER VII. De Eccles. Sacramentis; In Joann., cap. 3, lect. 1; De Verit., Q. 27, art. 4; Quodl. 12, art. 10; Ad Galat., cap. 2, lect. 4; In Joann., cap. 6, lect. 7.

CHAPTER VIII. De Eccles. Sacramentis; Ad Rom., cap. 7, lect. 1; Ad Hebr., cap. 11, lect. 7.

CHAPTER IX. De Symb. Apost; Cont. error. Graec., cap. 32; Quodl. 4, art. 10; Quodl. 11, art. 7; Quodl. 12, art. 19; S. Theol. Supplement., QQ. 34-40.

CHAPTER X. Quodl. 5, art. 6 & 11; De rat. fidei, cap. 8; Declarat. Q. 36, art. 31-35; Quodl. 7, art. 8-10; Ad Hebr., c. 10, lect. 1.

FINIS